A Socio-Legal Approach to Constitutional Law

CASES AND CONTROVERSIES

SECOND EDITION

EDITED BY

Jason Michael Leggett and
Helen-Margaret Nasser

Kingsborough Community College

SAN DIEGO

Bassim Hamadeh, CEO and Publisher
Carrie Baarns, Manager, Revisions and Author Care
Kaela Martin, Project Editor
Sara Watkins, Developmental Editor
Rachel Kahn, Production Editor
Jess Estrella, Senior Graphic Designer
Trey Soto, Licensing Specialist
Natalie Piccotti, Director of Marketing
Kassie Graves, Senior Vice President, Editorial
Jamie Giganti, Director of Academic Publishing

Printed in the United States of America.

3970 Sorrento Valley Blvd., Ste. 500, San Diego, CA 92121

CONTENTS

Preface v

UNIT I A Sociolegal Analysis of Constitutional Law 1

Epilogue: Law and Inequality in a Changing America 5

Originalism: The Lesser Evil 21

Chisholm, Ex'r v. Georgia (1793) 27

Korematsu v. United States (1944) 44

Johnson v. Mcintosh (1823) 47

Trump v. Hawaii (2018) 52

The Unbearable Lightness of Rights: On Sociolegal
  Inquiry in the Global Era 55

UNIT II Law and Difference through the Humanities 80

The Power of Self-Definition 84

Letter From a Birmingham Jail 93

Interview: "As a Latina, Sonia Sotomayor Says, 'You Have
  to Work Harder,'" 95

The Life and Success of Sonia Sotomayor 98

Futures of Social Movements 114

UNIT III Cases and Controversies 132

United States v. The Amistad (1841) 133

Scott v. Sandford 141

Plessy v. Ferguson (No. 210) 146

Brown v. Board of Education (1954) 148

Baker v. Carr (1962) 149

Gitlow v. New York (1925) 152

Garrity v. New Jersey (1967) 154

Powell v. Alabama (1932) 156

Furman v. Georgia (1972) 159

Gates v. Illinois (1983) 167

Roe v. Wade (1973) 169

Planned Parenthood of Southeastern Pa. v. Casey 173

Carhart v. Gonzalez (2007) 176

Griswold v. Connecticut (1965) 178

Miller v. California (1973) 180

Texas v. Lawrence (2003) 182

Loving v. Virginia (1967) 186

Wickard v. Filburn (1942) 187

Citizens United v. Federal Election Comm'n (2010) 190

Plyler v. Doe (1982) 195

E.P.A. v. EME Homer City Generation (2014) 200

UNIT IV ## Constitutional Contradiction

206

Confronting Class in the Classroom 207

Marbury v. Madison 217

Wards Cove v. Atonio (1989) 221

PREFACE

The motivation to write this textbook came from the Crucible Moment. Commissioned by the U.S. Department of Education, this major report documented the nation's anemic civic health and includes recommendations focused on campus culture, general education, and civic inquiry. One of your authors, Jason, is a law graduate and teaches Constitutional Law and the Judiciary in the criminal justice program at Kingsborough Community College. The other, Helen, is a Student Affairs administrator with a political science background. We both have extensive backgrounds in civic learning and democratic engagement. We both accepted the challenge of addressing the civic education gap.

From 2012–2016 we engaged in a curriculum redesign project sponsored by the National Endowment for the Humanities (NEH) grant "Bridging Cultures to Form a Nation: Difference, Community, and Democratic Thinking." Through that work we conducted intensive research and co-created learning materials that integrated co-curricular and traditional course work. As we engaged with community activists, civic leaders, educators and students we began to see that our approach was unique. We had effectively designed structured learning opportunities that empowered diverse individuals to engage with important social challenges and to develop agency in civic spaces across political lines. We have shared this work at national education conferences, through research articles, and through curriculum development.

But there was a limitation. We found an information gap about both historical processes and participatory politics that made learning constitutional law seem distant and irrelevant to students lived experiences. For example, our students make up one of the most diverse populations in the country. Most textbooks present a very white-washed perspective of constitutional law and fail to account for race, gender, or class in any meaningful way. In the first edition of this book we presented a variety of humanities-based readings to try to provide a context for analyzing legal cases that was culturally responsive. This was popular with students and peer reviewers found the readings helpful but the analysis was underdeveloped and the themes were not clearly organized.

In this edition we have provided a clearer thematic approach to integrate humanities-based perspectives and deepened our commitment to culturally responsive analysis. In the first section we present constitutional law as a way of framing historical social change. The dual nature of constitutionalism, individual rights against social control, is examined through competing conceptions of sovereignty. This helps the reader see how critical interpretation affects everyday application of constitutional law. This approach also lays out the foundation for the social production of intersectional injustice (race, gender, class) through the historical context of the constitution. The reader should see that the document and the political controversies are linked throughout U.S. history.

The second section digs deeper into how the social production of difference, made legal by the constitutional structure, is resisted by those experiencing injustice. The third section provides the reader the opportunity to apply the newly learned sociolegal framework to analyze cases organized by themes. These cases span racial injustice, criminal justice, gender and reproductive rights, privacy interests, property and commerce, political action committees and corporate influence, immigration and education rights, and climate change policy in a federalist system. The final section returns to the framing of the constitution as a contradictory document that both reflects and produces social inequality. The reader is introduced to a critical economic argument about constitutional law that posits the impossibility of resolving the inherent contradiction between rights and social control.

We are confident this edition will continue the call to civic learning and democratic engagement from a decade ago. A sociolegal framing of constitutional law is especially relevant when examining the most pressing civic challenges and controversies we see today. The approach is also more relevant to diverse learners and provides a roadmap for learning troublesome knowledge. We have found this has helped thousands of students engage with difficult concepts and to begin a dialogue with peers. Many times this had radiated out beyond the individual classroom, across the campus, and into our communities. This is the kind of civic ethos we think is important for the coming decades as we collectively work towards greater equity.

REFERENCE

The National Task Force on Civic Learning and Democratic Engagement. 2012. A Crucible Moment: College Learning and Democracy's Future. Washington, DC: Association of American Colleges and Universities. https://static1.squarespace.com/static/5409fd72e4b08734f6c05b4c/t6155c897879a6853b449 15f7/1633011865559/Crucible+Moment.pdf

A Sociolegal Analysis of Constitutional Law

LEARNING OUTCOMES _____

1. Students will be able to explain how variations in constitutional interpretations result in different systemic outcomes.
2. Students will be able to describe how judges interpret constitutional text.
3. Students will be able to challenge the idea that law is merely simple procedural rules.
4. Students will be able to better evaluate how social relations inform judicial decisions.
5. Students will be able to describe the tension between law as social control and law as rights.
6. Students will identify how groups use rights consciousness to mobilize against injustice.

It is generally agreed that an informed citizenry is necessary for a functioning democracy. And yet, there is much disagreement as to what constitutes reliable information and in recent times there has been a cacophony as to what constitutes "fake news." From the founding of the United States, there has been rigorous and often contentious rancor over what is true in the free press. In Federalist No. 85, Alexander Hamilton (Rossiter et al., 2003, 520) provided a defense for a free and vigorous exchange of ideas because he argued there was an enormous difficulty in balancing many competing ideas and interests in a democracy: the judgments of many must unite in the work; experience must guide their labor; time must bring it to perfection; and the feeling of inconveniences must correct the mistakes, which they inevitably fall into their first trials and experiments (520–527). During the constitutional convention, there were many who were against the national government and were circulating pamphlets and visiting their local places of worship and less reputable social spaces with what Hamilton deemed, "slender pretensions to consistency who can rail at the latter for imperfections which he finds no difficulty in excusing in the former" (521). Fake news today is similar to what Hamilton described as that which "rests merely on the verbal and nominal distinctions, entirely foreign from the substance of the thing" (515). Fake news, as such, has a history and continues to be a drag on democratic progress still today. If the ideals of democracy require an informed, honest, and transparent exchange of ideas, fake news is the tool of those who oppose this ideal.

Over the last few years, freedom of expression and misinformation have resulted in violence. One example of the way in which freedom of expression and misinformation has resulted in violence is the capital insurrection of 2021. Before this uprising, posts on social media promoted the belief that violent action was necessary in order to stop perceived injustices based on false claims. These were represented most often by the hashtags #stopthesteal and #youwillnot replace us.

The dilemma of fake news and violent action is not new to the field of law. "Fighting words" were described by the Supreme Court in *Chaplinsky v. New Hampshire* (1942), as those which by their very utterance inflict injury or tend to incite an immediate breach of the peace. It is obvious that there is indeed a relationship between rhetoric and behavior. Hindsight allows us to reconfigure the events of January 6, 2021, and to examine the time line of communication leading up to the insurrection, which suggests that violent language preceded violent behavior. It is harder however to determine how much influence violent rhetoric has on individual actors when deciding whether or not to commit violence. This is because the meaning behind fighting words varies based on a context and social group. Thus, many of the same supporters of the insurrection interpret #defundthepolice as an assault against the very same government but associate the hashtag with false claims of unleashed chaos and looting as rising to the legal definition of a riot. It is difficult to see where within the rhetoric a legal interpretation might resolve the linguistic conflict. In this section, you will examine how judges interpret constitutional text and principles when attempting to resolve social controversies and conflicts.

An Introduction to Sociolegal Analysis

A gap exists between what the actual text of the US Constitution is and how it influences the daily lives of most people in the United States. **Formalists** tend to focus on the words of the constitution and examine how well courts are able to meet the ideals presented in constitutional principles. Everyday people tend to focus on rights. Yet, the first seven articles of the text discuss very few individual rights and instead describe the construction of the federal governmental agencies and the routines of democratic governance including voting, running for office, and what could be described as a general collection of accepted conventions of self-government in the 18th century. It is widely believed that knowledge about this system of governance is critical to equitable treatment within the system. This gap between what is known about the system and what happens in everyday life is commonly referred to as a civic education gap (Hurtado 2019, 95). There is also a much larger contextual problem that tends to be overlooked: Different constituencies are speaking about law quite differently. This has ramifications for democratic governance founded on legitimacy of representation and ideals of participatory politics.

CONSTITUTION IN CRISIS: BEYOND LEGAL FORMALISM

The purpose of looking beyond legal formalism is to challenge the hegemony of property-based conceptions of citizenship and thus what it means to be a human with rights. Legal formalism reflects the belief that law can be separate from lived experience. Hegemony, in contrast, includes the various ways in which these beliefs limit the possibility for social change in everyday life. Legal formalism begins with the conception that those who own property are entitled to rights. This abstract-ideal limits the potentiality of other conceptions of both rights and citizenship including civil and human rights often at the expense of the most vulnerable and powerless.

Social theorist, Hannah Arendt, observed that declarations of rights following World War II embodied a contradiction—the declaration requires states to protect the "universal" and "inalienable" rights of all human beings, whereas the modern institution of the state is grounded on the principle of national and territorial sovereignty—rights that only apply to those recognized by a government as deserving subjects (Arendt 1973, 275). This contradiction requires that a person must be recognized as having the right to have rights. Today, those who are routinely marginalized and are subject to unjust power are also consistently excluded from the right to have rights.

Historically, most people have been explicitly excluded from the right to have rights. For example, one of the chief architects of the US Constitution, James Madison, wrote in Federalist Paper number ten that the first object of the new legal order was the protection of the different and unequal faculties for acquiring property. Thus, many of our common sense assumptions about citizenship are tied to the historical structure of property designed to exclude most people; some myths involve the idea that property owners are more responsible, more likely to participate in self-government, to vote, and less likely to engage in **free-riding**, an idea that some benefit from others without contributing. These myths circulate throughout media, education, and other social institutions and lead to a kind of common sense legality by which rights are imagined to be owned by the individual as a reward for hard work—work directed at acquiring property.

The problem of this myth, besides being inaccurate, is that it reduces human relationships to rights and responsibilities, one against the other, and denies other more meaningful ways of relating to one another (Medcalf 1978, 113). In response, a small but a growing number of legal scholars have examined how the **polyvocality of legality**, that is, the varieties of legal consciousness and the multiple schemas of and by which it is constituted, permits individuals' wide latitude in interpreting **social phenomena**, events by which we must make meaning, while at the same time still deploying signs of legality (Ewick and Silbey 1998). These differences matter because they influence how the constitutional law is taught and how it is understood in everyday settings.

On the one hand, we know there are many ways of thinking about law that differ a great deal from the idea that law is simply a set of rules. On the other hand, a brief survey of constitutional law and US government textbooks provides a sketch of common approaches to the instruction of law that focus solely on this view of formal law. These textbooks typically begin with framing today's constitutional controversies within the logic of framer's intent. This approach is understandable given that those who write educational materials about constitutional law were educated under the same system, employing similar approaches that embrace a formal law first approach. But this also reflects a problem of who gets to contribute to legal knowledge production. Historically, wealthy White males have dominated legal education and thus represent the same **social stratification** problems based on constructed hierarchies discussed in the reading excerpt below.

The focus on formal law is also a function of the **common law** itself, law written and interpreted by judges. Thus, in constitutional law you cannot practically avoid reading cases decided by the Supreme Court of the United States. These decisions are the educational products of a system based on **judicial review**, the judicial practice of determining whether a statute is consistent with the Constitution (Tushnet 2018). However, it is imperative that these cases, and the judicial practices, should be interrogated within a specific context of social stratification. The consequences of judicial decision-making are related to the inequalities we see in a society generally. In the reading excerpt that follows consider how systemic inequity shapes the controversies that end up in the courts.

EPILOGUE: LAW AND INEQUALITY
IN A CHANGING AMERICA

Steven Vago and Steven E. Barkan

The United States will soon be entering the third decade of the twenty-first century. Since the first settlers came to these shores some 400 years ago, America has been a land filled with inequality based on race and ethnicity, social class, gender, sexual orientation and gender identity, nationality, and religion. Although the relative importance of these factors has changed over the years, Americans remain more or less likely to achieve the American dream and to lead happy, healthy lives because of where they rank on these factors.

This harsh truth is a central message of sociology's emphasis on the **social stratification** found in every contemporary society (Andersen and Collins, 2016). Every society is stratified, meaning that some people enjoy many advantages based where they rank on the factors just listed, while other people suffer from many disadvantages.

The social inequality that has long beset American society has also beset its legal system. Historically, the American legal system has been filled with inequality, and it has also contributed to inequality in the larger society. The overall situation today is notably better than just a half-century ago, thanks to federal and state legislation and a host of rulings by the U.S. Supreme Court and other courts. [...] However, how the law plays out often differs from how it is supposed to play out. Despite the legislation and court rulings just mentioned, inequality continues to characterize the legal system, and the legal system continues to contribute to social inequality. We outline the major dimensions and dynamics of inequality in American law in the pages that follow. The bulk of our discussion focuses on race and ethnicity in view of the amount of research on this topic and its historical and contemporary significance in American life.

Race and Ethnicity

America was founded on two horrific examples of racial inequality that continue to stain the historic record: the slavery of African Americans and what many historians deem the near-genocide of Native Americans (Baptist, 2016;

Steven Vago and Steven E. Barkan, "Epilogue: Law and Inequality in a Changing America," *Law and Society*, pp. 303–315. Copyright © 2018 by Taylor & Francis Group. Reprinted with permission.

Dunbar-Ortiz, 2015). What is sometimes forgotten in remembering these two historic monstrosities is that American law at the federal, state, and local levels helped them to happen.

Regarding slavery, Article I of the U.S. Constitution allowed slaves to count as three-fifths of a person for electoral purposes. Earlier, the various colonies developed a body of so-called *slave law* that, among other things, regulated the buying and selling of slaves and stipulated that slaves could not own property or even marry (Friedman, 2004). In the South, a key aim of the criminal justice system was to help prevent slaves from escaping and to punish those who did try to escape (Walker, 1998). In 1850, the U.S. Congress passed the Fugitive Slave Act, which made it a federal crime to help slaves escape and to help escaped slaves remain free. Six years later, the U.S. Supreme Court ruled 7–2 in its notorious *Dred Scott* case that slaves and free blacks were not U.S. citizens and thus did not enjoy the legal protections given by the Constitution to citizens. The majority opinion said in part that African Americans have "for more than a century before been regarded as beings of an inferior order, and altogether unfit to associate with the white race ... ; and so far inferior, that they had no rights which the white man was bound to respect" (quoted in Burns, 1998:282). After the Civil War ended slavery, the South adopted the so-called Black Codes, which discriminated against freed slaves in many ways. Reconstruction in 1866 eliminated these codes, but legal racial discrimination and segregation returned to the South after Reconstruction ended in 1877.

Turning to Native Americans, American law provided the foundation for the activities over many decades that took land away from Native Americans and, worse, caused the deaths of untold numbers of their ranks. These efforts reduced the numbers of Native Americans from about 1 million in the early 1600s, when European settlers first arrived to these shores, to less than one-fourth that number by 1900, a fraction of what would have been expected through normal population growth (Venables, 2004). Beginning in the late eighteenth century, government authorities coerced Native Americans to sign legal treaties, in which they gave up their land and agreed to be confined to reservations (Samuels, 2006). The Congressional Removal Act of 1830 enabled the forced relocation of Native Americans from the Southeast to west of the Mississippi River. This relocation took the form of the heartbreaking *Trail of Tears*, as the relocated Native Americans had to walk for hundreds of miles, without thousands dying en route. In 1903, the U.S. Supreme Court ruled in *Lone Wolf v. Hitchcock* that Congress could nullify the land treaties and take land without compensation from Native Americans (Wildenthal, 2002).

These short summaries of African Americans' and Native Americans' histories only begin to illustrate the many ways that American law reinforced their maltreatment and subjugation. But as these summaries demonstrate, these two groups' distressing histories cannot be fully understood without appreciating the role that law played for many decades in the human suffering they experienced.

American history is replete with many legally caused injustices against other racial and ethnic groups. For example, federal legislation in 1882 banned immigration from China, and several states back then banned marriages between Chinese and whites (Friedman, 2004; Lee, 2003). During this era, fear of and hostility toward Chinese immigrants and African Americans fueled laws that banned opium and cocaine (Musto, 1999). Whites irrationally feared that the Chinese were using opium to lure young white children into sexual slavery and that African Americans who used cocaine could acquire super strength and become invulnerable to bullets. During the 1930s, fear by whites that marijuana use would make Mexican Americans rape and murder whites fueled federal legislation that banned marijuana use.

RACE/ETHNICITY AND THE LAW TODAY

History often repeats itself and thus helps us to understand the present and to predict the future. Even so, the past is not always prologue, as social change can and does occur [...]. Although law has played a fundamental role in establishing and reinforcing racial and ethnic inequality throughout American history, perhaps this role has diminished in recent decades. Perhaps American law has begun to achieve the ideal of **blind justice** promised by the familiar symbol of a blindfolded Lady Justice holding balanced scales. According to this symbol, the law should be impartial, and the chances of achieving justice under law should not depend on someone's race, ethnicity, wealth, or other nonlegal attributes.

What does the social science evidence say about racial and ethnic inequality in the legal system today? The answer here is less clear than it would have been more than a half century ago, for the law has improved in this regard during the past five decades, thanks to much legislation and many court rulings. However, the picture that emerges from the social evidence is still disturbing, because race and ethnicity still matter even if law itself is "officially" now blind when it comes to race and ethnicity. To recall what we stressed earlier [...] the law does not always work the way it is supposed to work. Supporting this harsh reality, there is ample evidence that race and ethnicity still influence many legal outcomes and that these outcomes in turn contribute to racial and ethnic inequality in the larger society.

Indirect and Direct Effects of Race and Ethnicity We have room here to summarize this evidence briefly, with fuller treatments available elsewhere (Johnson et al., 2015; Walker et al., 2018). To begin to summarize this evidence, we must first distinguish between the indirect effects of race and ethnicity on legal outcomes and their direct effects on legal outcomes. By *indirect* effects, we mean that people of color are generally much poorer and otherwise disadvantaged than whites and thus have worse legal outcomes than whites because of their lower socioeconomic status (SES). By *direct* effects, we mean that it is the race and ethnicity of people of color themselves that leads to their worse legal outcomes, because of bias against them by actors in the legal system.

Regarding indirect effects, low-income people of all racial and ethnic backgrounds are worse off in the legal system because, simply put, they lack money. The next section on social class discusses this dynamic further. Given this evidence, African Americans, Latinos, and Native Americans are indeed unequal within the legal system, regarding both civil cases and criminal cases, because of their lower SES. All things equal, these groups' lower SES renders them at a significant disadvantage in the civil and criminal justice arenas compared to whites facing similar legal issues.

Regarding direct effects, we must first acknowledge that there is actually little research on racial and ethnic bias in the *civil* legal system. However, because racial and ethnic prejudice exists in American society as a whole, it is reasonable to assume that it exists in the civil legal system and that it thus results in worse outcomes for people of color in this branch of the legal system. But much more research is needed on this matter before any firm conclusions can be drawn.

Fortunately, there is much research on the direct effects of race and ethnicity in the criminal justice system: the behavior of police, including the use of excess force and arrest; the various practices of prosecutors; and the sentencing practices of judges. Although this huge body of evidence is more complex than might be assumed, it does point to enduring and significant direct effects of race and ethnicity on legal outcomes at every stage of the criminal justice system. These effects stem from racial and ethnic bias by police, prosecutors, judges, and other criminal justice actors.

Implicit Bias Before discussing this evidence, we must comment on the nature of the bias just mentioned. A half century ago, racial and ethnic bias often took the form of "Jim Crow" racism, with whites holding blatantly racist views regarding African Americans and other people of color as biologically inferior, and with out-and-out racists occupying law enforcement, prosecutorial, and judicial positions in the South but also sometimes in the North (Litwack, 2009). Fortunately, that form of racism has largely faded, although too many Americans still hold such racist views. More to the point, Jim Crow racism has been replaced by what is called *modern* or *symbolic* racism that views African Americans and other people of color as culturally, if not biologically, inferior and blames them for their low SES (Quillian, 2006).

Responding to this change in the nature of racial and ethnic prejudice, social scientists have studied the extent and impact of implicit bias, the idea that many people hold unconscious racial and ethnic stereotypes (James et al., 2016; Lum, 2016). To the extent that people of color are at a key disadvantage today in the criminal justice system because of racial and ethnic bias by criminal justice professionals, social scientists think this bias reflects implicit bias rather than a conscious, shamelessly racist attempt of these professionals to oppress people of color (Walker et al., 2018). Some police and other criminal justice professionals, of course, may still be out-and-out racists, but overall the bias that operates in the criminal justice system is much more implicit and unconscious than explicit and conscious.

Evidence of Implicit Bias in the Criminal Justice System Because most evidence of this issue concerns African Americans, most of our discussion here will concern African Americans. That said, growing evidence indicates that Latinos and Native Americans also experience worse outcomes in the criminal justice system because of implicit bias against them. Our summary of the evidence that generally exists for these three groups will focus on decision making during major stages of criminal justice: law enforcement, prosecution, and conviction and sentencing.

Law Enforcement When Americans think about racial issues in criminal justice, the behavior of police probably comes most readily to mind. Are the police more likely to stop, frisk, and/or arrest African Americans and other people of color, whether they are walking, driving, or just standing around? Are the police more likely to use excessive force (*police brutality*) against these individuals? What does the evidence say?

As just noted, the evidence is complex, and not every study finds discrimination by police in all these dimensions of their behavior as they encounter the public. Overall, though, the picture that emerges from this evidence is disturbing, as it strongly suggests that African Americans are more likely, even if they have done nothing wrong, to be stopped for questioning if they are walking, driving, or just standing around, and more likely than whites to be arrested for suspicious behavior (Walker et al., 2018).

As also just noted, we do not have space to discuss all the evidence, but it is revealing to examine the results of a few specific studies. Let's begin with racial profiling of drivers and walkers. Anecdotally, African Americans often say that the police stopped them for no good reason while they were driving or walking, leading observers to sarcastically call these persons' alleged criminal behavior *DWB* (*driving while black*) or *WWB* (*walking while black*), respectively. Social science evidence backs up these drivers' and walkers' claims (Baker, 2010; Lundman and Kowalski, 2009; Rojek et al., 2012). For example, a Maryland study found that African Americans comprised more than three-fourths of all drivers stopped by state troopers on a particular highway, even though they comprised only 17% of the drivers on the highway. In locations such as New Jersey and St. Louis, studies have found state troopers or local police (depending on the study) much more likely to stop African American and Latino drivers than white drivers and also much more likely to search the cars of the drivers of color. In New York City, which for several years had an intensive "stop and frisk" policy of young males who were walking or standing around, studies have found that police were much more likely (i.e. out of proportion to their representation in the general population) to stop African American and Latino males and to frisk them after stopping them (Baker, 2010).

The evidence for racial bias in arrest is probably less clear than that for stopping, questioning, and frisking. Methodological problems make it difficult to study such bias, because social scientists would need to know, for example, how many black and white offenders are breaking the law, and what percentage of these offenders are arrested. But because much crime goes unreported, it is difficult to know how many offenders by race are breaking the law. To counter this problem, some social scientists have accompanied the police during their patrolling and recorded the race of possible suspects and whether the police arrest these suspects. Some of these observational studies find no racial bias in arrest, but other such studies do find racial bias (Walker et al., 2018). The best conclusion from these studies is probably that racial bias in arrest sometimes occurs, but that it is not nearly as extensive as a half-century ago.

In this regard, a more subtle form of police bias in arrest is possible. What if police tend to arrest white suspects only if the evidence against them is fairly strong, while arresting African American suspects even if the evidence against them is fairly weak? Some older evidence finds this is indeed the case (Hagan and Zatz, 1985; Petersilia, 1983), but newer evidence is needed to determine the extent to which this more subtle form of bias still exists.

Clear evidence exists of racial bias in arrests for one kind of criminal behavior, drug offenses. Although African Americans are not more likely than whites to use illegal drugs, they are arrested for illegal drug possession far beyond their proportion in the U.S. population (Mitchell and Caudy, 2015). To be more precise, African Americans comprise about 13% of the population, but accounted for 27% of all drug arrests in 2015 (Federal Bureau of Investigation, 2016), twice their "fair share" of arrests. The disparity for Latinos is smaller: Although Latinos comprise about 15% of the population, they accounted for 20% of drug arrests in 2015.

These disparities have existed ever since the nation began its legal war on drugs in the 1980s and have contributed to the overrepresentation of people of color in prisons and jails (Alexander, 2012). A former president of the American Society of Criminology warned of this situation in 1993, "What is particularly troublesome," he said, "is the degree to which the impact [of the drug war] has been so disproportionately imposed on nonwhites" (Blumstein, 1993:4–5). He added, "One can be reasonably confident that if a similar assault was affecting the white community, there would be a strong and effective effort to change either the laws or the enforcement priority."

Prosecution Researchers are becoming increasingly interested in the behavior of prosecutors, who must decide, among other things, whether to drop charges against arrested suspects or to continue to prosecute the case, whether to bring more serious or less serious charges against defendants, and whether to insist on incarceration as part of the plea-bargaining process (Pfaff, 2017). Despite this growing interest, research on race/ethnicity and prosecutorial decisions is still fairly scant, making it difficult to draw firm conclusions. Of the research that does exist, some studies do find racial bias in prosecutorial decision making, but other studies do not (Kutateladze et al., 2016). For example, New York prosecutors in marijuana cases are more likely during plea-bargaining discussions to demand incarceration of African American defendants than of white defendants; this difference manifested even after researchers took into account the strength of the evidence and other legal factors (Kutateladze et al., 2016).

Evidence of prosecutorial racial bias is clearer in homicide and rape cases (Myers, 2000). Some studies find that prosecutors in these cases bring more serious charges when the defendant is African American than when the defendant is white. The evidence for racial bias in these cases is even stronger when the race of the *victim* is considered, with prosecutors bringing more serious charges when the victim is white than when the victim is black. According to one criminologist, this latter evidence raises "the disturbing possibility that some prosecutors define the victimization of whites, especially when African Americans are perpetrators, as more serious criminal events than the comparable victimization of African Americans" (Myers, 2000:451).

Conviction and Sentencing   More than one-third of prison inmates are African American, and about one-fifth are Latino. These proportions exceed their representation in the U.S. population. Although this disparity may reflect heavier involvement in criminal behavior to some degree (Baumer, 2013; Spohn, 2015), a large amount of research does find that people of color are more likely than whites to be sentenced to prison for similar offenses and to receive longer prison terms once sentenced (Bales and Piquero, 2012; Franklin, 2015; Walker et al., 2018). This difference appears more often for African American than for Latino defendants, while some studies do not find racial disparities in sentencing. To the extent that racial differences in sentencing exist in the research, they are found more often for the decision by judges to incarcerate a convicted defendant (the "in/out" decision) than for the length of the prison term that judges determine.

Although the overall evidence on race/ethnicity and sentencing is somewhat inconsistent, it is clearer for death penalty cases and for drug cases. African Americans convicted of homicide are somewhat more likely than their white counterparts to be sentenced to death by juries, and this difference becomes stronger when the race of the victim is considered (Bohm, 2015). Echoing the findings for prosecutors in homicide cases, death sentences are more likely when a homicide victim is white than when the victim is black, and especially more likely when the victim is white and the defendant is black. Also echoing research on arrests for drug offenses, sentencing for drug offenses is harsher for African American and Latino defendants than for their white counterparts (Alexander, 2012).

A recent intriguing study uncovered an additional kind of racial bias in sentencing (Chokshi, 2017). This study examined 1,900 cases since 1989 where the defendant was convicted of murder, sexual assault, or drug offenses but later exonerated as evidence came to light pointing to the defendant's innocence. Exonerations stemmed from such reasons as mistaken identification by witnesses or police or prosecutorial misconduct. Of the 1,900 exonerations, 47% involved African American defendants. More to the point, the percentage of exonerated cases for these three crimes involving African American defendants exceeded the percentage of all convictions for these crimes involving African American defendants. As a news report summarized this evidence, "Black defendants convicted of murder or sexual assault are significantly more likely than their white counterparts to be later found innocent of the crimes" (Chokshi, 2017).

Social Class

Poor and low-income people experience many disadvantages in American society from infancy through old age. One significant set of disadvantages occurs in the legal system. Much evidence finds that the poor are much worse off than wealthier people in both the civil courts and in the criminal courts. This is because they do not have the money to afford a good attorney, or often any attorney, and because they do not have the knowledge base and "social capital" to succeed in the complex worlds of the civil and criminal courts. Although the Constitution requires effective counsel in criminal cases, in practice, this requirement is rather meaningless because the poor do not receive effective counsel, or at least do not receive counsel that is as skilled and effective as the counsel that a wealthy defendant can afford to hire.

In the civil court arena, [...] litigation can be very expensive, and that "one-shotters" are at a considerable disadvantage because they simply do not know the way of the courts. These twin problems combine to make it very difficult for low-income people to win justice in the civil courts. If they end up in these courts because of actions taken by a finance company or a landlord, they more often than not lose. If they have a legal problem, they cannot afford an attorney to take action on their behalf. Legal-aid societies help in this regard, but their staff is overworked, and they cannot give clients the same time and energy that wealthy clients receive from a private attorney they hire. For all these reasons, the "haves" come out ahead in the civil courts, and the "have-nots" come out behind, to paraphrase the title of Galanter's (1974) classic work that discussed this issue. Several studies from the past few decades find empirical support for Galanter's view that the poor come out behind in the civil courts (Carlin, et al., 1966; Farole, 1999; Songer et al., 1999).

The situation for low-income people in the criminal justice arena is perhaps even worse, if only because their physical freedom may be at stake. Political scientist Herbert Jacob (1978:185) observed long ago that the criminal courts are "fundamentally courts against the poor." This is because almost all the criminal cases these courts handle involve suspects and defendants who are poor or low-income. Wealthy defendants may commit white-collar crime, but they are much less likely to commit the "conventional" violent and property crimes that are the focus of the criminal courts.

Because almost all criminal suspects and defendants are poor or low-income, we do not really have enough wealthy people accused of violent and property crime to determine how disadvantaged poorer suspects and defendants are in the criminal justice system. Still, as Jacob (1978:185–186) also observed, "Those few defendants who are not poor can often escape the worse consequences of their [criminal] involvement." This is partly because, he said, they can afford bail, and they can afford to hire a skilled, private attorney who can devote much time to their case.

Two celebrated cases since Jacob made this observation illustrate his point. After O. J. Simpson, the former football player and movie celebrity, was arrested in 1994 for allegedly brutally murdering his ex-wife and her friend, he was able to afford a highly skilled legal defense team that cost him an estimated $10 million and won him a jury acquittal (Barkan, 1986). A decade later, star basketball player Kobe Bryant was prosecuted for alleged rape; his legal defense probably cost several million dollars and helped him to win his freedom after the alleged victim refused to testify and the prosecutor was forced to drop the charges (Saporito, 2004).

Beyond examples like these, many sociological and journalistic accounts since the 1960s confirm that indigent defendants typically do not enjoy effective counsel or even adequate counsel (Downie, 1972; Fritsch and Rohde, 2001; Strick, 1978; Sudnow, 1965). Criminal cases in the nation's urban courts are often called "factory-line justice" because overworked public defenders or assigned private counsel have so little time to handle any one case.

When we compare the sentencing of white-collar crime defendants, who can commit crime that is more serious than many violent and property crimes, we see ready evidence of social class bias in sentencing. When corporations pro- duce dangerous products or maintain dangerous workplaces, it is very rare that a single corporate executive is ever incarcerated, even though many people may be harmed or even killed by their companies' criminal behavior (Barak, 2017). One widely cited study found that California defendants convicted of grand theft were twice as likely as physicians convicted of Medicaid fraud to go to prison, even though the economic loss from the Medicaid fraud was ten times greater than the cost from the grand theft (Tillman and Pontell, 1992).

Gender

There was a time when women had no equality in the eyes of the legal system. They could not vote or own property, they could not sign contracts or serve on juries, and they could not even make a will. Employers were legally free to refuse to hire them. Thankfully those days are long gone, thanks to federal legislation and to various rulings by the Supreme Court and other courts. In today's world, women are formally equal in the eyes of the law, and they enjoy many more legal advantages than was true just a few decades ago.

In the juvenile justice and criminal justice arenas, some gender inequality still exists. Adolescent girls are more likely than boys to get into trouble with juvenile authorities for status offenses like sexual activity or running away from home (Chesney-Lind and Sheldon, 2014). In an opposite form of gender inequality, adult women are less likely than adult men convicted of similar crimes to be incarcerated, as judges and prosecutors evidently believe that women are less threatening than men to society and often have childcare responsibilities.

In another area, women who are victims of sexual assault, domestic violence, and other crimes targeting them as women still find that their allegations of criminal violence are taken less seriously than they should be by police, prosecutors, and judges. This is because many criminal justice professionals still believe that women are somehow to blame for the violence they suffer (Alderden and Ullman, 2012; Visher et al., 2008). To the extent these professionals continue to hold this belief and to accept other myths surrounding violence against women, the legal system contributes to women's inequality.

Sexual Orientation and Gender Identity

Same-sex sexual behavior used to be illegal in many states, and same-sex couples could not legally marry anywhere. Supreme Court rulings have abolished laws against same-sex sexual behavior and given same-sex couples the right to marry in every state and every community. Many Americans celebrated when these rulings occurred, and LGBTQ individuals enjoy many more legal advantages and much more legal equality than was true in just the recent past.

Despite these advances, the LGBTQ community continues to lack full legal equality. In particular, there is no federal law prohibiting employment or housing discrimination against LGBTQ people, and employers, landlords, and property owners are free in the majority of states to practice such discrimination. Because there is also no federal law prohibiting LGBTQ discrimination in public accommodations, restaurant owners, retail store managers, and hotel managers are also free in the majority of states to refuse to serve LGBTQ customers. In the area of the law, the United States still has a long road to travel before the LGBTQ community achieves full legal equality.

REFERENCES
Alderden, Megan A., and Sarah E. Ullman. 2012. "Creating a More Complete and Current Picture: Examining Police and Prosecutor Decision-Making When Processing Sexual Assault Cases," *Violence Against Women*, 18:525–551.

Alexander, Michelle. 2012. *The New Jim Crow: Mass Incarceration in the Age of Colorblindness*. New York: The New Press.

Andersen, Margaret L., and Patricia Hill Collins (eds.). 2016. *Race, Class, and Gender: An Anthology*. Belmont, CA: Wadsworth.

Baker, Al. 2010. "New York Minorities More Likely to be Frisked," *The New York Times* (May 13):A1.

Bales, William D., and Alex R. Piquero. 2012. "Racial/Ethnic Differentials in Sentencing to Incarceration," *JQ: Justice Quarterly*, 29(5):742–773.

Baptist, Edward E. 2016. *The Half Has Never Been Told: Slavery and the Making of American Capitalism*. New York: Basic Books.

Barak, Gregg. 2017. *Unchecked Corporate Power: Why the Crimes of Multinational Corporations Are Routinized Away and What We Can Do about It*. New York: Routledge.

Barkan, Steven E. 1986. "Interorganizational Conflict in the Southern Civil Rights Movement," *Sociological Inquiry*, 56:190–209.

Baumer, Eric P. 2013. "Reassessing and Redirecting Research on Race and Sentencing," *JQ: Justice Quarterly*, 30(2):231–261.

Blumstein, Alfred. 1993. "Making Rationality Relevant—The American Society of Criminology 1992 Presidential Address," *Criminology*, 31(1):1–16.

Bohm, Robert M. 2015. *Deathquest: An Introduction to the Theory and Practice of Capital Punishment in the United States*. New York: Routledge.

Burns, W. Haywood. 1998. "Law and Race in Early America." Pp. 279–284 in David Kairys (ed.), *The Politics of Law: A Progressive Critique*. New York: Basic Books.

Carlin, Jerome, Jan Howard, and Sheldon Messenger. 1966. "Civil Justice and the Poor," *Law & Society Review*, 1:9–90.

Chesney-Lind, Meda, and Randall G. Sheldon. 2014. *Girls, Delinquency, and Juvenile Justice*. Malden, MA: Wiley-Blackwell.

Chokshi, Niraj. 2017. "Black People More Likely to Be Wrongfully Convicted of Murder, Study Shows," *The New York Times* (March 7): //www.nytimes.com/2017/03/07/us/wrongful-convictions-race-exoneration.html?hp&action=click&pgtype=Homepage&clickSource=story-heading&module=first-column-region&region=top-news&WT.nav=top-news&_r=0.

Downie, Leonard, Jr. 1972. *Justice Denied: The Case for Reform of the Courts*. Baltimore, MD: Penguin Books.

Dunbar-Ortiz, Roxanne. 2015. *An Indigenous Peoples' History of the United States*. Boston, MA: Beacon Press.

Farole, Donald J., Jr. 1999. "Reexamining Litigant Success in State Supreme Courts," *Law & Society Review*, 33:1043–1057.

Federal Bureau of Investigation. 2016. *Crime in the United States, 2015*. Washington, DC: Federal Bureau of Investigation.

Franklin, Travis W. 2015. "Race and Ethnicity Effects in Federal Sentencing: A Propensity Score Analysis," *JQ: Justice Quarterly*, 32(4):653–679.

Friedman, Lawrence M. 2004. *Law in America: A Short History*. New York: The Modern Library.

Fritsch, Jane, and David Rohde. 2001. "Lawyers Often Fail New York's Poor," *The New York Times* (April 8):A1.

Galanter, Marc. 1974. "Why the 'Haves' Come Out Ahead: Speculations on the Limits of Legal Change," *Law & Society Review*, 9:95–160.

Hagan, John, and Marjorie S. Zatz. 1985. "The Social Organization of Criminal Justice Processing Activities," *Social Science Research*, 14:103–125.

Jacob, Herbert. 1978. *Justice in America: Courts, Lawyers, and the Judicial Process*. Boston, MA: Little, Brown and Company.

James, Lois, Lorie Fridell, and Frank Straub, Jr. 2016. "Psychosocial Factors Impacting Officers' Decisions to Use Deadly Force," *Police Chief*, 83(2):44–51.

Johnson, Devon, Amy Farrell, and Patricia Y. Warren (eds.). 2015. *Deadly Injustice: Trayvon Martin, Race, and the Criminal Justice System*. New York: NYU Press.

Kutateladze, Besiki Luka, Nancy R. Andiloro, and Brian D. Johnson. 2016. "Opening Pandora's Box: How Does Defendant Race Influence Plea Bargaining?" *JQ: Justice Quarterly*, 33(3):398–426.

Lee, Erika. 2003. *At America's Gates: Chinese Immigration During the Exclusion Era, 1882–1943*. Chapel Hill, NC: Univeristy of North Carolina Press.

Litwack, Leon F. 2009. *How Free Is Free? The Long Death of Jim Crow*. Cambridge, MA: Harvard University Press.

Lum, Cynthia. 2016. "Murky Research Waters: The Influence of Race and Ethnicity on Police Use of Force." *Criminology & Public Policy*, 15:453–456.

Lundman, Richard J., and Brian R. Kowalski. 2009. "Speeding While Black? Assessing the Generalizability of Lange et al.'s (2001, 2005) New Jersey Turnpike Speeding Survey Findings," *JQ: Justice Quarterly*, 26(3):504–527.

Mitchell, Ojmarrh, and Michael S. Caudy. 2015. "Examining Racial Disparities in Drug Arrests," *JQ: Justice Quarterly*, 32(2):288–313.

Musto, David F. 1999. *The American Disease: Origins of Narcotic Control*. New York: Oxford University Press.

Myers, Martha A. 2000. "The Social World of America's Courts." Pp. 447–471 in Joseph F. Sheley (ed.), *Criminology: A Contemporary Handbook*. Belmont, CA: Wadsworth.

Petersilia, Joan. 1983. *Racial Disparities in the Criminal Justice System*. Santa Monica: Rand Corporation.

Pfaff, John. 2017. *Locked In: The True Causes of Mass Incarceration and How to Achieve Real Reform*. New York: Basic Books.

Quillian, Lincoln. 2006. "New Approaches to Understanding Racial Prejudice and Discrimination," *Annual Review of Sociology*, 32:299–328.

Rojek, Jeff, Richard Rosenfeld, and Scott Decker. 2012. "Policing Race: The Racial Stratification of Searches in Police Traffic Stops," *Criminology*, 50(4):993–1024.

Samuels, Suzanne. 2006. *Law, Politics, and Society*. Boston, MA: Houghton Mifflin Company.

Saporito, Bill. 2004. "Kobe Rebounds," *Time* (September 13):72–73.

Songer, Donald R., Reginald S. Sheehan, and Susan Brodie Haire. 1999. "Do the 'Haves' Come Out Ahead over Time? Applying Galanter's Framework to Decisions of the U.S. Courts of Appeals, 1925–1988," *Law & Society Review*, 33:811–832.

Spohn, Cassia. 2015. "Race, Crime, and Punishment in the Twentieth and Twenty-First Centuries," *Crime and Justice*, 44(1):49–97.

Strick, Anne. 1978. *Injustice for All*. New York: Penguin.

Sudnow, David. 1965. "Normal Crimes: Sociological Features of the Penal Code in a Public Defender's Office," *Social Problems*, 12:255–276.

Tillman, Robert, and Henry N. Pontell. 1992. "Is Justice 'Collar-Blind'?: Punishing Medicaid Provider Fraud," *Criminology*, 30(4):547–573.

Venables, Robert W. 2004. *American Indian History: Five Centuries of Conflict & Coexistence*. Santa Fe, NM: Clear Light Publishers.

Visher, Christy A., Adele Harrell, Lisa Newmark, and Jennifer Yahner. 2008. "Reducing Intimate Partner Violence: An Evaluation of a Comprehensive Justice System-Community Collaboration," *Criminology & Public Policy*, 7(4):495–523.

Walker, Samuel. 1998. *Popular Justice: A History of American Criminal Justice*. New York: Oxford University Press.

Walker, Samuel, Cassia Spohn, and Miriam DeLone. 2018. *The Color of Justice: Race, Ethnicity, and Crime in America*. Belmont, CA: Wadsworth Publishing Company.

Wildenthal, Bryan H. 2002. "Fighting the Lone Wolf Mentality: Twenty-First Century Reflections on the Paradoxical State of American Indian Law," *Tulsa Law Review* 38:113–145.

Now that you have considered the relationship between social inequality and inequity in the legal system, it is helpful to examine what judges really do. Many frame what judges do as a simple review process. There is no discussion of judicial review in the text of article three of the US Constitution. Yet judges, at every level of the state and federal courts, hear individual cases that require both conflict resolution and application of some legal principles. These cases arise under multiple bodies of law and may or may not be clearly invoking a constitutional principle. Some have argued that a common sense reading of article three of the Constitution strongly supports the power of judges to say what the law is. Others argue that judges have arbitrarily abused their powers.

There is also reason to be skeptical that the original drafters of the constitution had a general agreement about what judges should do. Much of the US legal system is borrowed or adopted from the British system. However, the British use the term judicial review for the judicial practice of determining whether administrative action is consistent with statutory authorization. They refer to the US practice as constitutional review. These differences are not without practical distinction. They inform how different people think about governance and law based on the behaviors of judges. Legal scholars in Britain find it strange that judges should have the power to overrule the legislature. While US legal scholars rarely analyze the relationship between administrative law and legislative intent.

Differences among lawyers, judges, and legal scholars circulate out into the rest of society. Most people in the United States, when asked, think of judges as referees between all of the competing claims and as balancing the interests of other departments of government. They tend to say they prefer judges to be neutral and not politically motivated (Scheb and Lyons 2001). For example, each time a judicial nominee before the Supreme Court is questioned before the Senate, someone asks the judge to explain how they will maintain neutrality. Yet, this erroneous view that anyone could be free of implicit bias leaves the many nuances of governance and differences among legalities, constitutional, criminal, civil, legislative, and so on, largely left unexamined. As discussed in the excerpt, disparity in sentencing between property crimes committed by Black and White offenders reflects implicit bias of judges. There have been also reports that judges who have made decisions about cases involving companies in which they owned stocks failed to adhere to such a neutrality principle. In both examples, there is ample evidence to contradict that judges could withhold personal interests or bias from their reasoning processes.

How then should we think about interpreting what judges actually do? Scholars who study texts describe the close reading of these documents as the process of **exegesis**. This process requires what has been called a normative universe or the line of thinking that writers rely on when constructing a proposition. For example, Thomas Jefferson drew upon philosophers of natural law when he wrote all men are created equal. It is important to read the same writings that Jefferson read in order to understand what the phrase meant in that particular context. In other words, the phrase is not a statement of scientific fact as it is commonly understood today. Rather, it is a claim of moral truth; people should be treated equally. These natural law philosophers were using the language to support an argument to change the existing social order.

A close reading to determine a normative universe of the interpreter is especially important when analyzing constitutional principles. As a student of constitutional law, it is important to first consider the many possible ways one might interpret constitutional text and principles. Some judges believe that words in the constitution should be considered as changing with the times. They argue for a constitution that should reflect the living spirit of the general public in a specific time period. Hence, they are often association with the idea of a living constitution. In contrast, some judges argue that the words of the constitution should be read to give a plain meaning. These judges believe the principles should be strictly applied to uphold the meaning as constructed by those who wrote the legislation. This deference to legislatures is often called a textual approach. Other judges believe that the words in the constitution should be considered within the context of the legal case. In other words, what is the meaning that comes out of the controversy itself? This approach tries to include the meanings given by the opposing parties in the litigation, the meaning that has been given by previous courts, and the generally accepted principles in broader legal education. These judges are associated with term contextualists. Finally, there are those that argue that the plurality of judicial opinions over time must be framed within the logic of the meaning attributed to the framers of the constitution. They believe that this meaning can be found by considering the historical writings of the time. They argue a judge can then construct principles meant to survive to meet the needs of social problems today. These judges are commonly referred to as originalists.

Presently, the majority view of Supreme Court Justices is that of the originalists. Originalism is highly controversial and it has its critics. Originalists argue that social issues like same-sex marriage, abortion, and voting rights should be left to state politics and not issues that need constitutional protection. They believe that constitutional issues should only be considered when they explicitly refer to a right, like the right to own a gun in the second amendment. They argue that the so-called privacy rights should go through the amendment process to be considered by the courts or left to individual states to decide. The following excerpts explain why they reject the other approaches and adopt the historical meaning scheme.

From

ORIGINALISM: THE LESSER EVIL

Justice Antonin Scalia

It may surprise the layman, but it will surely not surprise the lawyers here, to learn that originalism is not, and had perhaps never been, the sole method of constitutional exegesis. It would be hard to count on the fingers of both hands and the toes of both feet, yea, even on the hairs of one's youthful head, the opinions that have in fact been rendered not on the basis of what the Constitution originally meant, but on the basis of what the judges currently thought it desirable for it to mean. That is, I suppose, the sort of behavior Chief Justice Hughes was referring to when he said the Constitution is what the judges say it is. But in the past, nonoriginalist opinions have almost always had the decency to lie, or at least to dissemble, about what they were doing—either ignoring strong evidence of original intent that contradicted the minimal recited evidence of an original intent congenial to the court's desires, or else not discussing original intent at all, speaking in terms of broad constitutional generalities with no pretense of historical support. [...]

The principal theoretical defect of nonoriginalism, in my view, is its incompatibility with the very principle that legitimizes judicial review of constitutionality. Nothing in the text of the Constitution confers upon the courts the power to inquire into, rather than passively assume, the constitutionality of federal statutes. That power is, however, reasonably implicit because, as Marshall said in Marbury v. Madison, (1) "[i]t is emphatically the province and duty of the judicial department to say what the law is," (2) "[i]f two laws conflict with each other, the courts must decide on the operation of each," and (3) "the constitution is to be considered, in court, as a paramount law." Central to that

Justice Antonin Scalia, "Originalism: The Lesser Evil," *University of Cincinnati Law Review*, vol. 57, pp. 852–855. Copyright © 1989 by University of Cincinnati/Law Review. Reprinted with permission.

analysis, it seems to me, is the perception that the Constitution, though it has an effect superior to other laws, is in its nature the sort of "law" that is the business of the courts–an enactment that has a fixed meaning ascertainable through the usual devices familiar to those learned in the law. If the Constitution were not that sort of a "law," but a novel invitation to apply current societal values, what reason would there be to believe that the invitation was addressed to the courts rather than to the legislature? One simply cannot say, regarding that sort of novel enactment, that "[i]t is emphatically the province and duty of the judicial department" to determine its content. Quite to the contrary, the legislature would seem a much more appropriate expositor of social values, and its determination that a statute is compatible with the Constitution should, as in England, prevail.

[...] If the law is to make any attempt at consistency and predictability, surely there must be general agreement not only that judges reject one exegetical approach (originalism), but that they adopt another. And it is hard to discern any emerging consensus among the nonoriginalists as to what this might be. Are the "fundamental values" that replace original meaning to be derived from the philosophy of Plato, or of Locke, or Mills, or Rawls, or perhaps from the latest Gallup poll? This is not to say that originalists are in entire agreement as to what the nature of their methodology is; [...] there are some significant differences. But as its name suggests, it by and large represents a coherent approach, or at least an agreed-upon point of departure. As the name "nonoriginalism" suggests (and I know no other, more precise term by which this school of exegesis can be described), it represents agreement on nothing except what is the wrong approach.

Transformative Learning, Legality Narratives, Threshold Concepts

Thus far you have been introduced to the multiple ways that constitution could be interpreted. This matters because people are treated differently in society and interpretation either maintains these unequal relations or works toward social change. Those with unequal power are less likely to be able to use rights effectively to protect themselves from harm. Inequality is maintained through a legal system that is divided: some judges interpret constitutional principles to promote inclusion, while others promote exclusion from participatory politics. Finally, traditional legal education tends to focus on formal law and discount others ways of making meaning around legality. You now need to consider how these social myths might be challenged so that you might better understand the

malleability of law—the idea that law changes based on competing arguments and interpretations.

Two educational theories must be kept in mind when learning about constitutional law and interpretation. The first is **threshold concepts**. The second is **transformative learning theory**. Within the context of the individual course, Meyer and Land's (2003, 412) notion of the **threshold concept** is defined as akin to a portal, opening up a new and previously inaccessible way of thinking about something that represents a transformed way of understanding, or interpreting or viewing something without which the learner cannot progress.

In order to cross a threshold toward a new way of thinking, a transformation must occur within your way of seeing the law. Educational theorist Jack Mezirow (1991, 35) summarized **transformative learning** as a process of learning involving five interacting contexts: a meaning perspective, the communication process, a line of action, a self-concept, and the external situation. Part of the process of transformative learning is that it is unique to the individual and the learning environment.

Imagination is strongly connected to our physical process that will help us understand the meaning of our experience. We rely upon recreations of these experiences to adapt what we know from the past to the present. Neuropsychologist, Lisa Feldman Barrett, explained why our culturally informed brains struggle with the myth of individual responsibility in criminal law. In criminal law, we consider two parts of responsibility: **mens rea**, an alleged mental state, and **actus reus**, an alleged illegal act. When we put these two legal concepts together, we imagine an individual who intentionally did not follow the set rules of society and acted with an intent to harm others. The myth influences our belief that there have always existed a set of clear rules for everyone to follow long before we ever organized into social relations.

Barrett, along with other scholars who study mind and behavior, explained that our brains do not work like that in the real world. Instead, every human is the sum of our concepts, which become the predictions that drive our behavior. These concepts come from our cultural influences; your brain is a function of other brains in your culture (Barrett 2017, 248). Simply, people from different cultural backgrounds have different experiences of what good behavior is, what they think the rules of society are, and what constitutes appropriate consequences for bad behavior. Our experiences are different, and so we have different meanings for intent, motive, and immoral behavior. This understanding of cultural relativity should provoke the learner to examine the concept of social responsibility in order to replace the myth of individual responsibility. We certainly owe an obligation to the social groups we participate in but we are also shaped by those social environments and they owe an obligation to us as well.

This understanding of cultural difference must also be reflected in the educational setting. In sum, the learning environment must be structured in such a way that learners engage in social organization to cocreate knowledge that begins with their own **identity**, or standpoint. This requires individuals to transform their point of view to accommodate multiple actors within an institution. This means that you first need to unpack your own implicit biases as well as your culturally informed values and beliefs. You then must consider these beliefs within a larger context of the college classroom. You are likely to attach different meanings to unexamined concepts like justice, equality, and law.

Further, individuals can only articulate a social identity that fosters **agency** by binding what is important to them with allies within the institution in a way that utilizes their existing skills and that constructs spaces with others for ongoing dialogue for change across difference. The development of critical reflection about your social identity and ability to be an agent of change theoretically leads to the potential for **advocacy**. In order to be an agent of change within a structure of inequality, one must understand how these unequal power relationships inform one's identity and how to use strategies of empowerment within institutions but also the potential agent must make the choice to act on behalf of oneself or others.

New students of law have been found to come with an understanding that law represents a set of rules that govern society and the ideas that those rules are malleable may be counter intuitive, alien, or event objectionable (Weresh 2014, 707). In order for you to cross the threshold toward understanding that law is more flexible and intentionally ambiguous you must be challenged to critically analyze two other previously unexamined beliefs: (1) existing assumptions about the legitimacy of centralized legal authority and (2) the usefulness of law as a tool for social control (Ricketts 2006, 53).

These unexamined assumptions are largely a product of civic education more generally but also reflect the American belief in the "myth of rights." Sociolegal scholar Stuart Scheingold identified the myth of rights as the ideological manifestation of law: it encourages us to associate rights with social justice (Scheingold 2004, 62). Over time, adults begin to realize and accept the fact the legal institutions will not always operate as they should. This understanding is based on personal experiences (identity), the inability or ability to initiate change (agency), and choices about whether to comply, protest, or resist (advocacy).

So far you have learned about the polyvocality of legality and the social process of interpretation as critical threshold concepts. You have now learned to examine your own assumptions about how law should be interpreted and to recognize patterns of unequal outcomes for people based on unequal power relationships. This should help you better understand how formal legal arrangements benefit those with more resources and more practice working within these institutions. While this is important to a deeper understanding of how law actually works in society, it is also helpful for your own practical needs.

In a society such as ours, constitutional law is central to how people experience the normative ideals of constitutional democracy. If we experience these norms differently, it is important for educators to first accept what a democratic community is and not to try to coerce learners to embrace ideals held by others. In order to move any group of participants in a diverse learning environment toward a more equitable social arrangement, a set of technical and practical skills (or tools) must be developed together over time (Leggett and King-Reilly 2020, 16). This construction is necessary for the theory of civic learning and the practice of democratic engagement to be integrated into a coherent theory and practice. These technical and practical skills are related to an ability to critically reflect and to engage in dialogue with others who hold different perspectives. The structured learning opportunities throughout this reader encourage you to self-reflect and to discuss with others how identity might lead to agency and advocacy.

In viewing the long arc of historical processes, people are better able to make meaning of the world around them—both existing and emerging. Civic identity then contains what the learner believes of herself in relation to the readings and the larger processes they will see in reflection all around them. This form of self-awareness is based on one's connection to civic institutions and processes including law and politics.

Agency is often best reflected in a paradox: although everyone supports some change, very few are engaged with change in their own lives and environments, particularly in thick social settings where norms, habits, and routines appear to be beyond the individual's control. Resistance to learning alternative ways of being is best overcome when learners can identify the challenge they wish to confront, are able to refer to others who have successfully overcome their own challenges, and are presented with the tools and resources necessary to locate allies, begin the process of naming their actions, and provide space for reflection leading to action.

Advocacy is captured in the moment of flow when the learner is able to apply their learning outside of the classroom, or activate that knowledge in the real world. Democracy is not a spectator sport. Whether you believe the major global problems we face may be solved politically or socially, or whether you believe they cannot, each individual deserves the opportunity to decide for herself in equal measure. This **fundamental right** of self-government is often taken for granted. The right is said to be fundamental because no one is supposed to be able to take it away; yet, many are excluded from participation through legal and extralegal means. This textbook aims to consistently challenge you to consider this assumption of autonomy within social structures from multiple points of view.

As you reflect upon on how your identity is constituted and contested within the legal system, it is helpful for you to consider your own standpoint. A key premise of **standpoint theory** is a commitment to bringing multiple points of view into dialogue with one another, especially the ones we hear less often, so that the social theory better explains the full breadth of social life (Wade 2022, 9). Within the historical structures of legality this involves bringing in majority discourses into conversation with a plurality of resistance narratives. This approach to narratives of legality has been framed as between the haves and the have nots (Galanter 1974). This framing should be kept in mind as you read through the readings provided.

A threshold concept helpful for comprehending the gravity of these philosophical differences in translation can be first illustrated through what it means to be **sovereign**. Sovereignty is a concept that is elusive yet critical to the framing of popular government. It is also brought into tension by the familiar dichotomy of liberty and social control. When conceived of as a right against the arbitrary action of government actors, sovereignty is seen as an individual protection. However, when conceived of as the power of the rationalized institution of the state, it is seen as a tool of control in violation of individual rights. This contradiction cannot be resolved within liberal conceptions of law and politics.

Black's Law Dictionary defines sovereignty as, Supreme dominion, authority, or rule (Garner 1996). However, Justice John Jay and Justice James Wilson, both founding members of the constitutional legal order, located sovereignty in the individual, a view that does not fit comfortably into the notion of popular sovereignty as a purely collective concept (Barnett 2007). The letter of the law that seems to refer to sovereign power as the ability to make decisions is contradicted by the spirit of the law that supports the idea of individual liberty. As you read the excerpts that follow consider how the letter and the spirit of the law inform the practice of law in everyday life, including your own.

CHISHOLM, EX'R V. GEORGIA (1793)

Opinion 1: Justice Iredell

With the advantage of the letter on our side, let us now advert to the spirit of the Constitution, or rather its genuine and necessary interpretation. I am aware of the danger of going into a wide history of the Constitution, as a guide of construction; and of the still greater danger of laying any important stress upon the preamble as explanatory of its powers. I resort, therefore, to the body of it; which shows that there may be various actions of States which are to be annulled. If, for example, a State shall suspend the priviledge of a writ of habeas corpus, unless when in cases of rebellion or invasion the public safety may require it; should pass a bill of attainder or ex post facto law; should enter into any treaty, alliance, or confederation; should grant letters of marque and reprisal; should coin money; should emit bills of credit; should make any thing but gold and silver coin a tender in payment of debts, should pass a law impairing the obligation of contracts; should, without the consent of Congress, lay imposts or duties on imports or exports, with certain exceptions; should, without the consent of Congress, lay any duty on tonnage, or keep troops or ships of war in time of peace; these are expressly prohibited by the Constitution; and thus is announced to the world the probability, but certainly the apprehension, that States may injure individuals in their property, their liberty, and their lives; may oppress sister States; and may act in derogation of the general sovereignty.

Are States then to enjoy the high privilege of acting thus eminently wrong, without controul; or does a remedy exist? The love of morality would lead us to with that some check should be found; if the evil, which flows from it, be not too great for the good contemplated. The common law has established a principle, that no prohibitory act shall be without its vindicatory quality; or, in other words, that the infraction of a prohibitory law, although an express penalty be omitted, is still punishable. Government itself would be useless, if a pleasure to obey or transgress with impunity should be substituted in the place of a function to its laws. This was a just cause of complaint against the deceased confederation. In our solicitude for a remedy, we meet with no difficulty, where the conduct of a State can be animadverted on through the medium of an individual. For

U.S. Supreme Court, "Chisholm, Ex'r versus Georgia," 1793.

instance, without suing a State, a person arrested may be liberated by habeas corpus; a person attainted and a convict under an ex post facto law, may be saved; those, who offend against improper treaties, may be protected, or who execute them, may be punished; the actors under letters of marque and reprisal may be mulested; coinage, bills of credit, unwarranted tenders, and the impairing of contracts between individuals, may be annihilated. But this redress goes only half way; as some of the preceeding unconstitutional actions must pass without censure, unless States can be made defendants. What is to be done, if in consequence of a bill of attainder, or an ex post facto law, the estate of a citizen shall be confiscated, and deposited in the treasury of a State? What, if a State should adulterate or coin money below the Congressional standard, emit bills of credit, or enact unconstitutional tenders, for the purpose of extinguishing its own debts? What if a State should impair her own contracts? These evils, and others which might be enumerated like them, cannot be corrected without a suit against the State. It is not denied, that one State may be sued by another; and the reason would seem to be the same, why an individual, who is aggrieved, should sue the State aggrieving. A distinction between the cases is supportable only on a supposed comparative inferiority of the Plaintiff. But, the framers of the Constitution could never have thought thus. They must have viewed human rights in their essence, not in their mere form. They had heard, seen- I will say felt; that Legislators were not so far sublimed above other men, as to soar beyond the region of passion. Unfledged as America was in the vices of old Governments, she had some incident to her own new situation: individuals had been victims to the oppression of States.

1st. I acknowledge, and shall always contend, that the States are sovereignties. But with the free will, arising from absolute independence, they might combine in Government for their own happiness. Hence sprang the confederation; under which indeed the States retained their exemption from the so rensic jurisdiction of each other, and, except under a peculiar modification, of the United States themselves. Nor could this be otherwise; since such a jurisdiction was no where (according to the language of that instrument) expressly delegated. This Government of supplication cried aloud for its own reform; and the public mind of America decided, that it must perish of itself, and that the Union would be thrown into jeopardy, unless the energy of the general system should be increased. Then it was the present Constitution produced a new order of things. It derives its origin immediately from the people; and the people individually are, under certain limitations, subject to the legislative, executive, and judicial authorities thereby established. The States are in fact assemblages of these individuals who are liable to process. The limitations, which the Federal Government is admitted to impose upon their powers, are diminutions of sovereignty, at least equal to the making of them defendants. It is not pretended, however, to deduce from these arguments alone, the amenability of States to judicial cognizance; but the result is, that there is nothing in the nature of sovereignties, combined as those of America are, to prevent the words of the Constitution, if they naturally mean, what I have affected, from receiving an easy and usual construction. But pursue the idea a step farther; and trace one, out of a multitude of examples, in which the General Government may be convulsed to its center without this judicial power, If a State shall injure an individual of another State, the latter must protect him by a remonstrance. What if this be ineffectual? To stop there would cancel his allegiance; one State cannot sue another for such a cause; acquiescence is not be believed. The crest of war is next raised; the Federal head cannot remain unmoved amidst these shocks to the public harmony. Ought then a necessity to be created for drawing out the general force on an occasion to replete with horror? Is not an adjustment by a judicial form far preferable? Are not peace and concord among the States two of the great ends of the Constitution? To be consistent, the opponents of my principles must say, that a State may not be sued by a foreigner.- What? Shall the tranquility of our country be at the mercy of every State? Or, if it be allowed, that a State may be sued by a foreigner, why, in the scale of reason, may not the measure be the same, when the citizen of another State is the complainant? Nor is the history of confederacies wholly deficient in analogy; although a very strict one is scarcely to be expected. A parade of deep research into the Amphyctionic Council, or the Achaean league, would be fruitless, from the dearth of historical monuments. With the best lights they would probably be found, not to be positively identical with our union. So little did they approach to a National Government, that they might well be destitute of a common judicatory. So ready were the ancient Governments to merge the injuries to individuals in a State quarrel, and so certain was it, that any judicial decree must have been enforced by arms, that the mild form of a legal discussion could not but be viewed with indifference, if not contempt. And yet it would not be extravagant to conjecture, that all civil causes were sustained before the Amphyctionic Council.

What we know of the Achaean confederacy, exhibits it as purely national, or rather consolidated.- They had common Magistrates taken by rotation, from the towns; and the amenability of the constituent cities to some Supreme Tribunal, is as probable as otherwise. But, in fact, it would be a waste of time, to dwell upon these obscurities. To catch all the semblances of confederacies, scattered through the historic page, would be no less absurd, than to search for light in regions of darkness, or a stable jurisprudence in the midst of barbarity and bloodshed.

Advancing then, into more modern times, the Helvetic Union presents itself; one of whose characteristics is, that there is no common judicatory. Stanyan, 117. Nor, does it obtain in Holland. But it cannot be concluded from hence, that the Swiss or the Dutch, the jealousy of whom would not suffer them to adopt a National Government, would deem it an abasement, to summon a State, connected as the United States are, before a National Tribunal. But our anxiety for precedents is relieved by appealing to the Germanic Empire. The jumble of fifty principalities together no more deserves the name of one body, than the incoherent parts of Nebuchadnazzar's image. The Princes wage war without the consent of their paramount sovereign; they even wage war upon each other; nay upon the Emperor himself; after which it will add but little to say, that they are distinct sovereignties. And, yet both the Imperial Chamber, and the Aulie Council hear and determine the complaints of individuals against the Princes.

It will not surely be required to assign a reason, why the Confederation did not convey a similar jurisdiction; since that scanty and strict paper was of so different a hue and feature from the Constitution, as scarely to appear the child of the same family.

Combine then into one view, the letter and the spirit of the Constitution; the relation of the several States to the union of the States; the precedents from other sovereignties; the judicial act, and process act; the power of forming executions; the little previous importance of this power to that of rendering of judgment; the influence under which every State must be to maintain the general harmony; and the inference, will, I trust, be in favor of the first proposition; namely, that a State may be sued by the citizen of another State.

With this discussion, though purely legal, it will be impossible to prevent the world from blending political considerations. Some may call this an attempt to consolidate. But before such an imputation shall be pronounced, let them examine well, if the fair intepretation of the Constitution does not vindicate my opinions. Above all, let me personally assure them, that the prostration of State-rights is no object with me; but that I remain in perfect confidence, that with the power, which the people and the Legislatures of the States indirectly hold over almost every movement of the National Government, the States need not fear an assault from bold ambition, or any approaches of covered stratagem.

A general question of great importance here occurs. What controversy of a civil nature can be maintained against a State by an individual? The framers of the Constitution, I presume, must have meant one of two things: Either 1. In the conveyance of that part of the judicial power which did not relate to the execution of the other authorities of the general Government (which it must be admitted are full and discretionary, within the restrictions of the Constitution itself), to refer to antecedent laws for the construction of the general words they use: Or, 2. To enable Congress in all such cases to pass all such laws, as they might deem necessary and proper to carry the purposes of this Constitution into full effect, either absolutely at their discretion, or at least in cases where prior laws were deficient for such purposes, if any such deficiency existed.

The Attorney-General has indeed suggested another construction, a construction, I confess, that I never heard of before, nor can I now consider it grounded on any solid foundation, though it appeared to me to be the basis of the Attorney-General's argument. His construction I take to be this: 'That the moment a Supreme Court is formed, it is to exercise all the judicial power vested in it by the Constitution, by its own authority, whether the Legislature has prescribed methods of doing so, or not.' My conception of the Constitution is entirely different. I conceive, that all the Courts of the United States must receive, not merely their organization as to the number of Judges of which they are to consist; but all their authority, as to the manner of their proceeding, from the Legislature only. This appears to me to be one of those cases, with many others, in which an article of the Constitution cannot be effectuated without the intervention of the Legislative authority. There being many such, at the end of the special enumeration of the powers of Congress in the Constitution, is this general one: 'To make all laws which shall be necessary and proper for carrying into execution the foregoing Powers, and all other powers vested by this Constitution in the Government of the United States, or in any department or officer thereof.' None will deny, that an act of Legislation is necessary to say, at least of what number the Judges are to consist; the President with the consent of the Senate could not nominate a number at their discretion. The Constitution intended this article so far at least to be the subject of a Legislative act. Having a right thus to establish the Court, and it being capable of being established in no other manner, I conceive it necessary follows, that they are also to direct the manner of its proceedings. Upon this authority, there is, that I know, but one limit; that is, 'that they shall not exceed their authority.' If they do, I have no hesitation to say, that any act to that effect would be utterly void, because it would be inconsistent with the Constitution, which is a fundamental law paramount to all others, which we are not only bound to consult, but sworn to observe; and, therefore, where there is an interference, being superior in obligation to the other, we must unquestionably obey that in preference. Subject to this restriction, the whole business of organizing the Courts, and directing the methods of their proceeding where necessary, I conceive to be in the discretion of Congress. If it shall be found on this occasion, or on any other, that the remedies now in being are defective, for any purpose it is their duty to provide for, they no doubt will provide others. It is their duty to legislate so far as is necessary to carry the Constitution into effect. It is ours only to judge. We have no reason, nor any more right to distrust their doing their duty, than they have to distrust that we all do ours. There is no part of the Constitution that I know of, that authorises this Court to take up any business where they left it, and, in order that the powers given in the Constitution may be in full activity, supply their omission by making new laws for new cases; or, which I take to be the same thing, applying old principles to new cases materially different from those to which they were applied before.

The only principles of law, then, that can be regarded, are those common to all the States. I know of none such, which can affect this case, but those that are derived from what is properly termed 'the common law,' a law which I presume is the ground-work of the laws in every State in the Union, and which I consider, so far as it is applicable to the Peculiar circumstances of the country, and where no special act of Legislation controls it, to be in force in each State, as it existed in England, (unaltered by any statute) at the time of the first settlement of the country. The statutes of England that are in force in America differ perhaps in all the States; and, therefore, it is probable the common law in each, is in some respects different. But it is certain that in regard to any common law principle which can influence the question before us no alteration has been made by any statute, which could occasion the least material difference, or have any partial effect. No other part of the common law of England, it appears to me, can have any reference to this subject, but that part of it which prescribes remedies against the crown. Every State in the Union in every instance where its sovereignty has not been delegated to the United States, I consider to be as completely sovereign, as the United States are in respect to the powers surrendered. The United States are sovereign as to all the powers of Government actually surrendered: Each State in the Union is sovereign as to all the powers reserved. It must necessarily be so, because the United States have no claim to any authority but such as the States have surrendered to them: Of course the part not surrenderred must remain as it did before. The powers of the general Government, either of a Legislative or Executive nature, or which particularly concerns Treaties with Foreign Powers, do for the most part (if not wholly) affect individuals, and not States: They require no aid from any State authority. This is the great leading distinction between the old articles of confederation, and the present constitution. The Judicial power is of a peculiar kind. It is indeed commensurate with the ordinary Legislative and Executive powers of the general government, and the Power which concerns treaties. But is also goes further. Where certain parties are concerned, although the subject in controversy does not relate to any of the special objects of authority of the general government, wherein the separate sovereignties of the States are blended in one common mass of supremacy, yet the general Governemnt has a Judicial Authority in regard to such subjects of controversy, and the Legislature of the United States may pass all laws necessary to give such Judicial Authority its proper effect. So far as States under the Constitution can be made legally liable to this authority, so far to be sure they are subordinate to the authority of the United States, and their individual sovereignty is in this respect limited. But it is limited no farther than the necessary execution of such authority requires. The authority externals only to the decision of controversies in which a State is a party, and providing laws necessary for that purpose. That surely can refer only to such controversies in which a State can be a part; in respect to which, if any question arises, it can be determined, according to the principles I have supported, in no other manner than by a reference either to pre-existent laws, or laws passed under the Constitution and in conformity to it.

The differences between such corporations, and the several States in the Union, as relative to the general Government, are very obvious in the following particulars. 1st. A corporation is a mere creature of the King, or of Parliament; very rarely of the latter; most usually of the former only. It owes its existence, its name, and its laws, (except such laws as are necessarily incident to all corporations merely as such) to the authority which create it. A State does not owe its origin to the Government of the United States, in the highest or in any of its branches. It was in existence before it. It derives its authority from the same pure and sacred source as itself: The voluntary and deliberate choice of the people. 2nd. A corporation can do no act but what is subject to the revision either of a Court of Justice, or of some other authority within the Government. A State is altogether exempt from the jurisdiction of the Courts of the United States, or from any other exterior authority, unless, in the special instances where the general Government has power derived from the Constitution itself. 3rd. A corporation is altogether dependant on that Government to which it owes its existence. Its charter may be forfeited by abuse. Its authority may be annihilated, without abuse, by an act of the Legislative body. A State, though subject in certain specified particulars to the authority of the Government of the United States, is in every other respect totally independent upon it. The people of the State created, the people of the State can only change, its Constitution. Upon this power there is no other limitation but that imposed by the Constitution of the United States; that it must be of the Republican form. I omit minuter distinctions. These are so palpable, that I never can admit that a system of law calculated for one of these cases is to be applied, as a matter of course, to the other, without admitting (as I conceive) that the distinct boundaries of law and Legislation may be confounded, in a manner that would make Courts arbitrary, and in effect makers of a new law, instead of being (as certainly they alone ought to be) expositors of an existing one. If still it should be insisted, that though a State cannot be considered upon the same footing as the municipal corporations I have been considering, yet, as relative to the powers of the General Government it must be deemed in some measure dependent; admitting that to be the case (which to be sure is, so far as the necessary execution of the powers of the General Government extends) yet in whatever character this may place a State, this can only afford a reason for a new law, calculated to effectuate the powers of the General Government in this new case: But it affords no reason whatever for the Court admitting a new action to fit a case, to which no old ones apply, when the application of law, not the making of it, is the sole province of the Court.

I have now, I think, established the following particulars. 1st. That the Constitution, so far as it respects the judicial authority, can only be carried into effect by acts of the Legislature appointing Courts, and prescribing their methods of proceeding. 2nd. That Congress has provided no new law in regard to this case, but expressly referred us to the old. 3rd. That there are no principles of the old law, to which, we must have recourse, that in any manner authorise the present suit, either by precedent or by analogy. The consequence of which, in my opinion, clearly is, that the suit in question cannot be maintained, nor, of course, the motion made upon it be complied with.

Opinion 2: Justice Wilson

I am, first, to examine this question by the principles of general jurisprudence. What I shall say upon this head, I introduce by the observation of an original and profound writer, who, in the philosophy of mind, and all the sciences attendant on this prime one, has formed an era not less remarkable, and far more illustrious, than that formed by the justly celebrated Bacon, in another science, not prosecuted with less ability, but less dignified as to its object; I mean the philosophy of matter. Dr. Reid, in his excellent enquiry into the human mind, on the principles of common sense, speaking of the sceptical and illiberal philosophy, which under bold, but false, pretentions to liberality, prevailed in many parts of Europe before he wrote, makes the following judicious remark: 'The language of philosophers, with regard to the original faculties of the mind, is so adapted to the prevailing system, that it cannot fit any other; like a coat that fits the man for whom it was made, and shews him to advantage, which yet will fit very aukward upon one of a different make, although as handsome and well proportioned. It is hardly possible to make any innovation in our philosophy concerning the mind and its operations, without using new words and phrases, or giving a different meaning to those that are received.' With equal propriety may this solid remark be applied to the great subject, on the principles of which the decision of this Court is to be founded. The perverted use of genus and species in logic, and of impressions and ideas in metaphysics, have never done mischief so extensive or so practically pernicious, as has been done by States and sovereigns, in politics and jurisprudence; in the politics and jurisprudence even of those, who wished and meant to be free. In the place of those expressions I intend not to substitute new ones; but the expressions themselves I shall certainly use for purposes different from those, for which hitherto they have been frequently used; and one of them I shall apply to an object still more different from that, to which it has hitherto been more frequently, I may say almost universally, applied. In these purposes, and in this application, I shall be justified by example the most splendid, and by authority the most binding; the example of the most refined as well as the most free nation known to antiquity; and the authority of one of the best Constitutions known to modern times. With regard to one of the terms State this authority is declared: With regard to the other sovereign the authority is implied only: But it is equally strong: For, in an instrument well drawn, as in a poem well composed, mence is sometimes most expressive.

To the Constitution of the United States the term SOVEREIGN, is totally unknown. There is but one place where it could have been used with propriety. But, even in that place it would not, perhaps, have comported with the delicacy of those, who ordained and established that Constitution. They might have announced themselves 'SOVEREIGN' people of the United States: But serenely conscious of the fact, they avoided the ostentatious declaration.

Having thus avowed my disapprobation of the purposes, for which the terms, State and sovereign, are frequently used, and of the object, to which the application of the last of them is almost universally made; it is now proper that I should disclose the meaning, which I assign to both, and the application, which I make of the latter. In doing this, I shall have occasion incidently to evince, how true it is, that States and Governments were made for man; and, at the same time, how true it is, that his creatures and servants have first deceived, next vilified, and, at last, oppressed their master and maker.

Man, fearfully and wonderfully made, is the workmanship of his all perfect Creator: A State; useful and valuable as the contrivance is, is the inferior contrivance of man; and from his native dignity derives all its acquired importance. When I speak of a State as an inferior contrivance, I mean that it is a contrivance inferior only to that, which is divine: Of all human contrivances, it is certainly most transcendantly excellent. It is concerning this contrivance that Gicero says so sublimely, 'Nothing, which is exhibited upon our globe, is more acceptable to that divinity, which governs the whole universe, than those communities and assemblages of men, which, lawfully associated, are denominated States.

Let a State be considered as subordinate to the People: But let every thing else be subordinate to the State. The latter part of this position is equally necessary with the former. For in the practice, and even at length, in the science of politics there has very frequently been a strong current against the natural order of things, and an inconsiderate or an interested disposition to sacrifice the end to the means. As the State has claimed precedence of the people; so, in the same inverted course of things, the Government has often claimed precedence of the State; and to this perversion in the second degree, many of the volumes of confusion concerning sovereignty owe their existence. The ministers, dignified very properly by the appellation of the magistrates, have wished, and have succeeded in their wish, to be considered as the sovereigns of the State. This second degree of perversion is confined to the old world, and begins to diminish, even there: but the first degree is still too prevalent, even in the several States, of which our union is composed. By a State I mean, a complete body of free persons united together for their common benefit, to enjoy peaceably what is their own, and to do justice to others. It is an artificial person. It has its affairs and its interests: It has its rules: It has its rights: And it has its obligations. It may acquire property distinct from that of its members: It may incur debts to be discharged out of the public stock, not out of the private fortunes of individuals. It may be bound by contracts; and for damages arising from the breach of those contracts. In all our contemplations, however, concerning this feigned and artificial person, we should never forget, that, in truth and nature, those, who think and speak, and act, are men.

Is the foregoing description of a State a true description? It will not be questioned but it is. Is there any part of this description, which intimates, in the remotest manner, that a State, any more than the men who compose it, ought not to do justice and fulfil engagements? It will not be pretended that there is. If justice is not done; if engagements are not fulfilled; is it upon general principles of right, less proper, in the case of a great number, than in the case of an individual, to secure, by compulsion, that, which will not be voluntarily performed? Less proper it surely cannotbe. The only reason, I believe, why a free man is bound by human laws, is, that he binds himself. Upon the same principles, upon which he becomes bound by the laws, he becomes amenable to the Courts of Justice, which are formed and authorised by those laws. If one free man, an original sovereign, may do all this; why may not an aggregate of free men, a collection of original sovereigns, do this likewise? If the dignity of each singly is undiminished; the dignity of all jointly must be unimpaired. A State, like a merchant, makes a contract. A dishonest State, like a dishonest merchant, wilfully refuses to discharge it: The latter is amenable to a Court of Justice: Upon general principles of right, shall the former when summoned to answer the fair demands of its creditor, be permitted, proteus-like, to assume a new appearance, and to insult him and justice, by declaring I am a Sovereign State? Surely not. Before a claim, so contrary, in it § first appearance, to the general principles of right and equality, be sustained by a just and impartial tribunal, the person, natural or artificial, entitled to make such claim, should certainly be well known and authenticated. Who, or what, is a sovereignty? What is his or its sovereignty? On this subject, the errors and the mazes are endless and inexplicable. To enumerate all, therefore, will not be expected: To take notice of some will be necessary to the full illustration of the present important cause. In one sense, the term sovereign has for its correlative, subject, In this sense, the term can receive no application; for it has no object in the Constitution of the United States. Under that Constitution there are citizens, but no subjects. 'Citizen of the United States*'. 'Citizens of another State.' 'Citizens of different States.' 'A State or citizen thereof*'. The term, subject,occurs, indeed, once in the instrument; but to mark the contrast strongly, the epithet 'foreign'* is prefixed. In this sense, I presume the State of Georgia has no claim upon her own citizens: In this sense, I am certain, she can have no claim upon the citizens of another State.

In another sense, according to some writers*, every State, which governs itself without any dependence on another power, is a sovereign State. Whether, with regard to her own citizens, this is the case of the State of Georgia; whether those citizens have done, as the individuals of England are said, by their late instructors, to have done, surrendered the Supreme Power to the State or Government, and reserved nothing to themselves; or whether, like the people of other States, and of the United States, the citizens of Georgia have reserved the Supreme Power in their own hands; and on that Supreme Power have made the State dependent, instead of being sovereign; these are questions, to which, as a Judge in this cause, I can neither know nor suggest the proper answers; though, as a citizen of the Union, I know, and am interested to know, that the most satisfactory answers can be given. As a citizen, I know the Government of that State to be republican;

and my short definition of such a Government is, one constructed on this principle, that the Supreme Power resides in the body of the people. As a Judge of this Court, I know, and can decide upon the knowledge, that the citizens of Georgia, when they acted upon the large scale of the Union, as a part of the 'People of the United States,' did not surrender the Supreme or Sovereign Power to that State; but, as to the purposes of the Union, retained it to themselves. As to the purposes of the Union, therefore, Georgia is NOT a sovereign State. If the Judicial decision of this case forms one of those purposes; the allegation, that Georgia is a sovereign State, is unsupported by the fact. Whether the judicial decision of this cause is, or is not, one of those purposes, is a question which will be examined particularly in a subsequent part of my argument.

There is a third sense, in which the term sovereign is frequently used, and which it is very material to trace and explain, as it furnishes a basis for what I presume to be one of the principal objections against the jurisdiction of this Court over the State of Georgia. In this sense, sovereignty is derived from a feudal source; and like many other parts of that system so degrading to man, still retains its influence over our sentiments and conduct, though the cause, by which that influence was produced, never extended to the American States. The accurate and well informed President Henault, in his excellent chronological abridgment of the History of France, tells us, that, about the end of the second race of Kings, a new kind of possession was acquired, under the name of Fief. The Governors of Cities and Provinces usurped equally the property of land, and the administration of justice; and established themselves as proprietary Seigniors over those places, in which they had been only civil magistrates or military officers. By this means, there was introduced into the State a new kind of authority, to which was assigned the appellation of sovereignty*. In process of time the feudal system was extended over France, and almost all the other nations of Europe: And every Kingdom became, in fact, a large fief. Into England this system was introduced by the conqueror: and to this era we may, probably, refer the English maxim, that the King or sovereign is the fountain of Justice. But, in the case of the King, the sovereignty had a double operation. While it vested him with jurisdiction over others, it excluded all others from jurisdiction over him. With regard to him, there was no superior power; and, consequently, on feudal principles, no right of jurisdiction. '*The law, says Sir William Blackstone, ascribes to the King the attribute of sovereignty: he is sovereign and independent within his own dominions; and owes no kind of objection to any other potentate upon earth. Hence it is, that no suit or action can be brought against the King, even in civil matters; because no Court can have jurisdiction over him: for all jurisdiction implies superiority of power.' This last position is only a branch of a much more extensive principle, on which a plan of systematic despotism has been lately formed in England, and prosecuted with unwearied assiduity and care. Of this plan the author of the Commentaries was, if not the introducer, at least the great supporter. He has been followed in it by writers later and less known; and his doctrines have, both on the other and this side of the Atlantic, been implicitly and generally received by those, who neither examined their principles nor their consequences, The principle is, that all human law must be prescribed by a superior. This principle I mean not now to examine. Suffice it, at present to say, that another principle, very different in its nature and operations, forms, in my judgment, the basis of sound and genuine jurisprudence; laws derived from the pure source of equality and justice must be founded on the CONSENT of those, whose obedience they require. The sovereign, when traced to his source, must be found in the man.

The next question under this head, is, Has the Constitution done so? Did those people mean to exercise this, their undoubted power? These questions may be resolved, either by fair and conclusive deductions, or by direct and explicit declarations. In order, ultimately, to discover, whether the people of the United States intended to bind those States by the Judicial power vested by the national Constitution, a previous enquiry will naturally be: Did those people intend to bind those states by the Legislative power vested by that Constitution? The articles of confederation, it is well known, did not operate upon individual citizens; but operated only upon states, This defect was remedied by the national Constitution, which, as all allow, has an operation on individual citizens. But if an opinion, which some seem to entertain, be just; the defect remedied, on one side, was balanced by a defect introduced on the other: For they seem to think, that the present Constitution operates only on individual citizens, and not on States. This opinion, however, appears to be altogether unfounded. When certain laws of the States are declared to be 'subject to the revision and controul of the Congress;'* it cannot, surely, be contended that the Legislative power of the national Government was meant to have no operation on the several States. The fact, uncontrovertibly established in one instance, proves the principle in all other instances, to which the facts will be found to apply. We may then infer, that the people of the United States intended to bind the several States, by the Legislative power of the national Government.

Opinion 3: Justice Jay

In determining the sense in which Georgia is a sovereign State, it may be useful to turn our attention to the political situation we were in, prior to the Revolution, and to the political rights which emerged from the Revolution. All the country now possessed by the United States was then a part of the dominions appertaining to the crown of Great Britain. Every acre of land in this country was then held mediately or immediately by grants from that crown. All the people of this country were then, subjects of the King of Great Britain, and owed allegiance to him; and all the civil authority then existing or exercised here, flowed from the head of the British Empire. They were in strict sense fellow subjects, and in a variety of respects one people. When the Revolution commenced, the patriots did not assert that only the same affinity and social connection subsisted between the people, of the colonies, which subsisted between the people of Gaul, Britain, and Spain, while Roman Provinces, viz. only that affinity and social connection which result from the mere circumstance of being governed by the same Prince; different ideas prevailed, and gave occasion to the Congress of 1774 and 1775.

The Revolution, or rather the Declaration of Independence, found the people already united for general purposes, and at the same time providing for their more domestic concerns by State conventions, and other temporary arrangements. From the crown of Great Britain, the sovereignty of their country passed to the people of it; and it was then not an uncommon opinion, that the unappropriated lands, which belonged to that crown, passed not to the people of the Colony or States within whose limits they were situated, but to the whole people; on whatever principles this opinion rested, it did not give way to the other, and thirteen sovereignties were considered as emerged from the principles of the Revolution, combined with local convenience and considerations; the people nevertheless continued to consider themselves, in a national point of view, as one people; and they continued without interruption to manage their national concerns accordingly; afterwards, in the hurry of the war, and in the warmth of mutual confidence, they made a confederation of the States, the basis of a general Government. Experience disappointed the expectations they had formed from it; and then the people, in their collective and national capacity, established the present Constitution. It is remarkable that in establishing it, the people exercised their own rights, and their own proper sovereignty, and conscious of the plenitude of it, they declared with becoming dignity, 'We the people of the United States, do ordain and establish this Constitution.' Here we see the people acting as sovereigns of the whole country; and in the language of sovereignty, establishing a Constitution by which it was their will, that the State Governments should be bound, and to which the State Constitutions should be made to conform. Every State Constitution is a compact made by and between the citizens of a State to govern themselves in a certain manner; and the Constitution of the United States is likewise a compact made by the people of the United States to govern themselves as to general objects, in a certain manner. By this great compact however, many prerogatives were transferred to the national Government, such as those of making war and peace, contracting alliances, coining money, etc. etc.

If then it be true, that the sovereignty of the nation is in the people of the nation, and the residuary sovereignty of each State in the people of each State, it may be useful to compare these sovereignties with those in Europe, that we may thence be enabled to judge, whether all the prerogatives which are allowed to the latter, are so essential to the former. There is reason to suspect that some of the difficulties which embarrass the present question, arise from inattention to differences which subsist between them.

It will be sufficient to observe briefly, that the sovereignties in Europe, and particularly in England, exist on feudal principles. That system considers the Prince as the sovereign, and the people as his subjects; it regards his person as the object of allegiance, and excludes the idea of his being on an equal footing with a subject, either in a Court of Justice or elsewhere. That system contemplates him as being the fountain of honor and authority; and from his grace and grant derives all franchises, immunities and privileges; it is easy to perceive that such a sovereign could not be amenable to a Court of Justice, or subjected to judicial controul and actual constraint. It was of necessity, therefore, that suability became incompatible with such sovereignty. Besides, the Prince having all the Executive powers, the judgment of the Courts would, in fact, be only monitory, not mandatory to him, and a capacity to be advised, is a distinct thing from a capacity to be sued. The same feudal ideas run through all their jurisprudence, and constantly remind us of the distinction between the Prince and the subject. No such ideas obtain here; at the Revolution, the sovereignty devolved on the people; and they are truly the sovereigns of the country, but they are sovereigns without subjects (unless the African slaves among us may be so called) and have none to govern but themselves; the citizens of America are equal as fellow citizens, and as joint tenants in the sovereignty.

From the differences existing between feudal sovereignties and Governments founded on compacts, it necessarily follows that their respective prerogatives must differ. Sovereignty is the right to govern; a nation or State-sovereign is the person or persons in whom that resides. In Europe the sovereignty is generally ascribed to the Prince; here it rests with the people; there, the sovereign actually administers the Government; here, never in a single instance; our Governors are the agents of the people, and at most stand in the same relation to their sovereign, in which regents in Europe stand to their sovereigns. Their Princes have personal powers, dignities, and pre-eminences, our rulers have none but official; nor do they partake in the sovereignty otherwise, or in any other capacity, than as private citizens.

You have just read three opinions by different justices of the court about the meaning of sovereignty less than 10 years following the **ratification of the US Constitution** and Congressional legislation of the **Federal Judiciary Act of 1789**. The **general semantic differences** of the justices reveal polyvocality. It is important to understand that these different interpretations lead to different consequences. As legal scholar, Robert Cover (1986, 1601) warned, "when interpreters have finished their work, the frequently leave behind victims whose lives have been torn apart by these organized, social practices of violence."

Polyvocality, Application and Legal Narratives: rights v. social control

You have now learned that many concepts have been taken for granted and unexamined. A close reading of legal cases reveals that judges have different normative universes that they draw from in order to make their decisions. These different approaches to norms come from their experiences, education, and linguistic environments. These differences are important because they have real-life consequences. Social theorist, Hannah Arendt (1973 279) argued the problem with human rights was that they are invoked at the precise moment, those rights of citizenship are stripped away, leaving one with "the abstract nakedness of being human and nothing but human." A framing of **rights-talk** and its critics is very important to understanding constitutional law. Social Movements scholar, Francesca Polletta (2000, 377) found that Southern civil rights organizers developed new understandings of the relations between rights and political representation. As they learned to assert their rights claims, they forged a political vision in contrast to that of mainstream civil right organizations as well as White segregationists. In other words, because rights are so ambiguous, they offer a way of contesting existing social orders.

On the other hand, critical legal studies scholars have argued that the indeterminacy of rights allows judicial decision makers to operate on the basis of idiosyncratic and ideological preferences and allows unmeritorious progressive interests to invoke legal rights with equal clout (Gabel 1984, 1566). In other words, the vague language of rights is left to judges to define. Some argue that this amount of **judicial discretion** is simply too much power.

These judges are more likely to frame all claims within the same logic of legal reasoning even when some claims are closer to reality than others. This means that some very serious rights abuses might not be taken seriously because there are so many rights claims that are being put forward to the courts. This tends to result in a balancing approach by judges where they try to balance one interest against the other.

Nowhere is this claim more accurate than in the justification for excluding members of the society based on the argument that cultural beliefs or national origin could pose a threat to national security. During World War II, the federal government, supported by the majority of voters, justified the internment of Japanese Americans in detention camps on the basis of a threat to national security. In reality, no Japanese Americans were prosecuted for espionage. Judges weighed the benefits of denying Japanese-Americans rights against the costs of potential acts of sabotage.

Many students are perplexed by this case because it goes against two unexamined assumptions. The first relates to the idea that the constitution provides for equal protection of the laws. This can be understood through the myth of rights: most people believe that the central legal authority will restore fairness to an unjust situation. They find it hard to accept that the central legal authority can be the institution that formalizes the social injustice. Further, there are textual examples that can be easily misunderstood or taken for granted in cases where balancing interested in based on the perception of threat to the social good.

The 15th Amendment, for example, includes, the right of citizens of the United States to vote shall not be denied or abridged by the United States or by any state on account of race, color, or previous condition of servitude. Students often overlook that this guarantee is tied to voting only. Second, students often mistake the principles stated in the opening phrases of the Declaration of Independence as constitutional legal commitments. Thus, "We hold these truths to be self-evident, that all men are created equal, that they are endowed by their Creator with certain unalienable Rights, that among these are Life, Liberty and the pursuit of Happiness," forms the basic foundation of most students belief in the rights myth.

Taken together these normative positions can be hard to confront when dealing with the rude reality. In *Korematsu v. United States*, the Supreme Court acknowledged they were not unmindful of the hardships imposed upon a large group of American citizens. On a purely textual level of analysis, you should now be able to analyze different interpretations of the spirit of the law in practice. There are those that read the words of the Constitution as providing a formal process of legal exclusion as a right of the federal government. On the other hand, there are those that see an unlawful abuse of power in practice. Both views are articulated in the case excerpt below.

KOREMATSU V. UNITED STATES (1944)

MR. JUSTICE BLACK delivered the opinion of the Court.

It should be noted, to begin with, that all legal restrictions which curtail the civil rights of a single racial group are immediately suspect. That is not to say that all such restrictions are unconstitutional. It is to say that courts must subject them to the most rigid scrutiny. Pressing public necessity may sometimes justify the existence of such restrictions; racial antagonism never can.

In the instant case prosecution of the petitioner was begun by information charging violation of an Act of Congress, of March 21, 1942, 56 Stat. 173, which provides that

> "... whoever shall enter, remain in, leave, or commit any act in any military area or military zone prescribed, under the authority of an Executive order of the President, by the Secretary of War, or by any military commander designated by the Secretary of War, contrary to the restrictions applicable to any such area or zone or contrary to the order of the Secretary of War or any such military commander, shall, if it appears that he knew or should have known of the existence and extent of the restrictions or order and that his act was in violation thereof, be guilty of a misdemeanor and upon conviction shall be liable to a fine of not to exceed $5,000 or to imprisonment for not more than one year, or both, for each offense."

Exclusion Order No. 34, which the petitioner knowingly and admittedly violated, was one of a number of military orders and proclamations, all of which were substantially based upon Executive Order No. 9066, 7 Fed. Reg. 1407. That order, issued after we were at war with Japan, declared that "the successful prosecution of the war requires every possible protection against espionage and against sabotage to national-defense material, national-defense premises, and national-defense utilities. ..."

U.S. Supreme Court, "Korematsu v. United States," 1944.

One of the series of orders and proclamations, a curfew order, which like the exclusion order here was promulgated pursuant to Executive Order 9066, subjected all persons of Japanese ancestry in prescribed West Coast military areas to remain in their residences from 8 p.m. to 6 a.m. As is the case with the exclusion order here, that prior curfew order was designed as a "protection against espionage and against sabotage." In *Hirabayashi* v. *United States*, 320 U.S. 81, we sustained a conviction obtained for violation of the curfew order. The Hirabayashi conviction and this one thus rest on the same 1942 Congressional Act and the same basic executive and military orders, all of which orders were aimed at the twin dangers of espionage and sabotage.

We uphold the exclusion order as of the time it was made and when the petitioner violated it. Cf. *Chastleton Corporation* v. *Sinclair*, 264 U.S. 543, 547; *Block* v. *Hirsh*, 256 U.S. 135, 154–5. In doing so, we are not unmindful of the hardships imposed by it upon a large group of American citizens. Cf. *Ex parte Kawato*, 317 U.S. 69, 73. But hardships are part of war, and war is an aggregation of hardships. All citizens alike, both in and out of uniform, feel the impact of war in greater or lesser measure. Citizenship has its responsibilities as well as its privileges, and in time of war the burden is always heavier. Compulsory exclusion of large groups of citizens from their homes, except under circumstances of direct emergency and peril, is inconsistent with our basic governmental institutions. But when under conditions of modern warfare our shores are threatened by hostile forces, the power to protect must be commensurate with the threatened danger.

It is said that we are dealing here with the case of imprisonment of a citizen in a concentration camp solely because of his ancestry, without evidence or inquiry concerning his loyalty and good disposition towards the United States. Our task would be simple, our duty clear, were this a case involving the imprisonment of a loyal citizen in a concentration camp because of racial prejudice. Regardless of the true nature of the assembly and relocation centers—and we deem it unjustifiable to call them concentration camps with all the ugly connotations that term implies—we are dealing specifically with nothing but an exclusion order. To cast this case into outlines of racial prejudice, without reference to the real military dangers which were presented, merely confuses the issue. Korematsu was not excluded from the Military Area because of hostility to him or his race. He *was* excluded because we are at war with the Japanese Empire, because the properly constituted military authorities feared an invasion of our West Coast and felt constrained to take proper security measures, because they decided that the military urgency of the situation demanded that all citizens of Japanese ancestry be segregated from the West Coast temporarily, and finally, because Congress, reposing its confidence in this time of war in our military leaders—as inevitably it must—determined that they should have the power to do just this. There was evidence of disloyalty on the part of some, the military authorities considered that the need for action was great, and time was short. We cannot—by availing ourselves of the calm perspective of hindsight—now say that at that time these actions were unjustified.

Legal Reasoning: Precedent and Ideology in Court Cases

Another key concept that students must learn to move past the threshold toward thinking like a lawyer or judge is **legal reasoning**. This tends to contradict many students' lived experience and once understood allows students to think differently about the legal, political, and social issues they hear about in the media and encounter in their daily lives. This involves the recognition that there is not one single answer and that the use of **judicial precedent** is required in order to use legal authority to support a position or to argue against it.

Precedent is an action or official decision that can be used as support for later actions or decisions, especially a decided case that furnishes a basis for determining later cases involving similar facts or issues (Garner 1996, 615).

This concept is extremely helpful in understanding the historical-structural power of the federal government to exclude members of society. Justice John Marshall articulated the power of the federal government to exclude American Indians from their ancestral lands as rooted in what is commonly referred to as the Doctrine of Discovery. Justice Marshall embraced this concept and made it a part of the law and judicial precedent in what are referred to at the trilogy cases by legal scholars. These cases include *Johnson v. McIntosh* (1823), *Cherokee Nation v. Georgia* (1831), and *Worcester v. Georgia* (1832).

Marshall defined the right for European men to take exclusive control of property as giving title to the government, acquired by discovery, by whose subjects, or by whose authority, it was made, against all other European governments, with title consummated by possession. A common saying, possession is 9/10 of the law is a remix of this idea. If one takes possession of a piece of property, they are presumed to be the superior claim holder. Marshall went on to explain that Native Americans were domestic, dependent nations, whose rights were diminished, and this framing of justified taking has been applied to legal concepts of **adverse possession** and **eminent domain** throughout history. This principle was also used to invade French lands in the South in the 18th century, Spanish and Native lands in the West in the 19th century, and continues to be used to take over land today for oil drilling, fracking, and water rights, to name a few examples. In ancient times, the motto *might makes right* would seem to be similar to this idea of fatherly strength or the duty to protect and thus there are references to Roman and Greek legal principles scattered throughout judicial opinions. It is important to remember that this interpretation builds upon a normative universe whereby the country is seen as the family and the government is seen as the protector of that family. Consider how the language supports this interpretation in the excerpt below.

JOHNSON V. MCINTOSH (1823)

Justice Marshall delivered the opinion of the Court,

On the part of the defendants, it was insisted, that the uniform understanding and practice of European nations, and the settled law, as laid down by the tribunals of civilized states, denied the right of the Indians to be considered as independent communities, having a permanent property in the soil, capable of alienation to private individuals. They remain in a state of nature, and have never been admitted into the general society of nations. All the treaties and negotiations between the civilized powers of Europe and of this continent, from the treaty of Utrecht, in 1713, to that of Ghent, in 1814, have uniformly disregarded their supposed right to the territory included within the jurisdictional limits of those powers. Not only has the practice of all civilized nations been in conformity with this doctrine, but the whole theory of their titles to lands in America, rests upon the hypothesis, that the Indians had no right of soil as sovereign, independent states. Discovery is the foundation of title, in European nations, and this overlooks all proprietary rights in the natives. The sovereignty and eminent domain thus acquired, necessarily precludes the idea of any other sovereignty existing within the same limits. The subjects of the discovering nation must necessarily be bound by the declared sense of their own government, as to the extent of this sovereignty, and the domain acquired with it. Even if it should be admitted that the Indians were originally an independent people, they have ceased to be so. A nation that has passed under the dominion of another, is no longer a sovereign state. The same treaties and negotiations, before referred to, show their dependent condition. Or, if it be admitted that they are now independent and

U.S. Supreme Court, "Johnson v. McIntosh," 1823.

foreign states, the title of the plaintiffs would still be invalid: as grantees from the *Indians*, they must take according to *their* laws of property, and as Indian subjects. The law of every dominion affects all persons and property situate within it; and the Indians never had any idea of individual property in lands. It cannot be said that the lands conveyed were disjoined from their dominion; because the grantees could not take the sovereignty and eminent domain to themselves.

Such, then, being the nature of the Indian title to lands, the extent of their right of alienation must depend upon the laws of the dominion under which they live. They are subject to the sovereignty of the United States. The subjection proceeds from their residence within our territory and jurisdiction. It is unnecessary to show, that they are not *citizens* in the ordinary sense of that term, since they are destitute of the most essential rights which belong to that character. They are of that class who are said by jurists not to be citizens, but perpetual inhabitants with diminutive rights. The statutes of Virginia, and of all the other colonies, and of the United States, treat them as an inferior race of people, without the privileges of citizens, and under the perpetual protection and pupilage of the government. The act of Virginia of 1662, forbade purchases from the Indians, and it does not appear that it was ever repealed. The act of 1779 is rather to be regarded as a declaratory act, founded upon what had always been regarded as the settled law. These statutes seem to define sufficiently the nature of the Indian title to lands; a mere right of usufruct and habitation, without power of alienation. By the law of nature, they had not acquired a fixed property capable of being transferred. The measure of property acquired by occupancy is determined, according to the law of nature, by the extent of men's wants, and their capacity of using it to supply them. It is a violation of the rights of others to exclude them from the use of what we do not want, and they have an occasion for. Upon this principle the North American Indians could have acquired no proprietary interest in the vast tracts of territory which they wandered over; and their right to the lands on which they hunted, could not be considered as superior to that which is acquired to the sea by fishing in it. The use in the one case, as well as the other, is not exclusive. According to every theory of property, the Indians had no individual rights to land; nor had they any collectively, or in their national capacity; for the lands occupied by each tribe were not used by them in such a manner as to prevent their being appropriated by a people of cultivators. All the proprietary rights of civilized nations on this continent are founded on this principle. The right derived from discovery and conquest, can rest on no other basis; and all existing titles depend on the fundamental title of the crown by discovery. The title of the crown (as representing the nation) passed to the colonists by charters, which were absolute grants of the soil; and it was a first principle in colonial law, that all titles must be derived from the crown. It is true that, in some cases, purchases were made by the colonies from the Indians; but this was merely a measure of policy to prevent hostilities; and William Penn's purchase, which was the most remarkable transaction of this kind, was not deemed to add to the strength of his title In most of the colonies, the doctrine was received, that all titles to land must be derived exclusively from the crown, upon the principle that the settlers carried with them, not only all the rights, but all the duties of Englishmen; and particularly the laws of property, so far as they are suitable to their new condition In New-England alone, some lands have been held under Indian deeds. But this was an anomaly arising from peculiar local and political causes.

As the right of society, to prescribe those rules by which property may be acquired and preserved is not, and cannot be drawn into question; as the title to lands, especially, is and must be admitted to depend entirely on the law of the nation in which they lie; it will be necessary, in pursuing this inquiry, to examine, not singly those principles of abstract justice, which the Creator of all things has impressed on the mind of his creature man, and which are admitted to regulate, in a great degree, the rights of civilized nations, whose perfect independence is acknowledged; but those principles also which our own government has adopted in the particular case, and given us as the rule for our decision.

On the discovery of this immense continent, the great nations of Europe were eager to appropriate to themselves so much of it as they could respectively acquire. Its vast extent offered an ample field to the ambition and enterprise of all; and the character and religion of its inhabitants afforded an apology for considering them as a people over whom the superior genius of Europe might claim an ascendency. The potentates of the old world found no difficulty in convincing themselves that they made ample compensation to the inhabitants of the new, by bestowing on them civilization and Christianity, in exchange for unlimited independence. But, as they were all in pursuit of nearly the same object, it was necessary, in order to avoid conflicting settlements, and consequent war with each other, to establish a principle, which all should acknowledge as the law by which the right of acquisition, which they all asserted, should be regulated as between themselves. This principle was, that discovery gave title to the government by whose subjects, or by whose authority, it was made, against all other European governments, which title might be consummated by possession.

The exclusion of all other Europeans, necessarily gave to the nation making the discovery the sole right of acquiring the soil from the natives, and establishing settlements upon it. It was a right with which no Europeans could interfere. It was a right which all asserted for themselves, and to the assertion of which, by others, all assented.

Those relations which were to exist between the discoverer and the natives, were to be regulated by themselves. The rights thus acquired being exclusive, no other power could interpose between them.

In the establishment of these relations, the rights of the original inhabitants were, in no instance, entirely disregarded; but were necessarily, to a considerable extent, impaired. They were admitted to be the rightful occupants of the soil, with a legal as well as just claim to retain possession of it, and to use it according to their own discretion; but their rights to complete sovereignty, as independent nations, were necessarily diminished, and their power to dispose of the soil at their own will, to whomsoever they pleased, was denied by the original fundamental principle, that discovery gave exclusive title to those who made it.

While the different nations of Europe respected the right of the natives, as occupants, they asserted the ultimate dominion to be in themselves; and claimed and exercised, as a consequence of this ultimate dominion, a power to grant the soil, while yet in possession of the natives. These grants have been understood by all, to convey a title to the grantees, subject only to the Indian right of occupancy.

The history of America, from its discovery to the present day, proves, we think, the universal recognition of these principles.

We will not enter into the controversy, whether agriculturists, merchants, and manufacturers, have a right, on abstract principles, to expel hunters from the territory they possess, or to contract their limits. Conquest gives a title which the Courts of the conqueror cannot deny, whatever the private and speculative opinions of individuals may be, respecting the original justice of the claim which has been successfully asserted. The British government, which was then our government, and whose rights have passed to the United States, asserted title to all the lands occupied by Indians, within the chartered limits of the British colonies. It asserted also a limited sovereignty over them, and the exclusive right of extinguishing the title which occupancy gave to them. These claims have been maintained and established as far west as the river Mississippi, by the sword. The title to a vast portion of the lands we now hold, originates in them. It is not for the Courts of this country to question the validity of this title, or to sustain one which is incompatible with it.

Although we do not mean to engage in the defense of those principles which Europeans have applied to Indian title, they may, we think, find some excuse, if not justification, in the character and habits of the people whose rights have been wrested from them.

The title by conquest is acquired and maintained by force. The conqueror pre-scribes its limits. Humanity, however, acting on public opinion, has established, as a general rule, that the conquered shall not be wantonly oppressed, and that their condition shall remain as eligible as is compatible with the objects of the conquest. Most usually, they are incorporated with the victorious nation, and become subjects or citizens of the government with which they are connected. The new and old members of the society mingle with each other; the distinction between them is gradually lost, and they make one people. Where this incorpora-tion is practicable, humanity demands, and a wise policy requires, that the rights of the conquered to property should remain unimpaired; that the new subjects should be governed as equitably as the old, and that confidence in their security should gradually banish the painful sense of being separated from their ancient connections, and united by force to strangers.

When the conquest is complete, and the conquered inhabitants can be blended with the conquerors, or safely governed as a distinct people, public opinion, which not even the conqueror can disregard, imposes these restraints upon him; and he cannot neglect them without injury to his fame, and hazard to his power.

But the tribes of Indians inhabiting this country were fierce savages, whose occupation was war, and whose subsistence was drawn chiefly from the forest. To leave them in possession of their country, was to leave the country a wilderness; to govern them as a distinct people, was impossible, because they were as brave and as high spirited as they were fierce, and were ready to repel by arms every attempt on their independence.

What was the inevitable consequence of this state of things? The Europeans were under the necessity either of abandoning the country, and relinquishing their pompous claims to it, or of enforcing those claims by the sword, and by the adoption of principles adapted to the condition of a people with whom it was impossible to mix, and who could not be governed as a distinct society, or of remaining in their neighborhood, and exposing themselves and their families to the perpetual hazard of being massacred.

If the discovery be made, and possession of the country be taken, under the authority of an existing government, which is acknowledged by the emigrants, it is supposed to be equally well settled, that the discovery is made for the whole nation, that the country becomes a part of the nation, and that the vacant soil is to be disposed of by that organ of the government which has the constitutional power to dispose of the national domains, by that organ in which all vacant territory is vested by law.

Roxanne Dunbar-Ortiz argued it is a troubling reality that most citizens of the United States have never heard of the doctrine of discovery, although it is honored annually on Columbus Day (Dunbar-Ortiz 2021, 32). It is troubling but not surprising when we consider how the hegemonic narrative of the myth of rights and the myth of individual responsibility coexist in the collective common sense. As a student you must challenge these unexamined assumptions and to recognize that judicial precedent has worked to rationalize colonial domination over indigenous peoples throughout history and to this day. Constitutional interpretation relies on precedent to legitimize both the doctrine of discovery and the right of judges to craft the common law citing to the Marshall court precedent as recently as 2005 in the US Supreme Court. This new knowledge of precedent and legal reasoning contrasts starkly to the myth of rights as a fair process held by most people before they study law more closely.

More recently, we have seen this power of social exclusion being extended from the legislature and courts to the executive through **Presidential executive order**. The Supreme Court held that the president had lawfully exercised the broad discretion granted to him under 8 U.S.C. §1182(f) to suspend the entry of aliens into the United States. While the political controversy debated through news media has largely subsided, the judicial precedent persists through case law. This power was never mentioned or granted in the Constitution and so once again judicial interpretation has produced dramatic consequences that affect life and death for many vulnerable populations.

TRUMP V. HAWAII (2018)

Chief Justice Roberts delivered the opinion of the Court

For more than a century, this Court has recognized that the admission and exclusion of foreign nationals is a "fundamental sovereign attribute exercised by the Government's political departments largely immune from judicial control." *Fiallo* v. *Bell*, 430 U. S. 787, 792 (1977); see *Harisiades* v. *Shaughnessy*, 342 U. S. 580, 588–589 (1952) ("[A]ny policy toward aliens is vitally and intricately interwoven with contemporaneous policies in regard to the conduct of foreign relations [and] the war power."). Because decisions in these matters may implicate "relations with foreign powers," or involve "classifications defined in the light of changing political and economic circumstances," such judgments "are frequently of a character more appropriate to either the Legislature or the Executive." *Mathews* v. *Diaz*, 426 U. S. 67, 81 (1976).

Nonetheless, although foreign nationals seeking admission have no constitutional right to entry, this Court has engaged in a circumscribed judicial inquiry when the denial of a visa allegedly burdens the constitutional rights of a U. S. citizen. In *Kleindienst* v. *Mandel*, the Attorney General denied admission to a Belgian journalist and self-described "revolutionary Marxist," Ernest Mandel, who had been invited to speak at a conference at Stanford University. 408 U. S., at 756–757. The professors who wished to hear Mandel speak challenged that decision under the First Amendment, and we acknowledged that their constitutional "right to receive information" was implicated. *Id.*, at 764–765. But we limited our review to whether the Executive gave a "facially legitimate and bona fide" reason for its action. *Id.*, at 769. Given the authority of the political branches over admission, we held that "when the Executive exercises this [delegated] power negatively on the basis of a facially legitimate and bona fide reason, the courts will neither look behind the exercise of that discretion, nor test it by balancing its justification" against the asserted constitutional interests of U. S. citizens. *Id.*, at 770.

The upshot of our cases in this context is clear: "Any rule of constitutional law that would inhibit the flexibility" of the President "to respond to changing world conditions should be adopted only with the greatest caution," and our inquiry into matters of entry and national security is highly constrained. *Mathews*, 426 U. S., at 81–82. We need not define the precise contours of that inquiry in this case. A conventional application of *Mandel*, asking only whether the policy is facially legitimate and bona fide, would put an end to our review. But the Government has suggested that it may be appropriate here for the inquiry to extend beyond the facial neutrality of the order. See Tr. of Oral Arg. 16–17, 25–27 (describing *Mandel* as "the starting point" of the analysis). For our purposes today, we assume that we may look behind the face of the Proclamation to the extent of applying rational basis review. That standard of review considers whether the entry policy is plausibly related to the Government's stated objective to protect the country and improve vetting processes. See *Railroad Retirement Bd. v. Fritz*, 449 U. S. 166, 179 (1980). As a result, we may consider plaintiffs' extrinsic evidence, but will uphold the policy so long as it can reasonably be understood to result from a justification independent of unconstitutional grounds.

Finally, the dissent invokes *Korematsu* v. *United States*, 323 U. S. 214 (1944). Whatever rhetorical advantage the dissent may see in doing so, *Korematsu* has nothing to do with this case. The forcible relocation of U. S. citizens to concentration camps, solely and explicitly on the basis of race, is objectively unlawful and outside the scope of Presidential authority. But it is wholly inapt to liken that morally repugnant order to a facially neutral policy denying certain foreign nationals the privilege of admission. [...] The entry suspension is an act that is well within executive authority and could have been taken by any other President—the only question is evaluating the actions of this particular President in promulgating an otherwise valid Proclamation.

The dissent's reference to *Korematsu*, however, affords this Court the opportunity to make express what is already obvious: *Korematsu* was gravely wrong the day it was decided, has been overruled in the court of history, and—to be clear "has no place in law under the Constitution." 323 U. S., at 248 (Jackson, J., dissenting).

Under these circumstances, the Government has set forth a sufficient national security justification to survive rational basis review. We express no view on the soundness of the policy. We simply hold today that plaintiffs have not demonstrated a likelihood of success on the merits of their constitutional claim.

While the Supreme Court decision did not surprise many legal experts, it did awaken the consciousness of many everyday people who joined activists in protest. From organized political groups like the American Civil Liberties Union to the Council on American–Islamic Relations a broad network of lawyers, faith-based organizers, and social workers were employed to deal with the dramatic fall out after the decision. Images of lawyers and activists crowded in airports spread across social media and news reports for weeks. In the final section of this introduction, you will learn how social groups respond to the unequal power revealed through formal legal processes.

Toward Legal Mobilization and Rights Consciousness: Injustice

As discussed above, immigration lawyers and advocates organized in response to the unjust action of the government to bring a legal case to try to right a wrong they claimed had been done to them. Sociolegal scholars refer to this awakening as **rights consciousness** and **legal mobilization**. Fundamental to an understanding of rights consciousness in action involves **structural analysis**: to the extent that individual personhood is subsumed within other social relationships, there is a possibility that these relationships are unequal and maintain existing social hierarchies (Chua and Engel 2019, 348). Awareness of unequal power relationships does not always produce mobilization, but it sometimes does. In addition to the civil rights activists mentioned previously, workers have often organized together in ways that move beyond individual rights toward collective protections in labor and equal pay movements. Michael McCann (1994, 261) found that organizers used litigation not only to mobilize women workers but also to pressure employers to negotiate contracts under the threat that judges might impose a new wage structure. Even though the courts were unreliable allies the strategies also included naming harms publicly and shaming wrong doers in the public media. In other words, there are additional reasons for mobilizing beyond rights consciousness alone. There are also material changes that can come about through the process of mobilization including negotiations for fair pay, better work conditions, or greater representation in private businesses and public offices.

In the excerpt that follows McCann provides an analytical framework for when and how such collective action forms in response to unequal power relationships and injustice.

2013 LSA Presidential Address

THE UNBEARABLE LIGHTNESS OF RIGHTS: ON SOCIOLEGAL INQUIRY IN THE GLOBAL ERA

Michael McCann

Paradox no. 1: What Rights Claims Count?

The first paradox regards the range of possibilities for meaningful claims facilitated by rights talk. In short, how light or heavy is rights as discourse? On the one hand, rights talk is very light in that language is indeterminate, malleable, variable, and polyvalent (Brigham 1996; Glendon 1993; Haskell 1988; McCann 1994; Milner 1989; Minow 1987; Scheingold 1974). Especially important in this regard is the recognition that rights language is not discrete and insular, but rather rights talk as a practice is inextricably interrelated with, contingent on, and transformable by contact with other discursive resources and normative traditions. And it is this contingency and interactive quality that makes rights dynamic, ever open to reconstruction as a discursive resource of aspiration.

This is, for example, the clear implication of Robert Cover's provocative thesis about *jurisgenesis*, about the persistent proliferation of claims about justice and rights that percolate up from communities and movements in civil society (Cover 1983). A key point of much sociolegal scholarship thus has been to demonstrate that such jurisgenetic proliferation of rights routinely emanates out of ordinary social life, often independent of direct influence from lawyers, judges, and state officials. This insight has been demonstrated repeatedly in research on everyday disputing among individuals (Zemans 1983). Perhaps no study has illustrated the dynamism and diversity in rights discourse as well as the recent book by my colleague George Lovell (2012). His research documents hundreds of letters by ordinary Americans to the new Civil Rights Division in the 1939–1941 period. The letters reveal an extraordinary range of rights claims and discourses, often merging moral, religious, and local norms into constructions of rights entitlement. Lovell documents how inherently light, volatile, and malleable rights talk can be. Scholarship on group mobilization around rights likewise has documented the ways that "novel rights claims," as Francesca Polletta (2000) labels them, frequently emerge from and animate social movements.

The lightness that permits such novelty to claimants also arguably signals a lack of weight as social power, however. Ronald Dworkin's (1978) famous claim that rights often "trump" other types of claims and values thus deserves qualification because rights in practice are far more limited in their inherent influence. After all, specific claims of rights are often met with opposing interpretations of that same right. Consider the long-standing, highly variable contests over the reach of freedom secured by property rights, or free speech rights, or rights against workplace discrimination. Moreover, claims of particular rights are often limited by claims of other rights, as when business owners claim property rights to hire whom they please as a limit on affirmative action for racial minorities or women. Finally, rights claims generally are often challenged by other social values, including democratic rule of the sovereign people, economic efficiency, or religious beliefs (Goldberg-Hiller 2004). In short, rights are never absolutes; rather, they simply confer authority to claims of entitlement whose restriction, modification, or denial is potentially subject to official legal procedures that assess and adjudicate the merits of competing claims (Stone 2010: 35).

And, hence, we shift toward the other hand of the analytical legacy. In short, the historical process of accumulated official actions legislating or adjudicating rights and their principled logics imposes weighty constraints on new rights claims. As historical contests over rights become settled for periods of time, dominant groups and their official representatives routinely police the boundaries of prevailing rights constructions to sustain status quo relationships, limiting the possibilities of practical rights claiming to the terms of what is legally permissible. And it is this enforced, institutionally embedded "common sense" of rights discourse that works, as John Brigham (1996) has put it, to "constitute citizen interests" and identities in routine ways. Rights become embedded in bounded, normalized discursive practices.[1]

This insight is central to much sociolegal scholarship. For example, Scheingold's myth of rights is not just a "figment of our imagination," but, as he says on his opening page of *The Politics of Rights,* it is "real" and material, enforced by dominant groups and institutions (1974: 3). A similar understanding is expressed in Robert Cover's (1983, 1986) argument that judges "kill" off far more than affirm visions of rights that bubble up from below, and that coordinated state "violence" necessarily enforces these narrow, select, traditionally bound constructions of rights on subjects. Law is words, but what makes words into law is the jurispathic violence that narrows the range of acceptable appropriations of rights talk in institutional practice and then systematically obscures or "forgets" the legal violence to both novel ideas and vulnerable bodies in the name of those circumscribed official norms. Cover's concepts of jurisgenesis and jurispathy together capture the interrelated lightness and heaviness of rights as convention.

Of course, judges are neither independent actors nor even primary sources of these constraints on meaningful, actionable rights constructions (McCann & Lovell, 2014). The webs of instrumental, institutional, and ideological power that delimit rights and contestation over rights are complex, diffuse, and interdependent. For one thing, other, nonjudicial state actors kill off rights claims in similar fashion. Lovell's (2012) aforementioned study is entitled *This Is Not Civil Rights,* because this is precisely what most administrative officials declared in denying appeals to rights by citizens in the pre-civil rights era. Equally important, organized social groups, including especially corporate actors, effectively neutralize many novel rights claims. In contests over basic rights, copious studies document, the "haves" usually "come out ahead" (Galanter 1974), or at least prevail until circumstances force or permit concessions to specific claims (Bell 1980). Scholars who focus on rights "counter mobilization" (Dudas 2005; Milner & Goldberg-Hiller 2003; Scheingold 1974) in particular have demonstrated how dominant groups stigmatize rights claims by

---

[1] On the implications of emphasizing rights as talk versus as a regulatory discourse, see McClure (1995).

marginalized groups—African-Americans, indigenous peoples, women, LGBT advocates, among others—as "special rights" that violate the principle of equal treatment or are otherwise rejected as alien to prevailing standards and values.[2]

Understood this way, rights constructions ensure order less because they dupe or brainwash ordinary people than because they are harnessed to constellations of group power, institutional arrangements, and state force supporting traditional constructions of rights that are difficult or costly for most people, and especially subaltern or disadvantaged groups, to challenge and change. And such practical understandings of ordinary persons about the difficulties or costs of challenging the status quo order then often ossify into resignation and routine. As Scheingold put it, "we learn to adapt—to endure … and to despair" as we yield to the perception that "the existing order is inevitable" (1974: 132). The status quo is inevitable less because most people, and especially those who are marginalized or oppressed, cannot imagine an alternative order than because they cannot perceive realistic ways to realize those alternatives without risking great loss, perhaps even death. Again, rights are light as talk, but they are often weighty as institutionalized cultural practices.

Paradox no. 2: The Contradictory Promise of Individual Freedom

One specific implication of the previous paradox is that, while basic, widely recognized rights long have been associated with the promise of freedom, that freedom is highly limited and limiting (Rose 1999). Indeed, more than a few sociolegal scholars have contended that the rhetoric of rights-based freedom in practice works as a weighty ideological force, not unlike what Kundera calls *kitsch* in the novel, that supports, legitimates, and authorizes deference to status quo hierarchies of wealth and influence. After all, the core rights enforced by dominant groups in the Western legal tradition have secured property, contracts, and other aggregations of unequal "private" power while individualizing subjects in ways that impede collective challenge to hierarchy in public life (McCann 1984, 1989). The entire apparatus of law, however liberal in pretense, supports a highly unequal social order, which makes some rights bearers far more free than the great many others. This logic was brilliantly outlined by the great German philosopher, who identified citizen rights as

---

[2] For a particularly dark story about how dominant groups crushed workers claiming their rights in one episode, see Brisbin (2002).

a "political lion's skin," an empty, abstract promise that held little power for emancipation from alienated, hierarchical market relations (Marx 1978; see Brown 1995; Goluboff 2007).

Moreover, classic liberal and neoliberal rights define mostly procedural rights that place selective limitations on arbitrary violence by discrete actors but do not limit routinized systemic violence—financial penalties, incarceration, solitary confinement, and the like[3]—and require few positive mandates for social equality and redistribution of power.[4] The latter point was nicely captured in Nancy MacLean's (2006) book on struggles for substantive rights against workplace discrimination; in short, the negative rights-based logic of individual *Freedom Is Not Enough* to redress centuries of exclusion and exploitation of African-Americans, Native Americans, Mexican-Americans, women, and other groups. In this perspective, rights discourse is a limited, arguably illusory promise of individualistic freedom that normalizes and naturalizes the historically evolved status quo enforced by the legal and political establishment.

Stuart Scheingold's (1974) classic argument about the "myth of rights" as an individualizing ideology that binds us to the status quo of inegalitarian liberal society owes much to this vision. Scholars following Foucault have recognized in different but complementary terms how the conferral of rights status works as a regulatory discourse that constructs disciplined subjects who internalize imperatives of rational self-governance. Rights and freedom again go hand in hand in this account, and they together often do provide nonconformists and

---

[3] One set of important examples include the due process rights revolution of the 1960s, which increased procedural restrictions on arbitrary police action but ended up empowering and legitimating police action and punishment in the mass incarceration state. See Murakawa and Beckett (2010). The Supreme Court's jurisprudence on capital punishment is a related example. The high court has ruled repeatedly on procedural questions reducing juror discretion in capital cases and involving the technologies of execution, but the Court has refused to consider seriously challenges to state killing as substantive manifestations of "cruel and unusual punishment" (Dayan 2011; McCann & Johnson 2009).

[4] For example, U.S. courts protect a women's right to choose abortion but do not mandate state funding to make that right available for all women. The SCOTUS likewise refused to recognize a substantive right to welfare subsidy or minimum income as a matter of due process or "new property" (McCann 1984). Or consider the individualistic terms of antidiscrimination rights that U.S. courts have supported while virtually abolishing remedies for claims of unequal impact of employer hiring, promotion, and wage policies (McCann 1994; McCann & Lovell, 2014).

even dissidents limited protections from compelled obedience to arbitrary power and violence. Rights do cut multiple ways. But, overall, the "power of freedom" (Rose 1999) that rights confer imposes a substantial burden of socially defined individual responsibility, a relentless weight that constructs subjects tethered to predetermined tracks of privatized deference to hierarchy. "While rights may operate as an indisputable force of emancipation at one moment in history," Wendy Brown (1995) has argued in an influential essay, "they may become at another time a regulatory discourse—a means of obstructing or co-opting more radical demands or simply the most hollow of empty promises."[5]

Kristin Bumiller's classic study of the dilemmas faced by minority citizens and women who experience injury well illustrates these dynamics. Her interviews reveal how claiming rights against race or sex discrimination individualizes the subject as a victim, discourages agency, and increases the sense of injury. "Individualization becomes a process of control—a mark of difference or a badge of stigma" (1990: 69; see also Brown 1995). David Engel's (1984) well-known study of Sander County shows convincingly how the pervasively enforced norm of "individual responsibility" discouraged adversarial rights claiming and enforced deference to community norms; respect for rights-bearing individuals ironically is won and sustained by forfeiting adversarial claims of rights. A book-length study that I conducted with William Haltom (2004) regarding the nationwide obsession with excessive rights claiming over personal injuries offered evidence that the same "common sense" ethic of individual responsibility was normalized through a complex mix of corporate advocacy and mass media practices. And John Gilliom (2001) likewise demonstrates how intensive state institutional surveillance forces welfare mothers to maintain, often by deception, appearances of morally "responsible," disciplined behavior to obtain the meager state support to

---

[5] Brown continues: "The paradox is ... expressed well *in* the irony that rights sought by politically defined *group* are conferred on depoliticized *individuals*: at the moment a particular 'we' succeeds in obtaining rights, it loses its we-ness and dissolves into individuals ... When does identity articulated through rights become production and regulation of identity through law and bureaucracy" (1995: 87). Kirstie McClure offers a different interpretation of Foucault that grants greater possibilities for "taking liberties" with rights (1995). Patricia Williams similarly recognizes how individualized subjects are at once both subjects of rights and agents who can reconstruct rights for struggle and change in prevailing relations (1992: 227). On the complex indeterminacy of rights "subjectivity," see Merry (2003).

which women are rightfully entitled.[6] In all these ways, the freedom conferred by basic rights is directly a product of complex regulatory mechanisms of responsibilization that weigh heavily on subjects.

Paradox no. 3: Who Can Claim Rights?

Rights not only confer a limited, paradoxical promise of freedom to citizens, but they are grounded in criteria that dominant groups use to justify exclusion of many persons and other entities from even this mixed promise of entitlement. This may seem counterintuitive, as rights are often hailed as a force of inclusive membership entitlement in the polity, and historically there is an element of truth to this claim. However, at every point in North American history, the standard of rights qualification also has been deployed as a normative force denying many people from even basic recognition and status as full citizens, i.e., as deserving the core "right to claim rights." It is relevant to recognize that Western nation states originally constructed rights as part of a bargain for ruling authority with dominant social groups. Specifically, as Charles Tilly (1985, 1992) has contended, modern nation states initially consolidated their power to make war, reduce or eliminate rivals, and extract resources by making deals with some established or potential rival groups. In developing capitalist regimes, states offered protections for bourgeois property rights to owning classes in return for the latter's support as clients of state rulers, revenue contribution through taxation (and plunder of others), and participation in policing for security. In the United States, the initial group extended recognition as rights bearers were white, property-owning males who contracted as subjects in the new political economy. The historical social contract securing rights status for citizens thus was exclusionary on the basis of race and gender, among other criteria, at its very core (Lovell & McCann 2004; Mills 2008; Pateman 1988).

These dominant groups who allied with the state became both the key actors and the normalized, unquestioned standard adjudicating entry for other groups seeking inclusion in the community of rights bearers over time.[7] The previously discussed premise that rights-bearing subjects must be disciplined, rational, and conventional to deserve rights has provided a justifying, even motivating logic

---

[6] In short, welfare mothers are "forced to be free." The responsibilizing rights paradigm that dominates American society advances "a hyper-individualistic image of social life that is both inaccurate and destructive," Gilliom (2001: 8) argues.

[7] It is tempting to label this historical baseline for rights qualification as the "unbearable whiteness of being" in America. See Mills (2008); Haney Lopez (1996).

for denying rights to select categories of people because they are allegedly incapable of, or resistant to, demonstrating such responsible self-governance. The liberal society of rights-bearing subjects thus did not abolish status and tribal distinctions; rather, the new order transformed status into individual terms of merit and character that have sustained hierarchies of lawful power and authority distinguishing *between* relative insiders and outsiders as well as *among* insiders to the community (Shklar 1989; Smith 1997; Stychin 1998). Dominant groups in North America—for several generations, white, mostly propertied males—interpreted those terms of discipline in different and often shifting ways over time, constructing ideas about race, ethnicity, gender, sexuality, family, education, and a host of other markers to determine the boundaries between deserving subjects entitled to rights and undeserving outsiders accorded few or no rights.[8]

This key point was well recognized by Dr. Martin Luther King, in his famous "Letter from a Birmingham Jail." King wrote that "We hold these truths to be self-evident, that all men are endowed by their creator with inalienable rights. That's a beautiful creed." As such, King celebrated rights, our creed, as an aspirational concept. Indeed, King appropriated rights claims to challenge not just the many manifestations of racial apartheid in the United States, but also the poverty and the deprivations it imposes on many. But it is vital to read what he said next: "America has never lived up to it" (King 1964). In short, his wise words suggest that it is not the language of rights so much as the larger institutional and ideological structures of exclusionary power and privilege, of "America," that most constrain who is respected as rights-bearing subjects and what rights structure our social lives. Again, recognition as a deserving rights-bearing subject requires the construction of subjectivities that fit, confirm, serve, and sustain dominant social relationships. And hence the history of struggles by various groups—indigenous peoples, people of color, women, immigrants, people with disabilities, LGBT persons, and other groups—to demand recognition of qualities ostensibly that match the baseline of rational, disciplined subjects.

Much historical sociolegal scholarship has documented these struggles over who can claim basic rights as well as the substantive reach of those rights. Sociolegal scholars have also interrogated the plight of those who intrinsically remain qualified for only limited rights status, like undocumented immigrants

---

[8] As Foucault (1978) and Agamben (1998) have alerted us, the flip side of the "biopolitics" that regulate deserving, rights-bearing citizens in the name of health and welfare is deprivation for those rightsless persons left to their own devices to sustain "mere life."

or children or the mentally ill, or from whom rights have been withdrawn, such as criminals and political subversives.[9] For these beings, failure to live up to the responsibilizing demands of freedom, as defined by dominant groups, threatens to doom subjects to forfeiture of rights and subjection to harsh forms of paternalistic control, repressively punitive law by the criminal justice system, or what Biehl (2005) calls "social abandonment" (see also Cover 1986).

But perhaps the most unique contribution of sociolegal scholarship has been in exploring the many ways that people who are formally recognized as deserving rights as citizens remain relatively rightsless in varying degrees in many spaces or dimensions of modern social life. Long-standing prejudices, assumptions, and stigmas about undeserving, untrustworthy character or lack of merit continue to disqualify or reduce the respect and freedom that rights are assumed to confer broadly. Again, studies demonstrating the gap between the promise and fulfillment of rights led the way, followed by many scores of studies exploring variations in rights consciousness, rights claiming, and the ways that rights do or do not matter in widely varying ways for differently situated and socially constructed subjects. Sociolegal studies of local community hostility toward "outsiders" in Engel's (1984) narrative, of poor welfare mothers (Gilliom 2001), of contemporary Native Americans resentfully relegated to un-American status (Dudas 2005), of disabled and mentally ill persons (Engel & Munger 2003; Failer 2001), of abused women who fail to qualify as "good victims" (Merry 2003), of people designated as "fat" (Kirkland 2008), and of many more subjects demonstrate this point about the exclusionary workings of rights in practice. All in all, rights remain unbearably light as sources of justice because many members of dominant groups in and beyond the state find that granting full respect to others as equals often is simply unbearable.

Paradox no. 4. Rights as a Potential Resource for Social Justice

The hope that rights can advance social justice and inclusive recognition returns us to the first paradox—that the inherent lightness of rights as talk has invited

---

[9] Of course, the walls of rights exclusion facilitated by the prevailing subject-centered conception of rights are even higher, when one considers nonhuman animals (Silverstein 1996; Rasmussen 2011–2012), natural resources (Stone 2010) and the like. A fascinating exploration of questions about who qualifies for rights is featured in the *Star Trek: Second Generation* episode, "The Measure of a Man," inspired by an essay by Martin Luther King. See Carter and McCann (2012).

one of the most persistent critiques of rights. In short, if rights are so light and supple, they must also mean very little and carry little weight as a challenge to the status quo; they are merely the superficial "um" and "ah" of social and political banter, mere talk rather than action with sufficient material consequence to compel respect. Such was the gist of Jeremy Bentham's challenge that human rights is "nonsense on stilts," of many critical legal theorists' challenges about indeterminacy of rights, and of some positivist empirical scholars assertions that rights are "just words" (Bartholomew & Hunt 1990; Horwitz 1988; McCann & Scheingold 2014; Rosenberg 1991; Tushnet 1984; Waldron 1987).

But rights, sometimes, can gain weight as a resource for egalitarian challenge and transformation when they animate organized collective challenge by exploited, excluded, needy, or righteous persons. This is the central point we came to identify with what Scheingold (1974) called the "politics of rights." At least two endeavors are necessary to add weight to rights claims that contest prevailing arrangements and open up possibilities for social justice to individuals and groups. The first of these has to do with constructions of rights themselves. Sometimes, of course, injustice follows from failure of settled rights to govern social practice, so struggles are simply aimed at reconciling promise and practice. But, quite often, rights must be reconstructed to fit new situations, aspirations, or claimants, and often joined to transformational visions of justice. In this regard, the polyvocality and indeterminacy of rights as (light) language can pose a "potential problem for, rather than a necessary product of, sovereignty" and regulatory discipline (McClure 1995: 164). In contexts where liberal rights talk is a dominant discourse, this reconstruction often entails turning some elements of rights, those offering a modest democratic and inclusionary nod to equality for all, against other elements, especially those more market-oriented, proprietarian elements protecting private power and social hierarchy as well as limits on state action.

This is the argument of Wendy Brown about the potential of rights as a limited but essential moderating force on unequal power in the neoliberal age (2003). It is important, though, that Brown further contends that liberal norms of equal respect alone do not go far enough, so they must be supplemented by ideas and values—such as care, fairness, mercy, or social justice—beyond liberalism to make rights serve more democratic ends.[10] Critical race scholar Patricia Williams (1992),

---

[10] Martin Luther King, Jr. agreed that empowerment required looking beyond liberal rights: "... the black revolution is much more than a struggle for the rights of Negroes. It is forcing America to face all its interrelated flaws—racism, poverty, militarism, and materialism ... It reveals systemic

in one of my favorite texts, imagines the challenge differently—as a process of alchemy, where the liberal principle of equal respect for interdependence actually can transform the proprietarian tradition of rights:

> The task ... , then, is not to discard rights but to see through or past them so ... that property regains its ancient connotation of being a reflection of the universal self. The task is to expand private property rights into a conception of civil rights, into the right to expect civility from other ... Society must give them away ... Give to all of society's objects and untouchables rights of privacy, integrity, and self assertion; give them distance and respect. (1991: 164)

Sociolegal scholars have demonstrated that simply constructing compelling rights claims and justifying standing as rights claimants is hardly enough, though. Discursive reconstructions of rights must be supported by material organizational power that poses an instrumental *counterweight* to status quo institutionalized hierarchies. This means, of course, that rights claimants must mobilize material resources and support networks—money, advocacy organizations, allies in other groups and the state, and experts, including lawyers. This mobilization of political and legal resources, whether by defiant individuals or groups, is how rights are made real, as Epp (2009) aptly puts it. Or, continuing my central metaphor, the issue is how rights sometimes help make social justice advocates into political *heavyweights*. To paraphrase A. Philip Randolph, "Rights are never given, they must be won, again and again" (Anderson 1973: v).

Whether as individuals or activist groups, those who challenge the status quo on behalf of new rights cannot just will their way to change, of course. Also required in most cases are changes in power relations beyond the control of rights claimants (Bell 1980). Indeed, advances in new rights claims usually require broad, often unexpected ruptures that render dominant groups, relationships, and practices vulnerable to challenge. And such fissures or faults in structures of subjugation often generate new "unruly" subjectivities and rights claims capable of challenging, perhaps even transforming, rather than being singularly produced by, power (McClure 1995: 187). My own work has drawn on social movement theory to explore how a host of broad social changes opened cracks in the prevailing patriarchal power structure to support

---

rather than superficial flaws and suggests that radical reconstruction of society itself is the real issue to be faced" (1968: 315).

a momentary challenge from gender-based pay equity activists in the 1980s (McCann 1994; see also Albiston 2010; Stryker 2007). Such opportunities and cracks are critical to change, but they are often small, short lived, and contradictory, severely limiting the possibilities for dramatic change, except in extraordinary moments.

Summary

All in all, then, rights as social practice are fraught with paradox and irony. Hence, the dominant lesson that we can take from decades of sociolegal study in the United States: what rights mean and how they do or do not matter as practices varies with the specific contexts in which they are embedded. Rights are contingent, at once unbearably light and fundamentally heavy in varying relationships.[12] And studying these variations of rights practice has defined a key theoretical and empirical challenge for a generation of scholars in the Law and Society Association.

REFERENCES

Abel, Richard L. (1995) *Politics by Other Means: Law in the Struggle against Apartheid, 1980–1994.* New York: Routledge.

Agamben, Giorgio (1998) *Homo Sacer: Sovereign Power and Bare Life.* (Daniel Heller-Roazen, Trans). Palo Alto, CA: Stanford Univ. Press.

Albiston, Catherine (2010) *Institutional Inequality and the Mobilization of the Family and Medical Leave Act: Rights on Leave.* New York, NY: Cambridge Univ. Press.

Anderson, Pervis (1973) *A. Philip Randolph: A Biographical Portrait.* Berkeley, CA: Univ. of California Press.

Atuahene, Bernadette (2014) *Dignity Restoration: South Africa's Post-Apartheid Attempt to Remedy Land Dispossession.* New York, NY: Oxford Univ. Press. Forthcoming.

Bartholomew, Amy, & Alan Hunt (1990) "What's Wrong with Rights?," 9 *Law & Inequality* 501–58.

Barzilai, Gad (2005) *Communities and Law: Politics and Cultures of Legal Identities.* Ann Arbor, MI: Univ. of Michigan Press.

Bell, Derrick (1980) "Brown vs. Board of Education and the Interest Convergence Dilemma," 93 *Harvard Law Rev.* 518–33.

Biehl, Joao (2005) *Vita: Life in a Zone of Social Abandonment.* Berkeley, CA: Univ. of California Press.

Bower, Lisa (1994) "Queer Acts and the Politics of Direct Address: Rethinking Law, Culture, and Community," 28 *Law & Society Rev.* 1009–33.

Brigham, John (1996) *The Constitution of Interests: Beyond the Politics of Rights.* New York, NY: New York Univ. Press.

Brisbin, Richard A., Jr (2002) *A Strike like No Other Strike: Law and Resistance during the Pittson Coal Strike of 1989–1990.* Baltimore, MD: Johns Hopkins Univ. Press.

Brown, Wendy (1995) "Rights and Identity in Late Modernity: Revisiting the 'Jewish Question'," in Sarat, Austin, & Thomas R. Kearns, eds., *Identities, Politics, and Rights.* Ann Arbor, MI: Univ. of Michigan Press.

——. (2003) "Neoliberalism and the End of Liberal Democracy," 7 *Theory & Event* 1–43.

Bumiller, Kristin (1990) *The Civil Rights Society: The Social Construction of Victims.* Baltimore, MD: Johns Hopkins Press.

Burke, Thomas F., & Jeb Barnes (2009) "Is There an Empirical Literature on Rights?," 48 *Studies in Law, Society, and Politics* 69–91.

Carter, Lief, & Michael McCann (2012) "Measuring Humanity: Rights in the 24th Century," in Robson, Peter, & Jessica Silbey, eds., *Law and Justice on the Small Screen.* Oxford, UK: Hart Publishing.

Cichowski, Rachel A. (2007) *The European Court and Civil Society: Litigation, Mobilization, and Governance.* New York, NY: Cambridge Univ. Press.

Comaroff, John (1996) "The Discourse of Rights in Colonial South Africa: Subjectivity, Sovereignty, Modernity," in Sarat, Austin, & Thomas R. Kearns, eds., *Identities, Politics, and Rights.* Ann Arbor, MI: Univ. of Michigan Press.

Cover, Robert (1983) The Supreme Court Term, Forward: Nomos and Narrative. Faculty Scholarship Series Paper #2705. Available at: http://digitalcommons.law.yale.edu/fss_papers/2705/ (Accessed 21 March 2014).

——. (1986) "Violence and the Word," 95 *Yale Law J.* 1601–29.

Crenshaw, Kimberlé, et al., ed. (1995) *Critical Race Theory: The Key Writings That Formed the Movement.* New York, NY: New Press.

Dayan, Colin (2011) *The Law is a White Dog.* Princeton, NJ: Princeton Univ. Press.

Delgado, Richard, & Jean Stefancic (2001) *Critical Race Theory: An Introduction,* 2nd ed. New York, NY: New York Univ. Press.

Dudas, Jeffrey (2005) "In the Name of Equal Rights: 'Special' Rights and the Politics of Resentment in Post-Civil Rights America," 39 *Law & Society Rev.* 723–57.

Dudziak, Mary (2011) *Cold War Civil Rights: Race and the Image of American Democracy,* 2nd ed. Princeton, NJ: Princeton Univ. Press.

Dworkin, Ronald (1978) *Taking Rights Seriously.* Cambridge, MA: Harvard Univ. Press.

Engel, David (1975) *Law and Kingship in Thailand during the Reign of King Chulalongkorn.* Ann Arbor, MI: Univ. of Michigan Center for South and Southeast Asian Studies.

_____. (1984) "The Oven Bird's Song: Insiders, Outsiders, and Personal Injuries in An American Community," 18 *Law & Society Rev.* 551–82.

_____. (1999) "Making Connections: Law and Society Researchers and Their Subjects," 33 *Law & Society Rev.* 3–16.

_____. (2012) "Vertical and Horizontal Perspectives on Rights Consciousness," 19 *Indiana J. of Global Legal Studies* 423–55.

_____, & Frank W. Munger (2003) *Rights of Inclusion: Life Stories of Identity, Disability, and Law.* Chicago, IL: Univ. of Chicago Press.

Englund, Harri (2006) *Prisoners of Freedom: Human Rights and the African Poor.* Berkeley, CA: Univ. of California Press.

Epp, Charles R. (1998) *The Rights Revolution: Lawyers, Activists, and Supreme Courts in Comparative Perspective.* Chicago, IL: Univ. of Chicago Press.

_____. (2009) *Making Rights Real: Activists, Bureaucrats, and the Creation of the Legalistic State.* Chicago, IL: Univ. of Chicago Press.

Ewick, Patricia, & Susan Silbey (1998) *The Common Place of Law.* Chicago, IL: Univ. of Chicago Press.

Failer, Judith (2001) *Who Qualifies for Rights? Homelessness, Mental Illness, and Civil Commitment.* Ithaca, NY: Cornell Univ. Press.

Feldman, Eric A. (2000) *The Ritual of Rights in Japan: Law, Society, and Health Policy.* New York, NY: Cambridge Univ. Press.

Fineman, Martha Albertson (2008) "The Vulnerable Subject: Anchoring Equality in the Human Condition," 20 *Yale J. of Law & Feminism* 1–24.

Fleury-Steiner, Benjamin, & Laura Beth Nielsen, eds. (2006) *The New Civil Rights Research: A Constitutive Approach.* Burlington, VT: Ashgate.

Foucault, Michel (1978) *The History of Sexuality, Volume One: An Introduction.* New York: Random House.

Fraser, Nancy (2000) "Rethinking Recognition," 3 *New Left Rev.* 107–20.

Galanter, Marc (1974) "Why the 'Haves' Come Out Ahead: Speculations on the Limits of Legal Change," 9 *Law & Society Rev.* 95–151.

_____(1989) *Law and Society in Modern India.* New York, NY: Oxford Univ. Press.

Garth, Bryant, & Joyce Sterling (1998) "From Legal Realism to Law and Society: Reshaping Law for the Last Stages of the Social Activist State," 32 *Law & Society Rev.* 409–72.

Gilliom, John (2001) *Overseers of the Poor: Surveillance, Resistance and the Limits of Privacy.* Chicago, IL: Univ. of Chicago Press.

Glendon, Mary Ann (1993) *Rights Talk: The Impoverishment of Political Discourse.* New York, NY: Free Press.

Godoy, Angelina (2013) *Of Medicines and Market: Intellectual Property and Human Rights in the Free Trade Era.* Stanford, CA: Stanford Univ. Press.

Goldberg-Hiller, Jon (2004) *The Limits to Union: Same-Sex Marriage and the Politics of Civil Rights.* Ann Arbor, MI: Univ. of Michigan Press.

Goluboff, Risa L. (2007) *The Lost Promise of Civil Rights.* New York, NY: Cambridge Univ. Press.

Goodale, Mark (2007) "The Power of Rights: Tracking Empires of Law and New Forms of Social Resistance," in Goodale, Mark, & Sally Engle Merry, eds., *The Practice of Human Rights.* New York, NY: Cambridge Univ. Press.

Gould, Jon, & Scott Barclay (2012) "Mind the Gap: The Place of Gap Studies in Sociolegal Scholarship," 8 *Annual Rev. of Law and Social Science* 323–35. Available at: http://www.annualreviews.org/doi/abs/10.1146/annurev-lawsocsci-102811-173833 (accessed 21 March 2014).

Haltom, William, & Michael McCann (2004) *Distorting the Law: Politics, Media, and the Litigation Crisis.* Chicago, IL: Univ. of Chicago Press.

Handler, Joel F. (1978) *Social Movements and the Legal System: A Theory of Law Reform and Social Change.* New York, NY: Academic Press.

Haskell, Thomas (1988) "The Curious Persistence of Rights in the Age of Interpretation," in Thelen, David, ed., *The Constitution and American Life.* Ithaca, NY: Cornell Univ. Press.

Havel, Vaclav (1994) "Acceptance Speech," National Constitution Center. Available at: http://constitutioncenter.org/libertymedal/recipient_1994_speech.html (accessed 20 October 2013).

Heyer, Katherina (2000) "From Welfare to Rights—Japanese Disability Law," 1 *Asia-Pacific Law and Policy J.* 1–21.

———. (2002) "The ADA on the Road: Disability Rights in Germany," 27 *Law and Social Inquiry* 723–62.

Horwitz, Morton (1988) "Rights," 23 *Harvard Civil Rights-Civil Liberties Rev.* 393–406.

Hussin, Iza (2012) "Circulations of Law: Colonial Precedents, Contemporary Questions," 2 *Oñati Socio-Legal Series* 18–32.

Kairys, David, ed. (1998) *The Politics of Law: A Progressive Critique*, 3rd ed. New York, NY: Basic Books.

King, Martin Luther, Jr (1964) "Letter from Birmingham Jail," in King, Martin Luther, Jr, ed., *Why We Can't Wait.* New York: New American Library (Harper & Row).

———. (1968) *A Testament of Hope*. New York: Harper Collins Publishers.

Kirkland, Anna (2008) *Fat Rights: Dilemmas of Difference and Personhood*. New York, NY: New York Univ. Press.

Klug, Heinz (2005) "Campaigning for Life: Building a New Transnational Solidarity in the Face of HIV/AIDS and TRIPS," in Santos, Boaventura de Sousa, & Cesar Rodriguez-Garavito, eds., *Law and Globalization from Below*. New York, NY: Cambridge Univ. Press.

Kundera, Milan (1984) *The Unbearable Lightness of Being*. (Michael Henry Heim, Trans.). New York, NY: Harper & Row.

———. (1990) *Immortality*. (Peter Kussi, Trans.). New York, NY: Harper Collins.

Lake, Milli (2014) "Organizing Hypocrisy: Providing Legal Accountability for Human Rights Violations in Areas of Limited Statehood," 58 *International Studies Quarterly* Forthcoming.

Lopez, Ian Haney (1996) *White by Law: The Legal Construction of Race*. New York: NYU Press.

Lovell, George (2012) *This Is Not Civil Rights: Discovering Rights Talk in 1939 America*. New York, NY: Cambridge Univ. Press.

———, & Michael McCann (2004) "A Tangled Legacy: Federal Courts and the Politics of Democratic Inclusion," in Wolbrecht, Christina, & Rodney Hero, with Peri E. Arnold & Alvin Tillery (Eds.), *The Politics of Democratic Inclusion*. Philadelphia, PA: Temple Univ. Press.

MacLean, Nancy (2006) *Freedom Is Not Enough: The Opening of the American Workplace*. Cambridge, MA: Harvard Univ. Press.

Marx, Karl (1978) "On the Jewish Question," in Tucker, Robert, ed., *The Marx-Engels Reader*, 2nd ed. New York: Norton.

Massoud, Mark Fathi (2013) *Law's Fragile State: Colonial, Authoritarian, and Humanitarian Legacies in Sudan*. New York, NY: Cambridge Univ. Press.

McCann, Michael (1984) "Resurrection and Reform: Perspectives on Property in the American Constitutional Tradition," 13 *Politics and Society* 143–76.

———. (1989) "Equal Protection for Social Inequality: Race and Class in American Constitutional Ideology," in McCann, Michael W., & Gerald L. Houseman, eds., *Judging the Constitution: Critical Essays on Judicial Lawmaking*. Boston, MA: Little, Brown.

———. (1994) *Rights at Work: Pay Equity Reform and the Politics of Legal Mobilization*. Chicago, IL: Univ. of Chicago Press.

———, & David Johnson (2009) "Rocked but Still Rolling: The Enduring Institution of Capital Punishment in Historical and Comparative Perspective," in

Sarat, Austin, & Charles Ogletree, eds., *Where Are We on the Road to Abolition?* New York, NY: New York Univ. Press.

———, & George Lovell (2014). A Union by Law: Filipino Cannery Workers and the Transnational Struggle for Human Rights. Funded by NSF grant #SES-1060698. Presented at the Annual Meetings of the Midwest Political Science Association, Chicago, IL, April 4, 2014.

———, & Stuart Scheingold (2014) "Rights: Legal Aspects," in Smelser, Neil J., & Paul, B. Baltes, ed., 2nd ed. *International Encyclopedia of the Social & Behavioral Sciences*. London, UK: Elsevier Forthcoming.

McClure, Kirstie M. (1995) "Taking Liberties in Foucault's Triangle: Sovereignty, Discipline, Governmentality, and the Subject of Rights," in Sarat, Austin, & Thomas R. Kearns, eds., *Identities, Politics, and Rights*. Ann Arbor, MI: Univ. of Michigan Press.

Merry, Sally Engle (1990) *Getting Justice and Getting Even: Legal Consciousness among Ordinary Americans*. Chicago, IL: Univ. of Chicago Press.

———. (1995) "Resistance and the Cultural Power of Law," 29 *Law & Society Rev.* 11–26.

———. (2000) *Colonizing Hawaii: The Cultural Power of Law*. Princeton, NJ: Princeton Univ. Press.

———. (2003) "Rights Talk and the Experience of Law: Implementing Women's Human Rights to Protection from Violence," 25 *Human Rights Q.* 243–81.

———. (2006) *Human Rights and Gender Violence*. Princeton, NJ: Princeton Univ. Press.

Miller, Richard, & Austin Sarat (1980–81) "Grievances, Claims, & Disputes: Assessing the Adversary Culture," 15 *Law & Society Rev.* 525–66.

Mills, Charles (2008) "Racial Liberalism," *Proceedings of the Modern Language Association* 1380–97. Available at: http://www.havenscenter.org/files/Mills-Racial%20Liberalism.pdf (accessed 30 March 2014).

Milner, Neal (1989) "The Denigration of Rights and the Persistence of Rights Talk: A Cultural Portrait," 14 *Law & Social Inquiry* 631–75.

———, & Jon Goldberg-Hiller (2003) "Rights As Excess: Understanding the Politics of Special Rights," 28 *Law & Social Inquiry* 1075–125.

Minow, Martha (1987) "Interpreting Rights: An Essay for Robert Cover," 96 *Yale Law J.* 1860–915.

Munger, Frank (2001) "Inquiry and Activism in Law and Society," 35 *Law & Society Rev.* 7–20.

Murakawa, Naomi, & Katherine Beckett (2010) "The Penology of Racial Innocence," 44 *Law & Society Rev.* 695–730.

Osanloo, Arzoo (2009) *The Politics of Women's Rights in Iran*. Princeton, NJ: Princeton Univ. Press.

Pateman, Carole (1988) *The Sexual Contract*. Palo Alto, CA: Stanford Univ. Press.

Polletta, Francesca (2000) "The Structural Context of Novel Rights Claims: Rights Innovation in the Southern Civil Rights Movement, 1961–1966," 34 *Law & Society Rev.* 367–406.

Rasmussen, Claire (2011–2012) "Are Animal Rights Dead Meat?," 41 *Southwestern Law Rev.* 253–64.

Rodriguez-Garavito, Cesar A. (2005) "Nike's Law: The Anti-Sweatshop Movement, Transnational Corporations, and the Struggle over International Labor Rights in the Americas," in Santos, Boaventura de Sousa, & Cesar Rodriguez-Garavatio, eds., *Law and Globalization from Below: Towards A Cosmopolitan Legality*. New York, NY: Cambridge Univ. Press.

Rose, Nicholas (1999) *The Powers of Freedom: Reframing Political Thought*. Cambridge, MA: Cambridge Univ. Press.

Rosenberg, Gerald (1991) *The Hollow Hope: Can Courts Bring About Social Change?* Chicago, IL: Univ. of Chicago Press.

Santos, Boaventura de Sousa (1995) "Three Metaphors for A New Conception of Law: The Frontier, the Baroque, and the South," 29 *Law & Society Rev.* 569–84.

———. (2002) *Towards A New Legal Common Sense*. London: Elsevier.

———. (2005) "Beyond Neoliberal Governance: The World Social Forum and Subaltern Cosmopolitan Politics and Legality," in Santos, Boaventura de Sousa, & Cesar Rodriguez-Garavito, eds., *Law and Globalization from Below: Towards a Cosmopolitan Legality*. New York, NY: Cambridge Univ. Press.

Sarat, Austin (1990) " '... The Law Is All Over': Power, Resistance and the Legal Consciousness of the Welfare Poor," 2 *Yale J. of Law & the Humanities* 343–80. Available at: http://digitalcommons.law.yale.edu/yjlh/vol2/iss2/6http://digitalcommons.law.yale.edu/yjlh/ (accessed 31 March 2014).

Scheingold, Stuart A. (1965) *The Rule of Law in European Integration*. New Haven: Yale Univ. Press.

———. (1974) *The Politics of Rights: Lawyers, Public Policy, and Social Change*. New Haven, CT: Yale Univ. Press.

Shklar, Judith. (1989) *American Citizenship: The Quest for Inclusion. The Tanner Lectures on Human Values*. Salt Lake, UT: Univ. of Utah.

Silbey, Susan (1997) " 'Let Them Eat Cake': Globalization, Postmodern Colonialism, and the Possibilities of Justice," 31 *Law & Society Rev.* 207–35.

Silverstein, Helena (1996) *Unleashing Rights: Law, Meaning, and the Animal Rights Movement.* Ann Arbor, MI: Univ. of Michigan Press.

Simmons, Beth (2009) *Mobilizing for Human Rights.* New York, NY: Cambridge Univ. Press.

Smith, Rogers (1997) *Civic Ideals: Conflicting Visions of Citizenship in U.S. History.* New Haven, CT: Yale Univ. Press.

Stone, Christopher (2010) *Should Trees Have Standing? Law, Morality, and the Environment,* 3rd ed. New York, NY: Oxford Univ. Press.

Stryker, Robin (2007) "Half Empty, Half Full, or Neither: Law, Inequality, and Social Change in Capitalist Democracies," 3 *Annual Rev. of Law and Social Science* 69–97.

Stychin, Carl (1998) *A Nation By Rights: National Cultures, Sexual Identity Politics, and the Discourse of Rights.* Philadelphia, PA: Temple Univ. Press.

Tilly, Charles (1985) "War Making and State Making as Organized Crime," in Evans, Peter, Dietrich Rueschemeyer, & Theda Skocpol, eds., *Bringing the State Back In.* New York, NY: Cambridge Univ. Press.

_____. (1992) "Where Do Rights Come From?," Mjoset, Lars, ed., *Contributions to the Comparative Study of Development (Vol. 2: Proceedings Form the Vilhelm Aubert Memorial Symposium).* Oslo: Institute for Social Research.

Tushnet, Mark (1984) "Essay on Rights," 62 *Texas Law Rev.* 1363–403.

Waldron, Jeremy, ed. (1987) *Nonsense Upon Stilts: Bentham, Burke, and Marx on the Rights of Man.* London, UK: Metheun.

West, Tim (2009) "Destiny as Alibi: Milan Kundera, Vaclav Havel, and the 'Czech Question' after 1968," 87 *The Slavonic and East European Rev.* 401–28.

Williams, Patricia (1992) *The Alchemy of Race and Rights.* Cambridge, MA: Harvard Univ. Press.

Zemans, Frances Kahn. (1983) "Legal Mobilization: The Neglected Role of Law in the Political System," 77 *American Political Science Rev.* 690–703.

This introduction to sociolegal analysis of constitutional law has been intended to help you reframe how you approach the study of constitutions to broaden the point of view beyond so-called landmark cases. This should help you complicate the idealistic narratives of law as a mere formalism, or simple procedural rules, and to help you better understand how social relations inform these decisions and the consequences of injustice. We will certainly examine historical and structural elements of the constitution in the pages that follow.

These readings will include influential cases; however, this reader reframes the concept of constitutional law to focus on structural injustice, persistent controversies, and the mobilization of groups as they use rights consciousness to resist domination and construct new claims and advocacy for social change.

SUMMARY

1. A small but a growing number of legal scholars have examined how the polyvocality of legality, that is, the varieties of legal consciousness and the multiple schemas of and by which it is constituted, permits individuals' wide latitude in interpreting social phenomena, while at the same time still deploying signs of legality.

2. Different constituencies are speaking about law quite differently. This has ramifications for democratic governance founded on legitimacy of representation and ideals of participatory politics. These differences matter because they influence how constitutional law is taught and how it is understood in everyday settings.

3. Judges engage in close reading of legal texts as the process of exegesis. This process requires what has been called a normative universe or the line of thinking that writers rely on when constructing a proposition.

4. On a purely textual level of analysis, you should be able to analyze different interpretations of the spirit of the law in practice. There are those that read the words of the Constitution as providing a formal process of legal exclusion as a right of the federal government. On the other hand, there are those that see an unlawful abuse of power in practice.

5. Lawyers recognize that there is not one single answer and that the use of judicial precedent is required in order to use legal authority to support a position or to argue against it.

6. The malleability of law challenges two previously unexamined beliefs: (1) existing assumptions about the legitimacy of centralized legal authority and (2) the usefulness of law as a tool for social control.

7. There are dramatic consequences that follow from legal interpretation: the process frequently leaves behind victims whose lives have been torn apart by these organized, social practices of violence.

8. While rights-talk leads to an awareness of injustice, it reveals that without the implementation of rights in practice, one is left with the abstract nakedness of being human and nothing but human, vulnerable to abuse.

9. This introduction to sociolegal analysis of constitutional law has been intended to help you reframe how you approach the study of constitutions to broaden the point of view beyond so-called landmark cases.

10. This reader reframes the concept of constitutional law to focus on structural injustice, persistent controversies, and the mobilization of groups as they use rights consciousness to resist domination and construct new claims and advocacy for social change.

KEY TERMS AND CONCEPTS

actus reus. An element of proving guilt in a criminal case needed to show the act of the accused was in violation of the criminal code.

adverse possession. When one's claim to hold property conflicts with another's claim to hold the same property; possession is granted to the claim that was proved to be continuous, exclusive, hostile, open, and conspicuous.

advocacy. Your ability to act against injustice on behalf of one's self or another group of people based on an understanding of the structures and constraints of one's environment.

agency. Your ability to navigate structures of inequality with others to defend yourself against injustice or to construct consent or compliance.

civic education gap. The belief that those who hold more power or authority have greater knowledge about sociopolitical processes than those without power, which is then used against the interests of the powerless and democratic society more broadly.

common law. Law derived from judicial opinions over time.

eminent domain. Power of government actor to take privately owned property for a public use through due process.

exegesis. A close reading of a text with a critical perspective to find the meaning within a larger context.

Federal Judiciary Act of 1789. A legislative act of Congress to establish the design, structure, jurisdiction, and processes of the federal court system.

formalists. Theorists who believe law is separate from social reality and composed of rules composed by legislatures that are uniformly applied by judges without regard to context.

free-riding. A theory developed originally from economics that claims that person might profit from the actions of others without having to participate.

general semantic differences. How different perceptions of what is reality are formed by experiences and linguistic patterns of one's environment.

hegemony. Structural processes that maintain unequal power relationships through myths that make those relations less visible.

human with rights. As contrasted from human rights as an ideal—a human must be legally recognized to have the right to have rights. Many people have not been recognized as being fully legal human beings, including the stateless, undocumented, homeless, chattel and slaves, and victims of human trafficking.

identity. How your sense of self is derived from your experiences in social relations and how you are perceived by institutions in your environment.

judicial discretion. A result of the adversarial system of common law, where judges are left with interpretations of legal controversies based on education, experience, and professional values.

judicial precedent. The belief that judges make law through the convention of common law whereby judges review whether the court's application of statute or action to a new situation.

judicial review. The judicial practice of determining whether a statute is consistent with the Constitution.

legal mobilization. A diverse set of ideas that relate to the process of individuals and groups using legality as a means to pursue strategies toward a more equitable social order including but not limited to litigation, but also rights claiming through protest, organizing activities, and raising awareness.

legal reasoning. A method of finding reasons for a proposition based on previous uses of the legal rule or principle that tends to support a conclusion consistent with other cases or that deviates from other cases that show the rule or principle to be inapplicable.

malleability of law. The integrative function of law with other concepts such as jurisdiction, precedent, stare decisis, the preference of predictability, and stability in the principle of a rule of law as well as the role of the lawyer or legal advocate to shape an argument in the institution of law.

mens rea. An element of proving guilt in a criminal case needed to show intent, motive, or the state of mind of the accused.

myth of rights. Encourages us to associate rights with social justice and to believe that the ideals of social justice can be obtained through a belief in rights without further action.

polyvocality of legality. An empirical finding that people hold many ideas about legality that include law as a game, as an ideal, and as a tool that can be abused and resisted.

Presidential executive order. The ability of the president of the United States to adopt policy unilaterally without having to compromise with the Congress, the courts, or state governments.

property-based citizenship. A historical orientation that favors the rights of property holders over those without property and the myth that property holders are more likely to be model citizens due to self-interest.

ratification of the US Constitution. A process over several years whereby delegates to the constitutional convention returned to colonial governments to offer the federal constitutional document to each of the 13 legislatures for approval and adoption, or rejection.

rights consciousness. A process where individuals and groups imagine an alternative social order based on rights yet to be formally recognized or implemented fully by government actors.

rights talk. A critical theory of rights that argues that talking about rights shifts the burden of confronting inequality away from the state or private offender to a broader commitment of rights awareness that tends to mask or hide unequal power relationships.

self-government as a fundamental right. A historical political theory that a social group has a natural right to self-determination or to govern themselves without interference by other social groups.

social responsibility. Framework of obligations and actions by members of social groups in the interest of working toward an equitable society.

social stratification. Societal ordering of humans where unequal power relationships result in advantages to some social groups and disadvantages to others.

sovereign. A legal fiction whereby a thing is constructed to hold absolute authority.

sovereignty. A complicated sociopolitical concept that has been historically related to the power of command, compact, or counsel over the rightful behavior of individuals.

standpoint theory. In societies stratified by gender and other categories, such as race and class, one's social positions shape what one actually knows.

structural analysis. Awareness that individualism is constituted because of other social relations, especially those roles that create unequal power relationships.

territorial sovereignty. Land and water over which a state has legal jurisdiction including the power to exclude or deport enforced the use of geographical boundaries.

threshold concept. Akin to a portal, opening up a new and previously inaccessible way of thinking about something that represents a transformed way of understanding, or interpreting or viewing something without which the learner cannot progress.

transformative learning. An educational theory that argues learning occurs through a process of self-reflection, the development of new skills, a new outlook that constructs new adaptive behaviors.

REFERENCES

Annenberg Public Policy Center. Rozansky, Michael. "Amid pandemic and protests, civics survey finds Americans know more of their rights." September 16, 2020. https://penntoday.upenn.edu/news/amid-pandemic-and-protests-civics-survey-finds-americans-know-more-their-rights. Accessed May 26, 2022.

Annenberg Public Policy Center. Most Americans Trust the Supreme Court, But Think It Is 'Too Mixed Up in Politics.' October 16, 2019. https://www.annenbergpublicpolicycenter.org/most-americans-trust-the-supreme-court-but-think-it-is-too-mixed-up-in-politics/. Accessed May 26, 2022.

Arendt, H. (1906–1975) 1973. *The Origins of Totalitarianism*. New York: Harcourt Brace Jovanovich.

Barnett, R. E. 2007. "The People or the State? Chisholm v. Georgia and Popular Sovereignty." *Virginia Law Review*, 93, no. 7 (November): 1729–58.

Barrett, L. F. 2017. *How Emotions Are Made: The Secret Life of the Brain*. New York: Houghton Mifflin Harcourt. 248.

Chua, Lynette J., and David M. Engel. 2019. "Legal Consciousness Reconsidered." *Annual Review of Law and Social Science* 15: 335–53.

Cover, R. M. 1986. "Violence and the Word." *The Yale Law Journal* 95 (8): 1601–29.

Dunbar-Ortiz, Roxanne. 2021. *Not "A Nation of Immigrants": Settler Colonialism, White Supremacy, and a History of Erasure and Exclusion*, 33–34. Beacon Press.

Ewick, P., and S. S. Silbey 1998. *The Common Place of Law: Stories from Everyday Life*. Chicago: University of Chicago Press. 28

Gabel, P. 1984. "The Phenomenology of Rights-Consciousness and the Pact of the Withdrawn Selves." *Texas Law Review* 62: 1563–98.

Galanter, M. 1974. "Why the 'Haves' Come Out Ahead: Speculations on the Limits of Legal Change." *Law and Society Review* 9 (1): 95–160.

Garner, Bryan. 1996. *Black's Law Dictionary*, 6th Pocket ed., Saint Paul, MN: Thomson Reuters. 615, 735.

Hurtado, S. 2019. "Now Is the Time": Civic Learning for a Strong Democracy." *Daedalus*, 148 (4): 94–107.

Leggett, Jason M., and Reabeka King-Reilly. 2020. "In the Age of Fake News: Shifting Citizenry, Shifting Thresholds." Currents in Teaching and Learning 12 (1). 6–18.

Medcalf, L. 1978. *Law and Identity: Lawyers, Native Americans, and Legal Practice*. Beverly Hills, California: SAGE.

Meyer, J., and R. Land. 2003. *Threshold Concepts and Troublesome Knowledge: Linkages to Ways of Thinking and Practicing within the Disciplines.* 412–24. Edinburgh: University of Edinburgh.

Mezirow, J. 1991. *Transformative Dimensions of Adult Learning*, 35. San Francisco: Jossey-Bass.

McCann, M. 1994. Rights at Work: Pay Equity Reform and the Politics of Legal Mobilization. Chicago: University of Chicago Press.

Polletta, F. 2000. "The Structural Context of Novel Rights Claims: Southern Civil Rights Organizing, 1961–1966." *Law & Society Review* 34 (2): 367–406.

Ricketts, A. 2006. "Threshold Concepts in Legal Education, 26 Directions." *Journal of Education Studies* 2 (6).

Rossiter, C. R., A. Hamilton, J. Madison, J. Jay, and C. R. Kesler. 2003. *The Federalist Papers*. New York, NY: Signet Classics.

Scheb, J. M., and W. Lyons. 2001. "Judicial Behavior and Public Opinion: Popular Expectations Regarding the Factors That Influence Supreme Court Decisions." *Political Behavior*, 23 (2): 181–94.

Scheingold, Stuart. 2004. *The Politics of Rights: Lawyers, Public Policy, and Political Change*. Ann Arbor: University of Michigan Press.

Tushnet, Mark. 2018. *Advanced Introduction to Comparative Constitutional Law*. Cheltenham, UK: Elger.

Wade, Lisa. 2022. *Terrible Magnificent Sociology*. New York, NY: Norton & Company.

Weresh, Melissa H. 2014. "Stargate Malleability as a Threshold Concept in Legal Education." *Journal of Legal Education* 63, no. 4 (May): 689–728.

UNIT II

Law and Difference through the Humanities

LEARNING OUTCOMES _____

1. Students will be able to explain how philosophical differences derive from experience with legal institutions.
2. Students will contrast the belief in one universal moral law against three stories about what law means in everyday life.
3. Students will be able to describe how law is used as a tool for social change.
4. Students will be able to better evaluate how individual and structural elements influence resistance.
5. Students will identify how groups might use rights consciousness to mobilize against injustice in the future.
6. Students will be able to describe how the humanities position different identities as an important interpretive mechanism.

During the Supreme Court confirmation hearings of Ketanji Brown Jackson, Senator Ted Cruz, a Republican from Texas, held up a copy of a children's book he wrongly accused of teaching babies to be racist. The controversy around whether critical race theory should be taught reflects the tensions you have read about in this textbook so far. On the one hand, those who benefit from the historical exclusion of women and people of color are afraid that critical analysis will be used to take away their power or to question their judgment. On the other hand, others argue that critical analysis should shed light on the contradictions of the most pressing controversies that persist throughout history and erupt again today.

It is helpful to acknowledge that in these stories of historical power, there exist different philosophies. These philosophies have to deal with what constitutes reality. There are those that claim that reality can be deduced through reason, logic, and mathematics. They point to advances in technology, medicine, and physics as examples that laws can be universal. In contrast, there are those that argue that reality is relative to one's position and experience. They also point to other advances in technology, medicine, and physics that question so-called universal laws. Different perspectives of what constitutes reality serve as a foundation for the interpretation of sovereignty.

Lawyers and judges are trained in a process termed abductive reasoning, which includes constructing a major premise, minor premise, and a conclusion. Generally speaking, judges draw upon previous cases, a process referred to as stare decisis, for case rules that extend beyond individual facts and the seek to embody broad constitutional principles. Given what you have already read in the introduction you should be able to see that judges have relied extensively on the cases where Justice John Marshall defined the role of judges in a constitutional democracy: to say what the law is. Marshall also points out that judges are put to the test when two or more laws are in conflict with one another. How then do we interpret how judges use constitutional interpretation in their work?

This kind of a question must be considered within a larger social context. Sometimes textbooks and professors tend to focus on formal law, or what they think the law says, and forget that these words have meanings that vary across social groups. In the humanities, this understanding has been termed exegesis, or close reading, that has a long history and requires the reader to consider varying contexts when applying meaning to a text. This sociocultural context of what law means requires drawing upon the humanities to better understand how sociopolitical decisions, including laws and judicial interpretations, affect people with different standpoints and relative power.

As discussed earlier in the text, judges have struggled trying to balance individual interests and social control. These challenges also extend into the different treatment of different groups. In other words, some individuals have received greater freedom from the courts than entire groups. In this section, you will be introduced to how philosophical differences explain competing approaches to legal change. In the readings that follow you will consider intersectional injustices of race, gender, and class. Identity is not a one-size-fits-all concept and there is much fluidity between different identities we may possess. You will also learn how individuals and groups have used legal institutions to resist and to construct new social relations. Finally, you will consider what social movements might look like in the future.

Philosophical Differences and Empirical Experience

Legal scholar Ronald Dworkin argued that truth about what is just is obtained through a process of reflection that oscillates between consideration of beliefs or convictions about particular examples of paradigm cases of justice and a general theoretical structure that shows those beliefs to constitute a unified and justifiable body of convictions, with the expectation that both the particular beliefs and general theory will be refined until a satisfactory point of equilibrium is reached (Dworkin 2006). For example, one can read legal cases that outline general moral principles and compare those principles to logical propositions about right and wrong. Such a belief is built upon the major premise that human law can contain a set of consistent and objective moral truths.

In contrast to Dworkin's belief, as you have seen in the previous section, law is experienced differently by people with different access to power. The narrative of objective moral truths has largely been determined in Western law by Anglo-Saxon propertied White males. These truths have been discussed by men in power but they tend to be resisted by women of color and other marginalized groups. What is more, law incorporates countless, varied, and often ambiguous rules; it refers to a host of official actors and organizations ranging from the supreme court to the local traffic enforcement officer. These actors have different routines, ways of seeing the value of their work, and purposes that are sometimes in contradiction with logical arguments about law and moral truths. In short, law is many things to many different people, meaning that Dworkin's argument should be understood as normative, an argument about the way the legal world should be rather than as it really is.

Ewick and Silbey (1998) identified three types of stories people tell about law in their interviews and field observations with everyday people. The first type, before the law, imagined and treated legality as an objective realm of disinterested action: formerly ordered, rational, and hierarchical system of rules and procedures. The second, with the law, described legality as a game to be played, where rules can be bent or invented by self-interested actors set out to win. The third narrative, up against the law, where law is seen as the product of unequal power and is used arbitrarily and capriciously against the interests of the most vulnerable.

All three of these narratives coexist within the same spaces and within both groups and individuals. This is because legal language is used in places that are not strictly defined as legal. The language appears in street interactions, pick-up basketball games, relationships among family and friends, and a variety of other social spaces. Thus, the normative belief in a universal objective moral code can damage or exclude other ways of knowing.

One example of how stories about law differ based on unequal power is how American Indians have been treated over the last 300 years. Sociolegal scholar Linda Medcalf (1978) concluded, "One of the major expectations of Law in the United States is that it contribute to social change. But given that the Law as practiced is consistent with and reflective of liberalism, the only change possible through its utilization is change consistent with liberal definitions." In her study of liberal lawyers advocating for Native Americans in the state of Washington, she found that Native Americans believed they were being coerced by lawyers to abandon their own cultural traditions and take on that of liberal westerners. This was akin to a second colonization from their point of view. They argued that settlers first drove them off their lands and onto reservations and now hundreds of years later they were being told to change their cultural beliefs and practices.

Medcalf believed that the law is often best understood through experiences of different groups rather than as a set of written rules that are supposedly universal and objective. Although the relationship with American Indians has been complicated, there has been a stability in behavioral expectations that center on what the law is and how we can act within the legal framework through a series of legal cases from the Marshall Trilogy up through the 21st century. For example, in 2005, the Supreme Court in *City of Sherrill v. Oneida Indian Nation of New York*, that state and federal legal standards of the federal Indian law and federal equity precluded the tribe from unilaterally reviving its ancient sovereignty over the land at issue. American lawyers, in these cases, have pursued a strategy of legal sovereignty for American Indians: the ability to look and act like a government with other state and federal government agencies. The assumption that the lawyers make is that power can be earned by giving up nonlegal cultural practices and behaviors. If the law is like a river flowing around us, then this assumption of assimilation is akin to jumping in headfirst without thinking. A fundamental question must be examined as you continue through this section: As one goes through the steps toward legal sovereignty does this process alter the state of mind or constitution of the individual and the group? In other words, what aspects of your cultural identities must you give up in order to gain legal sovereignty and be recognized by government officials?

In the next reading, Patricia Hill Collins presents a powerful argument for the age-old problem of defining knowledge and who gets to participate in the naming process. The power to write, from an authentic point of view, is a form of resistance that can transform civic institutions and serve as a reminder to the collective of the importance of individual protections. As Black women as a group continue to fight for social and political equality, what universal truths of self-definition and individual expression arise from the struggle for freedom? What steps have writers taken in the past that can help guide individuals who feel excluded, who have been denied access, or who have unequal power in formal civic institutions? You should begin to integrate this reading into the dialogues you have about law and stereotypes as you explore the different meanings of community in a democratic republic.

From

THE POWER OF SELF-DEFINITION

Patricia Hill Collins

The voices of Black women writers

During the summer of 1944, recent law school graduate Pauli Murray returned to her California apartment and found the following anonymous note from the "South Crocker Street Property Owner's Association" tacked to her door: "We ... wish to inform you the flat you now occupy ... is restricted to the white or Caucasian race only. ... We intend to uphold these restrictions, therefore we ask that you vacate the above mentioned flat ... within seven days" (1987, 253). Murray's response was to write. She remembers: "I was learning that creative expression is an integral part of the equipment needed in the service of a compelling cause; it is another form of activism. Words poured from my typewriter" (p. 255).

Though a Black women's written tradition existed (Christian 1985; Carby 1987), it was available primarily to educated women. Denied the literacy that enabled them to read books and novels, as well as the time to do so, working-class Black women struggled to find a public voice. Hence the significance of the blues and other dimensions of Black oral traditions in their lives. In this class-segmented context, finding Black women's writing that transcends these divisions among written and oral traditions is noteworthy. In this regard, because it fits neither solely within the Black women's blues tradition nor within equally important traditions of Black women's writers, the work of Alice Childress (1956) remains exemplary. Childress created the character of Mildred, a fictional working-class, Black woman domestic worker. Through short monologues to her friend Marge, Mildred, a domestic worker, speaks out on a range of topics. Mildred's 62 monologues, each two or three pages in length, constitute provocative statements of Childress's Black feminist theory (Harris 1986). Take, for example, Mildred's rendition to Marge of what she said to her boss in response to hearing herself described to her boss's luncheon friends as a quasi-family member:

> I am *not* just like one of the family at all! The family eats in the dining room and I eat in the kitchen. Your mama borrows your lace tablecloth for her company and your son entertains his friends in your parlour, your daughter takes her afternoon nap on the living room couch and the puppy sleeps on your satin spread ... so you can see I am not *just* like one of the family.

> (Childress 1956, 2)

In this passage, Childress creates a fictional version of what many Black women domestic workers have wanted to say at one time or another. She also advances a biting critique of how the mammy image has been used to justify Black women's bad treatment.

Foreshadowing Barbara Neely's creation of the character of Blanche, Mildred's ideas certainly ring true. But Childress's Mildred also illustrates a creative use of Black women's writing that is targeted not just to educated Black women, but to a wider Black women's community. The character of Mildred first appeared in a series of conversations that were originally published in Paul Robeson's newspaper, *Freedom*, under the title "Conversations from Life." They continued in the *Baltimore Afro-American* as "Here's Mildred." Since many of Childress's readers were themselves domestic workers, Mildred's bold assertions resonated with the silenced voices of many of these readers. Moreover, Mildred's identity as a Black working-class domestic and the form of publication of these fictionalized accounts illustrates an increasingly rare practice in Black intellectual production—a Black author writing to an African-American, working-class audience, using a medium controlled by Black people (Harris 1986).[5]

Since the 1970s, increased literacy among African-Americans has provided new opportunities for U.S. Black women to expand the use of scholarship and literature into more visible institutional sites of resistance. A community of

Black women writers has emerged since 1970, one in which African-American women engage in dialogue among one another in order to explore formerly taboo subjects. Black feminist literary criticism has documented the intellectual and personal space created for African-American women in this emerging body of ideas (Washington 1980, 1982; Tate 1983; Evans 1984; Christian 1985; O'Neale 1986). Especially noteworthy are the ways in which many Black women writers build on former themes and approaches of the Black women's blues tradition (Williams 1979) and of earlier Black women writers (Cannon 1988).

How "safe" are safe spaces?

Historically, safe spaces were "safe" because they represented places where Black women could freely examine issues that concerned us. By definition, such spaces become less "safe" if shared with those who were not Black and female. Black women's safe spaces were never meant to be a way of life. Instead, they constitute one mechanism among many designed to foster Black women's empowerment and enhance our ability to participate in social justice projects. As strategies, safe spaces rely on exclusionary practices, but their overall purpose most certainly aims for a more inclusionary, just society. As the work of Black women blues singers and Black women writers suggests, many of the ideas generated in such spaces found a welcome reception outside Black women's communities. But how could Black women generate these understandings of Black women's realities without first talking to one another?

Since the 1970s, U.S. Black women have been unevenly incorporated into schools, jobs, neighborhoods, and other U.S. social institutions that historically have excluded us. As a result, African-American women have become more class stratified than at any period in the past. In these newly desegregated settings, one new challenge consists of building "safe spaces" that do not become stigmatized as "separatist." U.S. Black women who find ourselves integrating corporations and colleges encounter new forms of racism and sexism that require equally innovative responses. A new rhetoric of colorblindness that reproduces social inequalities by treating people the same (Crenshaw 1997) makes it more difficult to maintain safe spaces at all. Any group that organizes around its own self-interests runs the risk of being labeled "separatist," "essentialist," and antidemocratic. This protracted attack on so-called identity politics works to suppress historically oppressed groups that aim to craft independent political agendas around identities of race, gender, class, and/or sexuality.

Within this climate, African-American women are increasingly asked why we want to "separate" ourselves from Black men and why feminism cannot speak for all women, including us. In essence, these queries challenge the need for distinctive Black women's communities as *political* entities. Black women's organizations devoted to cooking, nails, where to find a good babysitter, and other apolitical topics garner little attention. But how do Black women as a collectivity resist intersecting oppressions as they affect us without organizing as a group? How do U.S. Black women identify the specific issues associated with controlling images of Black womanhood without safe spaces where we can talk freely?

One reason that safe spaces are so threatening to those who feel excluded, and so routinely castigated by them, is that safe spaces are free of surveillance by more powerful groups. Such spaces simultaneously remove Black women from surveillance and foster the conditions for Black women's independent self-definitions. When institutionalized, these self-definitions become foundational to politicized Black feminist standpoints. Thus, much more is at stake here than the simple expression of voice.

A broader climate that aims to suppress political speech among African-American women, among others, has affected the organization of historically safe spaces within Black civil society. Relationships among Black women, within families, and within Black community organizations all must contend with the new realities and rhetoric that characterize an unfulfilled racial and gender desegregation in the context of increasingly antagonistic class relationships.

The blues tradition in Black women's music also remains under assault under these new social conditions. Traditionally, Black women blues singers drew upon traditions of struggle in order to produce "progressive art." Such art was emancipatory because it fused thought, feeling, and action and helped Black women among others to see their world differently and act to change it. More recently, commodification of the blues and its transformation into marketable crossover music have virtually stripped it of its close ties to African-American oral traditions. Considerable controversy surrounds the issue of how to assess the diverse genres of contemporary Black music. As Angela Davis observes, "Some of the superstars of popular-musical culture today are unquestionably musical geniuses, but they have distorted the Black music tradition by brilliantly developing its form while ignoring its content of struggle and freedom" (1989, 208). Black literary critic Sondra O'Neale suggests that similar processes of depoliticization may be affecting Black women's writing. "Where are the Angela Davises, Ida B. Wellses, and Daisy Bateses of black feminist literature?" she asks (1986, 144).

Contemporary African-American musicians, writers, cultural critics, and intellectuals function in a dramatically different political economy than that of any prior generation. It remains to be seen whether the specialized thought generated by contemporary Black feminist thinkers in very different institutional locations is capable of creating safe spaces that will carry African-American women even further.

CONSCIOUSNESS AS A SPHERE OF FREEDOM

Traditionally, when taken together, Black women's relationships with one another, the Black women's blues tradition, and the work of Black women writers provided the context for crafting alternatives to prevailing images of Black womanhood. These sites offered safe spaces that nurtured the everyday and specialized thought of African-American women. In them Black women intellectuals could construct ideas and experiences that infused daily life with new meaning. These new meanings offered African-American women potentially powerful tools to resist the controlling images of Black womanhood. Far from being a secondary concern in bringing about social change, challenging controlling images and replacing them with a Black women's standpoint constituted an essential component in resisting intersecting oppressions (Thompson-Cager 1989). What have been some of the important ideas that developed in these safe spaces? Moreover, how useful are these ideas in responding to the greatly changed social context that confronts U.S. Black women?

The importance of self-definition

"Black groups digging on white philosophies ought to consider the source. Know who's playing the music before you dance," cautions poet Nikki Giovanni (1971, 126). Her advice is especially germane for African-American women. Giovanni suggests: "We Black women are the single group in the West intact. And anybody can see we're pretty shaky. We are ... the only group that derives its identity from itself. I think it's been rather unconscious but we measure ourselves by ourselves, and I think that's a practice we can ill afford to lose" (1971, 144). When Black women's very survival is at stake, creating independent self-definitions becomes essential to that survival.

The issue of the journey from internalized oppression to the "free mind" of a self-defined, womanist consciousness has been a prominent theme in the works of U.S. Black women writers. Author Alexis DeVeaux notes that there is a "great exploration of the self in women's work. It's the self in relationship with an intimate other, with the community, the nation and the world" (in Tate 1983, 54). Far from being a narcissistic or trivial concern, this placement of self at the center of analysis is critical for understanding a host of other relationships. DeVeaux continues, "you have to understand what your place as an individual is and the place of the person who is close to you. You have to understand the space between you before you can understand more complex or larger groups" (p. 54).

Black women have also stressed the importance of self-definition as part of the journey from victimization to a free mind in their blues. Sherley Anne Williams's analysis of the affirmation of self in the blues makes a critical contribution in understanding the blues as a Black women's text. In discussing the blues roots of Black literature, Williams notes, "The assertion of individuality and the implied assertion—as action, not mere verbal statement—of self is an important dimension of the blues" (1979, 130).

The assertion of self usually comes at the end of a song, after the description or analysis of the troublesome situation. This affirmation of self is often the only solution to that problem or situation. Nina Simone's (1985) classic blues song "Four Women" illustrates this use of the blues to affirm self. Simone sings of three Black women whose experiences typify controlling images: Aunt Sarah, the mule, whose back is bent from a lifetime of hard work; Sweet Thing, the Black prostitute who will belong to anyone who has money to buy; and Saphronia, the mulatto whose Black mother was raped late one night. Simone explores Black women's objectification as the Other by invoking the pain these three women actually feel. But Peaches, the fourth woman, is an especially powerful figure, because Peaches is angry. "I'm awfully bitter these days," Peaches cries out, "because my parents were slaves." These words and the feelings they invoke demonstrate her growing awareness and self-definition of the situation she encountered. They offer to the listener not sadness and remorse, but an anger that leads to action. This is the type of individuality Williams means—not that of talk but self-definitions that foster action.

While the theme of the journey also appears in the work of Black men, African-American women writers and musicians explore this journey toward freedom in ways that are characteristically female (Thompson-Cager 1989). Black women's journeys, though at times embracing political and social issues, basically take personal and psychological forms and rarely reflect the freedom of movement of Black men who hop "trains," "hit the road," or in other ways physically travel in order to find that elusive sphere of freedom from racial oppression. Instead, Black women's journeys often involve "the transformation of silence into language and action" (Lorde 1984, 40). Typically tied to children and/or community, fictional Black women characters, especially those created prior to the 1990s, search for self-definition within close geographical boundaries. Even though physical limitations confine the Black heroine's quest to a specific area, "forming complex personal relationships adds depth to her identity quest in lieu of geographical breadth" (Tate 1983, xxi). In their search for self-definition and the power of a free mind, Black heroines may remain "motionless on the outside … but inside?"

Given the physical limitations on Black women's mobility, the conceptualization of self that has been part of Black women's self-definitions is distinctive. Self is not defined as the increased autonomy gained by separating oneself from others. Instead, self is found in the context of family and community—as Paule Marshall describes it, "the ability to recognize one's continuity with the larger community" (Washington 1984, 159). By being accountable to others, African-American women develop more fully human, less objectified selves. Sonia Sanchez points to this version of self by stating, "We must move past always focusing on the 'personal self' because there's a larger self. There's a 'self' of black people" (Tate 1983, 134). Rather than defining self in opposition to others, the connectedness among individuals provides Black women deeper, more meaningful self-definitions.[6]

This journey toward self-definition has political significance. As Mary Helen Washington observes, Black women who struggle to "forge an identity larger than the one society would force upon them … are aware and conscious, and that very consciousness is potent" (1980, xv). Identity is not the goal but rather the point of departure in the process of self-definition. In this process Black women journey toward an understanding of how our personal lives have been fundamentally shaped by intersecting oppressions of race, gender, sexuality, and class. Peaches's statement, "I'm awfully bitter these days because my parents were slaves," illustrates this transformation.

This particular expression of the journey toward self-definition offers a powerful challenge to the externally defined, controlling images of African-American women. Replacing negative images with positive ones can be equally problematic if the function of stereotypes as controlling images remains unrecognized. John Gwaltney's (1980) interview with Nancy White, a 73-year-old Black woman, suggests that ordinary Black women can be acutely aware of the power of these controlling images. To Nancy White the difference between the controlling images applied to African-American and White women is one of degree, not of kind:

> My mother used to say that the black woman is the white man's mule and the white woman is his dog. Now, she said that to say this: we do the heavy work and get beat whether we do it well or not. But the white woman is closer to the master and he pats them on the head and lets them sleep in the house, but he ain't gon' treat neither one like he was dealing with a person.

(p. 148)

Although both groups are objectified, albeit in different ways, the images function to dehumanize and control both groups. Seen in this light, it makes little sense in the long run for Black women to exchange one set of controlling images for another even if positive stereotypes bring better treatment in the short run.

The insistence on Black women's self-definitions reframes the entire dialogue from one of protesting the technical accuracy of an image—namely, refuting the Black matriarchy thesis—to one stressing the power dynamics underlying the very process of definition itself. By insisting on self-definition, Black women question not only what has been said about African-American women but the credibility and the intentions of those possessing the power to define. When Black women define ourselves, we clearly reject the assumption that those in positions granting them the authority to interpret our reality are entitled to do so. Regardless of the actual content of Black women's self-definitions, the act of insisting on Black female self-definition validates Black women's power as human subjects.

REFERENCES

———. 1988. *Black Womanist Ethics*. Atlanta: Scholars Press.

Carby, Hazel. 1987. *Reconstructing Womanhood: The Emergence of the Afro-American Woman Novelist*. New York: Oxford University Press.

Childress, Alice. [1956] 1986. *Like One of the Family: Conversations from a Domestic's Life*. Boston: Beacon.

Christian, Barbara. 1985. *Black Feminist Criticism, Perspectives on Black Women Writers*. New York: Pergamon.

———. 1997. "Color Blindness, History, and the Law." In *The House That Race Built*, ed. Wahneema Lubiano, 280–88. New York: Pantheon.

———. 1989. *Women, Culture, and Politics*. New York: Random House.

Evans, Sara. 1979. *Personal Politics*. New York: Vintage.

Giovanni, Nikki. 1971. *Gemini*. New York: Penguin.

Gwaltney, John Langston. 1980. *Drylongso, A Self-Portrait of Black America*. New York: Vintage.

———. 1986. "Introduction." In *Like One of the Family: Conversations from a Domestic's Life*, by Alice Childress, xi–xxxviii. Boston: Beacon.

———. 1984. *Sister Outsider*. Trumansberg, NY: Crossing Press.

———. 1987. *Song in a Weary Throat: An American Pilgrimage*. New York: Harper and Row.

O'Neale, Sondra. 1986. "Inhibiting Midwives, Usurping Creators: The Struggling Emergence of Black Women in American Fiction." In *Feminist Studies/Critical Studies*, ed. Teresa de Lauretis, 139–56. Bloomington: Indiana University Press.

Simone, Nina. 1985. *Backlash*. Portugal: Movieplay Portuguesa Recording.

Tate, Claudia, ed. 1983. *Black Women Writers at Work*. New York: Continuum Publishing.

Thompson-Cager, Chezia. 1989. "Ntozake Shange's *Sassafras, Cypress and Indigo*: Resistance and Mythical Women of Power." *NWSA Journal* 1 (4): 589–601.

———. 1983. *In Search of Our Mother's Gardens*. New York: Harcourt Brace Jovanovich.

———, ed. 1980. *Midnight Birds*. Garden City, NY: Anchor.

———. 1982. "Teaching *Black-Eyed Susans*: An Approach to the Study of Black Women Writers." In *But Some of Us Are Brave*, ed. Gloria T. Hull, Patricia Bell Scott, and Barbara Smith, 208–17. Old Westbury, NY: Feminist Press.

———. 1984. "I Sign My Mother's Name: Alice Walker, Dorothy West and Paule Marshall." In *Mothering the Mind: Twelve Studies of Writers and Their Silent Partners*, ed. Ruth Perry and Martine Watson Broronley, 143–63. New York: Holmes & Meier.

Williams, Sherley A. 1979. "The Blues Roots of Afro-American Poetry." In *Chant of Saints: A Gathering of Afro-American Literature, Art and Scholarship*, ed. Michael S. Harper and Robert B. Steptoe, 123–35. Urbana: University of Illinois Press.

Empirical Experience: Segregation

Another practical example that severely questions the universal moral nature of law is that of segregation. Throughout the US history, there have been different legal standards for different social groups. This should not be surprising given that the US Constitution was born out of chattel slavery, inequality, and the unjust laws that supported these different power relationships.

In the excerpt that follows, Dr. Martin Luther King Jr. defined an unjust law as a code that a numerical or power majority group compels a minority group to obey but does not make binding on itself. He continued that this reality is difference made legal. His story about law provided a framework for us to analyze the process of law and politics whereby a political group uses law and the institutions of government to exclude another person. The politics of legal exclusion is not based on a natural or fundamental law but is rather a perversion of this process to strictly benefit the group using power over others. This power of an arbitrary nature is precisely what the doctrine of separation of powers was intended to thwart in order to protect individual liberty. Individual liberty, as you read in the introduction, is the basis for legal sovereignty.

Much legislative and judicial change occurred throughout the many years of the civil rights movement. We see this change as a collective process of over 100 years of realizing civic identity and practicing agency for those who were denied citizenship in the *Dred Scott* case and as a legacy of a slavery economy. As we see today, issues of civic conflict still emanate from the unequal access to participation. From voting to running for office or from education to opportunity in the workplace, there are many stinging examples of unfair treatment. Dr. Martin Luther King Jr. provided a clear rationale for civic change in this short excerpt arguing we cannot wait.

From

LETTER FROM A BIRMINGHAM JAIL

1964

Martin Luther King, Jr.

I just referred to the creation of tension as a part of the work of the nonviolent resister. This may sound rather shocking. But I must confess that I am not afraid of the word tension. I have earnestly worked and preached against violent tension, but there is a type of constructive nonviolent tension that is necessary for growth. Just as Socrates felt that it was necessary to create a tension in the mind so that individuals could rise from the bondage of myths and half-truths to the unfettered realm of creative analysis and objective appraisal, we must see the need of having nonviolent gadflies to create the kind of tension in society that will help men rise from the dark depths of prejudice and racism to the majestic heights of understanding and brotherhood. So the purpose of the direct action is to create a situation so crisis packed that it will inevitably open the door to negotiation. We, therefore, concur with you in your call for negotiation. Too long has our beloved Southland been bogged down in the tragic attempt to live in monologue rather than dialogue.

One of the basic points in your statement is that our acts are untimely. Some have asked, "Why didn't you give the new administration time to act?" The only answer that I can give to this inquiry is that the new administration must be prodded about as much as the outgoing one before it acts. We will be sadly mistaken if we feel that the election of Mr. Boutwell will bring the millennium to Birmingham. While Mr. Boutwell is much more articulate and

Martin Luther King Jr., Selection from "Letter from Birmingham Jail," 1964.

gentle than Mr. Connor, they are both segregationists dedicated to the task of maintaining the status quo. The hope I see in Mr. Boutwell is that he will be reasonable enough to see the futility of massive resistance to desegregation. But he will not see this without pressure from the devotees of civil rights. My friends, I must say to you that we have not made a single gain in civil rights without determined legal and nonviolent pressure. History is the long and tragic story of the fact that privileged groups seldom give up their privileges voluntarily. Individuals may see the moral light and voluntarily give up their unjust posture; but as Reinhold Niebuhr has reminded us, groups are more immoral than individuals.

We know through painful experience that freedom is never voluntarily given by the oppressor; it must be demanded by the oppressed. Frankly I have never yet engaged in a direct action movement that was "well timed," according to the timetable of those who have not suffered unduly from the disease of segregation. For years now I have heard the word "Wait!" It rings in the ear of every Negro with a piercing familiarity. This "wait" has almost always meant "never." It has been a tranquilizing thalidomide, relieving the emotional stress for a moment, only to give birth to an ill-formed infant of frustration. We must come to see with the distinguished jurist of yesterday that "justice too long delayed is justice denied." We have waited for more than three hundred and forty years for our constitutional and God-given rights.

Empirical Experience: Race, Class, and Gender

When we look at successful people, we may often be quick to judge or assume that their journey to success was easy and that a similar ascent to success is not available to regular people like us. Supreme Court Justice Sonya Sotomayor, appointed in 2009, holds the distinction of being the first justice of Hispanic heritage, the first Latina, the court's third female justice, and its 12th Roman Catholic justice. This history making distinction was not handed to her—as she explains, she had to work harder given her marginalized upbringing in the Bronx, New York, and being able to avoid the violence and addition that plagued other members of her family. How did she do it? It starts early, according to Sotomayor, "each child has to have within them a desire to achieve something."

Justice Sotomayor refers to the ability to do something. That something for you can be anything—small or big. But that something starts it all. Your community, country, and world need you and the unique gifts and talents you bring. Don't sell yourself short, don't say you can't possibly achieve anything. You have seen throughout history that individuals have the power to create momentous change. Who says that can't be you?

From

INTERVIEW: "AS A LATINA, SONIA SOTOMAYOR SAYS, 'YOU HAVE TO WORK HARDER,'"

National Public Radio, January 13, 2014.
Sonia Sotomayor

Like most sitting Supreme Court justices, Sonia Sotomayor is circumspect when talking about the court; but she has written intimately about her personal life—more so than is customary for a Supreme Court justice.

"When I was nominated by the president for this position, it became very clear to me that many people in the public were interested in my life and the challenges I had faced," she tells Fresh Air's Terry Gross. "... And I also realized that much of the public perception of who I was and what had happened to me was not quite complete."

In her memoir, *My Beloved World*, Sotomayor recounts growing up poor in the South Bronx; living with juvenile diabetes, a chronic disease; being raised by a single mother after her father, who was an alcoholic, died; and struggling to get a good education in spite of the odds. It became a best-seller when it was published last year and has just come out in paperback.

> I watched my father, who I knew loved me, kill himself with alcohol; I watched a cousin [Nelson] whom I adored ... this person who had an enormous talent and a great intelligence ... destroy himself and affect his family with a great deal of pain by ultimately killing himself with drug use.

That has always permitted me ... as a judge ... to understand that the people who came before me as defendants were human beings with good and potentially very bad things within them. It was not unusual for defendants to have families who depended on them, who loved them, who thought the world of them, even though they had done horrific things. ...

When I was being nominated to the [U.S.] Court of Appeals, I was asked [by] the Senate to give them a record of how often I had departed from the then-mandatory sentencing guidelines. And judges were permitted under certain circumstances to depart downward, give a lesser sentence, or depart upwards, give a higher sentence than the guidelines called for. I was shocked to find that I gave less downward departures, lesser sentences, and more greater sentences than the national average. ...

I think because of my experiences, however, I could treat that person in my courtroom as an individual and not as a nonentity and at the same time hold them responsible for their acts.

On how she was able to succeed while her cousin Nelson didn't, despite growing up in the same neighborhood:

I think there's always a discussion about nature versus nurturing, but I do believe that it's always a combination of the two that impacts what happens to a person. For me, I was blessed, unlike my cousin Nelson, with being a girl. My family was more protective of me. I wasn't permitted to play outside alone. It was a different world for the boys in the family: They were permitted to go out. ...

I also think that each child has to have within them a desire to achieve something. For me, my initial goals were just to graduate from college because nobody in my family had done it. But the idea of having a mark that I wanted to achieve helped me. Nelson couldn't find that in his life. He loved being a musician. Regrettably, his father wanted him to be a doctor and their dreams clashed and I think Nelson never found the support that he needed to give reality to his dreams.

On missing certain cultural references:

One day talking to my first-year roommate ... I was telling her about how out of place I felt at Princeton, how I didn't connect with many of the experiences that some of my classmates were describing, and she said to me, "You're like Alice in Wonderland."

And I said, "Who is Alice?"

And she said, "You don't know about Alice?"

And I said, "No, I don't."

And she said, "It's one of the greatest book classics in English literature. You should read it."

I recognized at that moment that there were likely to be many other children's classics that I had not read. ... Before I went home that summer, I asked her to give me a list of some of the books she thought were children's classics and she gave me a long list and I spent the summer reading them. That was perhaps the starkest moment of my understanding that there was a world I had missed, of things that I didn't know anything about. ... [As an adult] there are moments when people make references to things that I have no idea what they're talking about.

On being Latina and her responsibility to her community:

You have to work harder. ... In every position that I've been in, there have been naysayers who don't believe I'm qualified or who don't believe I can do the work. And I feel a special responsibility to prove them wrong. I think I work harder than a lot of other people because of that sense of responsibility.

Does it mean that I think that I have an obligation to any particular group including Latinos? No. My job is my job and, particularly being a judge, I would be doing a disservice to the Latino community if I ruled on the basis of a preference for any group. ... I have to rule as I do on the basis of the law ... but I do feel that I have a special responsibility to work harder to prove myself because I am the first of a group that has been perceived as being incapable of doing whatever it is that I've had the benefit of becoming a part of.

On women trying to "have it all":

This whole continuing question about whether women can "have it all"—I think it's the wrong question. I think the right question should be, "What makes you happy as a person? Do you want to not 'have it all' but to have both in your life in an imperfect way?" Because if the question presupposes that you're going to do both and be equally happy at every moment, it's a false question.

It's a compromise; it's a balance; it's figuring out what's the most important thing you have to give at that moment and to what. All of that is a constant work in progress.

There are also structural elements one must consider when confronting unequal power relationships. These ongoing elements are largely beyond our individual control. They are products of our social relations. However, these structural elements can also be seen as opportunities for social change and direct action. In the reading that follows think about how Justice Sotomayor's environment and relationships led to her awareness that law school could be a tool for legal change.

THE LIFE AND SUCCESS OF SONIA SOTOMAYOR

Perseverance and Productive Giftedness

Susan J. Paik, Kenya R. Marshall-Harper, Charlina Gozali, and Tammy Johnson

Research Methods

In studying the lives of eminent individuals, biographical research methods have been commonly used in various talent domains (Cox, 1926; Freeman & Walberg, 1999; Goertzel et al., 2004; Walberg & Stariha, 1992; Wallace & Walberg, 1987). Biographical studies are useful in examining the childhoods of notable individuals (Goertzel et al., 2004). Becoming more popular in social science and educational research, biographical methods uniquely allow a deeper study of the life history or "lived" experiences of a single person (Creswell, 2012; Cridel, 2016; Roberts, 2002). Personal, social, or other lived experiences are carefully reviewed to develop life narratives (Creswell, 2012).

Susan J. Paik, Kenya R. Marshall-Harper, and Charlina Gozali, "The Life and Success of Sonia Sotomayor: Perseverance and Productive Giftedness," *High-Achieving Latino Students: Successful Pathways Toward College and Beyond*, ed. Susan J. Paik, Stacy M. Kula, and Jeremiah J. Gonzalez, pp. 184–196. Copyright © 2020 by Information Age Publishing. Reprinted with permission.

Sotomayor's (2013a) memoir *My Beloved World* was extensively studied to understand what contributed to her success. Most of the findings were taken from her memoir, but additional biographical sources and recorded interviews supplemented our findings (See list for biographical sources). She was selected because of her notable accomplishments as the first Latina Supreme Court Justice. Several researchers conducted content analysis to determine key themes from her autobiography. Using the theoretical framework as a guide, the researchers read each chapter carefully, identified key factors through "evidence" of lived experiences, and discussed each finding carefully until consensus was reached.

Since the purpose of biographical studies is to capture the life history of a single individual, this study is limited in its generalizability; however, we can learn a great deal from Sotomayor's life story. Through the lens of research and collection reflections, the illustrations of our key findings are described below.

Results and Discussion: Key Findings

CONTEXT

Born in the U.S. on June 25, 1954, Sotomayor was the oldest of two children born to Puerto Rican parents. Sotomayor and her younger brother, Juan Jr., were raised in a community adversely affected by drugs and violence. However, these environmental conditions existed on the periphery of her home which was often occupied by extended family members ("Sonia Sotomayor," 2017). Her aunt, grandmother, and cousins lived in close proximity and visited often, sharing many family gatherings ("Sonia Sotomayor," 2017; Sotomayor, 2002). The closeness and support of family grounded her in Puerto Rican culture, serving as a buffer against challenging circumstances.

During her childhood, her parents frequently argued, which was usually fueled by her father's alcoholism ("Sonia Sotomayor," 2017). Her father's drinking eventually led to a fatal alcohol-induced heart attack when Sotomayor was in high school (Bernier-Grand, 2010). In order to meet the family's financial needs, Sotomayor's mother added school to her already full parenting and work schedule, and Sotomayor herself also began to work (Bernier-Grand, 2010). Despite the barriers she experienced, Sotomayor remained dedicated and committed to pursuing a career in law.

As a young child, Sotomayor also struggled with Type 1 diabetes (Stein, 2017). At age 7, she learned how to sterilize needles and regularly administered insulin to herself (McElroy, 2010). This experience taught her to be responsible from a young age and serves as an early example of the strength and independence she would display as an adult.

INDIVIDUAL APTITUDE

Ability. Throughout Sotomayor's life, she had high academic achievement. She excelled in her early school years (Felix, 2011; "Sonia Sotomayor," 2017), received full marks on the Regents geometry exam in high school, and later graduated as the valedictorian of her high school ("Sonia Sotomayor," 2017). With acceptance to several Ivy League universities and a full scholarship to Princeton, she was the first person in her family to attend college. At college, she was awarded Phi Beta Kappa and the Pyne Prize, served as editor of the *Yale Law Review*, published, and graduated summa cum laude. Sotomayor's early ambition to become a lawyer and judge not only came to fruition, but her professional career culminated into the highest position as Supreme Court Justice, making her the first Latina and only third female Justice.

Development. Sotomayor developed her talent throughout life; she saw every experience as a learning opportunity. As a young child, she advanced her cognitive and social-emotional skills by always listening to adult conversations. Nicknamed "Aji" or hot pepper (Sotomayor, 2013a, p. 5), she was a curious and quick learner. For example, she was able to calculate numbers and work the cash register at her *Tío* Mayo's bakery in Puerto Rico.

As an aspiring lawyer, Sotomayor learned to develop skills she would need later. For example, Sotomayor recited the Bible at church to practice public speaking and eventually won a high school speech competition. She also participated in the Forensics Club to improve her debating skills. Her early preparation and achievements helped her to get into Princeton and Yale, where she continued to flourish academically.

As a district attorney, Sotomayor managed a hundred cases at a time, developing her skills as a tough lawyer. At Pavia and Harcourt, her colleagues recognized her talent, promoted her as partner and supported her as a judge.

Motivation. As a highly motivated individual, Sotomayor also had *focused motivation*, "undeterred, intentional perseverance with an end goal in mind" (Paik, 2013, p. 106). Becoming a lawyer, and ultimately a judge, was Sotomayor's childhood goal. She was further motivated by the injustice and inequality she witnessed in her Bronx community.

Young Sotomayor was also self-regulated and independent. For example, her childhood diabetes taught her to become responsible, giving herself insulin shots ("Sonia Sotomayor," 2017). Living with an overworked mother and an alcoholic father also taught her to become extremely self-reliant. For instance, she kept the house clean and well-stocked. Sotomayor managed to take care of herself as well as household responsibilities.

Sotomayor demonstrated a growth mindset throughout her life (Dweck, 2006). For example, as a Princeton freshman, she read grammar and vocabulary books independently to improve her writing (Academy of Achievement, 2017; "Sonia Sotomayor," 2017). As a Latina from a low-income community, she also realized that she was underprepared academically relative to her peers. She reflects "that many of the gaps in my knowledge and understanding were simply limits of class and cultural background, not lack of aptitude or application" (Sotomayor, 2013a, p. 171). The recently-enacted affirmative action policy meant that Sotomayor was one of the few students of color at Princeton. As a racial minority, she felt tremendous pressure to succeed, as failure "would be proving the critics right, and the doors that had opened just a crack to let us in would be slammed shut again" (p. 183). At times, Sotomayor struggled with being "an imposter" even as a judge, but she was never afraid of hard work (p. 378). She learned the value of hard work from her mother, who modeled a "surplus of effort" in "overcom[ing] a deficit of confidence" (p. 145). Throughout her life, both her abilities and effort leveraged her into new opportunities (Paik, 2013, 2015).

INSTRUCTION

Learning Climate. Sotomayor experienced rigorous school communities. She attended Blessed Sacrament and Cardinal Spellman schools for elementary and secondary education. Catholic schools not only brought resources to an impoverished neighborhood, but they instilled structure and discipline, "virtually an eighth sacrament" (Sotomayor, 2013a, p. 38). Consequently, students were not distracted by inappropriate behavior and could focus on their work. Learning occurred despite some of the negative attitudes held by nuns or other school administrators toward students from poor neighborhoods (pp. 38, 147). Still, teachers created positive school climates. For example, at Blessed Sacrament, Sotomayor enjoyed Mrs. Reilly's fifth grade class. She created a positive learning environment by awarding gold stars to deserving students ("Sonia Sotomayor," 2017). At Cardinal Spellman, Miss Katz, her junior year history teacher created an engaging and challenging class.

Princeton continued to provide a conducive learning environment and it was also a safe space where she could explore her ethnic heritage and identity (Sotomayor, 2013a). She took courses that deepened her understanding of

Puerto Rican history and culture. Ethnic classes and other social justice courses supported diversity, but the overall climate was challenging at times due to over-arching white middle-class perspectives. However, change slowly occurred due to activist students and professors, eventually diversifying the student body and faculty. For example, Acción Puertorriqueño, an activist student group, encouraged Princeton's president to establish a faculty that reflected the student body. Consequently, they hired a Hispanic dean of student affairs.

Yale Law School consisted of stellar faculty and peers who challenged each other. She also found Yale to have a "commitment to fostering a supportive environment on a human scale" (Sotomayor, 2013a, p. 217). Sotomayor saw her peers as "the most brilliant, dazzlingly articulate, and hard-charging people I'd ever met" (p. 170). Surrounded by "ultra-high wattage classmates," peer learning was helpful (p. 220). She especially appreciated learning with her "compadres" in school (p. 223).

Quality of Instruction. In the private schools, Sotomayor received a solid education through rigorous curriculum and quality teachers. For example, Mrs. Reilly encouraged her to excel by rewarding good performance with gold stars. She recalls "I was a sucker for those gold stars! I was determined to collect as many as I could" (Sotomayor, 2013a, p. 90). While her earlier learning involved more direct instruction and rote learning, high school teachers offered more challenging courses. Miss Katz, in particular, taught Sotomayor that "education could be for something other than opening the doors of job opportunity" (p. 133). Through teaching methods and student projects, Miss Katz encouraged critical thinking. She challenged "us against getting stuck in rote learning, about how we needed to master abstract, conceptual thinking" (p. 132).

Sotomayor's higher education experiences continued toward an upward trend. Princeton provided supportive teachers who created a space for Sotomayor to embrace her cultural heritage (e.g., Professor Peter Winn's course on Puerto Rican history). Similarly, classes at Yale were taught by exceptional instructors who were "established giants in their fields" (Sotomayor, 2013a, p. 219).

Quantity of Instruction. From her early years at Blessed Sacrament School to professional training at Yale Law School, Sotomayor spent much time in school, learning and studying. Aside from the typical school day in elementary school, Sotomayor and her brother were observed studying several hours after school. Her mother remarked, "they study four, five hours every night, and they bring home good grades" (Sotomayor, 2013a, p. 104). Sotomayor continued to be devoted to her studies throughout high school. At Princeton, she spent a considerable amount of time in tutorial sessions and studying independently to catch up with more academically advanced peers.

ENVIRONMENT

Home. Sotomayor's home, culture, language, and family support influenced her life. Although school officials encouraged English at home during elementary school, her family members "spoke virtually no English," allowing her to practice Spanish (Sotomayor, 2013a, p. 14). During high school, she developed more skills in her honors Spanish course, but her fluency strengthened during her Puerto Rico trips. Sotomayor's bilingualism not only reinforced her own cultural values and ethnic identity, but they became key skills as she later served the community.

Sotomayor deeply valued family relationships. Her family supported her through her father's death and later on, her divorce from Kevin Noonan, her high school sweetheart. During high school, *Titi* Aurora also lived with them to help care for them. At Princeton, her mother and cousins visited every year, and the entire family "en masse" always came to celebrate her milestones (Sotomayor, 2013a, p. 206). Although they may not have always understood her educational or career experiences (e.g., being the first to attend college), they remained supportive.

Her mother and *abuelita* (grandmother) were her most influential family members. Largely absent during Sotomayor's childhood, her mother worked hard to pay for private schooling and avoid the father's alcoholism; however, their relationship transformed after her father's death. Despite their limited means, her mother valued education and purchased encyclopedias for her children (Sotomayor, 2013b). Holding high expectations, her mother made it clear they were expected to attend college, since "It's the only way to get ahead in the world" (Sotomayor, 2013a, p. 89). After her father's death, her mother returned for her nursing degree during Sotomayor's high school years. Her mother's determination to succeed in school and life "instilled" values of "compassion, hard work, and courage to face the unknown" (p. 384).

Abuelita was the embodiment of "healer and protector, with her overflowing generosity of spirit" (Sotomayor, 2013a, p. 323). She always reinforced the importance of family and provided unconditional love to her "favorite" grandchild (Academy of Achievement, 2017). *Abuelita* also modeled independence, extraversion, and intelligence. For example, she had the practical intelligence and skills to negotiate with grocers and neighbors. *Abuelita* also helped Sotomayor to appreciate diversity in social, cultural and economic classes.

Kevin Noonan, her high school sweetheart turned spouse, played an essential role in Sotomayor's life during their courtship and marriage. Although they later divorced, they had supported each other through critical years of their development.

Mentors. Sotomayor valued and learned from each of her relationships. She especially "sought out mentors, asking guidance from professors, or colleagues, and in every friendship soaking up eagerly whatever that friend could teach me" (Sotomayor, 2013a, p. 91).

Two school friends served as peer mentors: Donna Renella and Kenny Moy. In primary school, Sotomayor asked Renella, one of the brightest students, how she studied ("Sonia Sotomayor," 2017). Kenny Moy, high school student coach for the Forensics Club, helped her debate skills. He also encouraged her to "try for the Ivy League" (Sotomayor, 2013a, p. 147), a decision that set her trajectory to become a lawyer. Sotomayor appreciated Moy's friendship and mentorship, since he was one of the first fellow Spellman students to make it into an elite college (Academy of Achievement, 2017; "Sonia Sotomayor," 2017).

At Princeton, Sotomayor met fellow Puerto Rican Jose Cabranes, her *"true mentor"* and role model (Sotomayor, 2013a, p. 224). Cabranes embraced his ethnic identity and served as a "citizen-lawyer" for the Puerto Rican community (p. 226). As his research assistant, Sotomayor learned about Puerto Rican history and U.S. citizenship. Bureau Chief John Fried was another key mentor who Sotomayor admired for his fairness and integrity. When Sotomayor struggled with when to try cases, he helped analyze them. Fried encouraged and supported her (p. 263).

Other key influences and role models included some of her colleagues. Role model Judge Harold Rothwax was a "black-robed presence, the first embodiment of an ideal I would be able to observe up close" (Sotomayor, 2013a, p. 267). In her efforts to become a federal judge, Senator Daniel Patrick Moynihan, David Botwinik, and Fran Bernstein became key supporters (p. 370). Senator Moynihan later nominated Sotomayor to her current position.

Peers. Peers played a critical role in Sotomayor's development. She viewed her classmates and colleagues as invaluable resources, who provided guidance and support throughout different times.

Cousins Nelson, Miriam, Eddie, Charlie and Tony were her closest peers while growing up. Her closest cousin Nelson was a "genius and [her] best friend" (Sotomayor, 2013a, p. 26), who battled a drug addiction, eventually ending his life. Outside of the family, Gilmar was her best friend until he moved away.

In primary school, Donna Renella helped her to study more effectively by sharing her study habits ("Sonia Sotomayor," 2017). During high school, Sotomayor hosted student council and Forensics Club meetings at her home, which allowed her to socialize with high-achieving peers such as Kenny Moy (Sotomayor, 2013a, p. 130).

At Princeton, she met other students of color who shared similar sentiments and insecurities about being there such as roommate Dolores Chavez (Sotomayor, 2013a, p. 184). Another friend, Margarita Rosa, introduced her to Acción Puertorriqueño, where they shared concerns for social justice and developed a support network (Biography.com Editors, 2019). Her roommate, Felice Shea, also played a role by affirming Sotomayor's academic ability.

At Yale, she respected her peers who all worked hard. Sotomayor developed deep friendships with "four older brothers I'd never had"—Felix Lopez, Drew Ryce, Rudy Aragon and George Keys (Sotomayor, 2013a, p. 222). Charlie Hey-Maestre, another male friend introduced, Sotomayor to Cabranes, who would eventually become her future mentor.

Professionally, colleagues also played a significant role during her career. For example, public defender and lifelong friend Dawn Cardi taught Sotomayor about mercy and using discretion in her profession.

Extracurricular Time. From childhood through adulthood, Sotomayor spent most of her time studying and reading. Reading became an escape from her childhood diabetes and father's death: "Books had seen me through an earlier time of trouble, and their presence all around me was both a comfort and an answer to the question of why I had come here [Princeton]" (Sotomayor, 2013a, p. 162). She was a voracious reader and found solace in libraries (Biography.com Editors, 2019). As a child, she read Nancy Drew mystery books, who she admired for her "character and courage" (Sotomayor, 2013b). Sotomayor also enjoyed reading the Encyclopedia Britannica "for an hour a day ... for almost a year. It was a universe opener" (Sotomayor, 2013b).

Although television is generally viewed as being less constructive, if it were not for television, Sotomayor would never have discovered *Perry Mason* (Biography.com Editors, 2019). The show inspired her to become a lawyer and judge. While Sotomayor's mother was criticized for her children watching television while doing homework, "It seemed lost on everyone that television helped broaden our horizons beyond the Bronx" (Sotomayor, 2013a, p. 104). Television also served as a form of escape from the challenges at home for Sotomayor and her brother.

She also enjoyed traveling, especially to Puerto Rico where she learned more about her culture, family, and identity. Other hobbies while growing up included ballet, guitar, piano, and self-defense. In high school, Sotomayor also worked at a Jewish bakery and participated in afterschool programs (e.g., cadet program, Forensics Club). At Princeton, she was a key operator for her work-study position. If Sotomayor was not studying or working, she participated in student organizations and volunteerism such as Acción Puertorriqueño, Discipline Committee, and the governance board at the Third World Center, which supported minority students (Biography, 2019). At Yale, Sotomayor served as co-chair of LANA (Latino, Asian, and Native American student association) and managing editor of a student-run journal called *Yale Studies in World Public Order*.

Summary of Key PGM Findings

INDIVIDUAL APTITUDE: ABILITY, DEVELOPMENT, & MOTIVATION

From childhood to her current position, Sotomayor displayed productive giftedness. Her early ability and effort over time influenced her educational and career trajectories. Sotomayor was undoubtedly motivated throughout her life. Rather than seeing adversity as a barrier, she took on the challenge and viewed it as an opportunity, motivating her to work even harder. Sotomayor's character traits of perseverance and resilience are evident in her self-regulation and growth mindset (Dweck, 2006; Paik, 2012, 2013).

Development and learning occur throughout life; accumulative learning over time increases productive outcomes (Merton, 1968; Paik, 2015; Walberg, 1984). For Sotomayor, her talent and skills developed from childhood to adulthood. At a young age, with the goal of becoming a lawyer and judge, she developed her skills by studying hard, practicing public speaking at church and debate club, and leading as an activist during college and graduate school. Sotomayor was motivated to learn, accomplishing her endeavors.

INSTRUCTION: LEARNING CLIMATE, QUALITY & QUANTITY OF INSTRUCTION

Sotomayor enjoyed school and sought refuge in educational institutions throughout her life. Her private school education gave her a solid foundation and key skills. Teachers at all levels took great interest in Sotomayor and she received many educational opportunities along the way. Attending Princeton and Yale gave her more social and cultural capital, providing even more opportunities for her career. Throughout her education, she experienced overall conducive learning climates, supportive teachers, rigorous curriculum, high expectations, and engaging school communities. While school wasn't always easy for her, she continued to work hard and excel in her education.

ENVIRONMENT: HOME, MENTORS, PEERS, & EXTRACURRICULAR TIME

Home and family support played a critical role for Sotomayor. Although her upbringing had its challenges, she drew strength from her family connections, especially her mother and grandmother. Culture, language, and ethnic identity were validated at home through family relationships and visits to Puerto Rico.

Mentors provided Sotomayor with academic, career, and psychosocial skills from early peers to her true mentor, Cabranes. Navigating school or career without mentors or role models would have been difficult for her. Key mentors provided more access and opportunity, support as well as resources to help her become successful.

Peers were essential in developing academic and career success. Sotomayor's support network consisted of high-achieving peers throughout her life. These friendships also opened doors for her, providing the socio-emotional connections that she needed in her different worlds.

Sotomayor was conscientious on how she spent her time. If she wasn't studying or working, she was involved in constructive extracurricular activities that equipped her with skills. For Sotomayor, even watching television helped her to envision her career goals. Most time, however, was spent on reading, participating in school clubs, volunteering, and travel.

Conclusion

The Productive Giftedness Model provides a comprehensive and systematic perspective to understand individual, instructional, and environmental factors that influence success. The model highlighted key factors that examine the life and success of Sonia Sotomayor from her childhood throughout adulthood. There are a number of key implications we can learn from this work:

First, what are the factors that influence success? Research shows that individual, instructional, and environmental factors have bearing on learning and development (Paik, 2013, 2015; Paik et al., 2019; Walberg, 1984). Success is often explained or predicted by one factor, but Sotomayor's life helps us to understand that many factors work in concert with each other (Bloom, 1985: Paik, 2013, 2015; Paik, et al., 2019; Walberg, 1984). Life's complications require more than one perspective. In Sotomayor's case, her early ability and motivation (individual factors) were enhanced through quality education and schools (instructional factors), and key relationships and time well spent (environmental factors) continued to sustain her. Since home and family life was not always easy, Sotomayor sought resources and opportunities outside, oftentimes through school, teachers, peers and mentors. Sotomayor's initiative to find additional support and resources provided more access and opportunities in her schooling and career.

Second, why does context matter in understanding outcomes? Context matters because it helps us to understand the whole person at that point in time. Historical, socio-cultural, demographic, and other factors provide insight into Sotomayor's upbringing, identity development, and how key experiences merge together. Altogether, they help us to understand who she is as an individual. Context gives meaning to one's overall experiences. For Sotomayor, her life story and success are even more compelling because of her contextual factors. Growing up in adverse conditions, navigating multiple worlds, and learning "new" languages within each respective world require individual strength. However, without role models and key relationships inferred in Sotomayor's quote at the beginning of this [reading], even gifted-ness alone cannot open doors. Context also sheds light on the availability of opportunities, which are not always afforded to every individual (Paik; 2013, 2015; Paik et al., 2018).

Third, we can't always change context, but then what can we change? Alterable factors within the model emphasize the importance of "altering" (or optimizing) conditions. For example, individual agency can facilitate more effort towards high achievement. In the same vein, parents', teachers', peers', and mentors' atti-tudes and practices should also not be underestimated. Individual motivation did indeed make a difference for Sotomayor. Without her growth mindset, she would have not sought help. Advocating an "effort-ability" approach, the model emphasizes the importance of both effort and ability, which Sotomayor embod-ied in her life. However, the burden cannot be on the individual herself; what can parents, teachers, mentors, and others alter? They can change their attitudes and practices to encourage and support more children of various abilities. High expectations, support, and caring can go a long way for all children, especially from under-served populations.

Recommendations
Based on the findings, this [reading] offers some key recommendations:

1. Support learning and development with key *individual, instructional, and environmental factors*; accumulative learning can support high achieve-ment over time.

2. Know that *contextual factors* provide greater understanding of the whole child; awareness of the child's context can provide more insight and better align support.

3. Help students, parents, and teachers to optimize *alterable factors*; changing attitudes, behaviors, and practices will increase the likelihood of positive change.

4. Encourage both *effort* and *ability*; ability when fueled with effort can sustain high performance over time.

5. Find mentors for students; peer and adult mentors can be game changers for academic, career, and psychosocial skills.

6. Provide opportunities, support, and resources; no child can move forward without it.

7. Believe in all children; high expectations can make a world of difference.

BIOGRAPHICAL SOURCES

Academy of Achievement. (2017, March 24). *Sonia Sotomayor: The power of words*. Retrieved from: http://www.achievement.org/achiever/sonia-sotomayor/

Bernier-Grand, C. (2010). *Sonia Sotomayor: Supreme court justice*. New York, NY: Marshall Cavendish Children.

Biography.com Editors. (2019, Jan. 16). *Sonia Sotomayor biography*. Retrieved from: https://www.biography.com/people/sonia-sotomayor-453906

Felix, A. (2011). *Sonia Sotomayor: The true American dream*. New York, NY: Penguin Group.

McElroy, L. (2010). *Sonia Sotomayor: First Hispanic U.S. Supreme Court Justice*. Minneapolis, MN: Lerner Publication Company.

Sotomayor, S. (2002). A Latina Judge's Voice. *Berkeley La Raza LJ, 13*(1), 87–93.

Sotomayor, S. (2013a). *My beloved world*. New York, NY: Vintage Books.

Sotomayor, S. (2013b, Jan. 19). *For Justice Sotomayor, books unlocked imagination* (N. Totenberg, Interviewer), NPR. Retrieved from: https://www.npr.org/2013/01/19/169772287/for-justice-sotomayor-books-unlocked-imagination

Sotomayor, S. (2017, March 21). *Sonia Sotomayor: Power of words* (A. Winkler, Interviewer). Academy of Achievement. Retrieved from: http://www.achievement.org/achiever/sonia-%20%20%20%20sotomayor/#interview

Stein, M. (2017). *Who is Sonia Sotomayor?* New York, NY: Penguin Random House LLC.

REFERENCES

Albert, R. S. (1994). The achievement of eminence: A longitudinal study of exceptionally gifted boys and their families. In R. F. Subotnik & K. D. Arnold

(Eds.), *Beyond Terman: Contemporary longitudinal studies of giftedness and talent* (pp. 282–315). Norwood, NJ: Ablex Publishing Co.

Allen, T. D., Eby, L. T., & Lentz, E. (2006). Mentorship behaviors and mentorship quality associated with formal mentoring programs: closing the gap between research and practice. *Journal of Applied Psychology, 91*(3), 567.

Bloom, B. S. (Ed.). (1985). *Developing talent in young people.* New York, NY: Ballantine.

Burke, M. A., & Sass, T. R. (2013). Classroom peer effects and student achievement. *Journal of Labor Economics, 31*(1), 51–82. Retrieved from: https://doi.org/10.1086/666653

Busato, V. V., Prins, F. J., Elshout, J. J., & Hamaker, C. (2000). Intellectual ability, learning style, personality, achievement motivation and academic success of psychology students in higher education. *Personality and Individual Differences, 29*(6), 1057–1068.

Clasen, D. R., & Clasen, R. E. (2003). Mentoring the gifted and talented. In N. Colangelo & G. A. Davis (Eds.), *Handbook of gifted education* (pp. 254–267). Boston, MA: Pearson Education.

Collinson, V. (1996). *Becoming an exemplary teacher: Integrating professional, interpersonal, and intrapersonal knowledge.* In Paper presented at the annual meeting of the Japan-United States Teacher Education Consortium (p. 17). Retrieved from: http://eric.ed.gov/?id=ED401227

Cox, C. M. (1926). *The early mental traits of three hundred geniuses.* Stanford, CA: Stanford University Press.

Creswell, J. W. (2012). *Educational research: Planning, conducting, and evaluation quantitative and qualitative Research.* Boston, MA: Pearson Education.

Cridel, C. (2016). *An introduction to biographical research.* Retrieved from: http://www.aera.net/SIG013/Research-Connections/Introduction-to-Biographical-Research

Crisp, G., & Cruz, I. (2009). Mentoring college students: A critical review of the literature between 1990 and 2007. *Research in higher education, 50*(6), 525–545.

Csikszentmihalyi, M. (1992). Motivation and creativity. In R. S. Albert (Ed.), *Genius and eminence* (pp. 19–33). New York, NY: Pergamon Press.

Csikszentmihalyi, M., Rathunde, K., & Whalen, S. (1993). *Talented teenagers: The roots of success and failure.* Cambridge, UK: Cambridge University Press.

Dweck, C. (2006). *Mindset: The new psychology of success.* New York, NY: Random House

Eccles, J. S., & Barber, B. L. (1999). Student council, volunteering, basketball, or marching band what kind of extracurricular involvement matters? *Journal of Adolescent Research, 14*(1), 10–43.

Fairweather, E., & Cramond, B. (2010). Infusing creative and critical thinking into the curriculum together. In R. A. Beghetto & J. C. Kaufman (Eds.), *Nurturing creativity in the classroom* (pp. 113–141). New York, NY: Cambridge University Press.

Fraser, B. J., Walberg, H. J., Welch, W. W., & Hattie, J. A. (1987). Syntheses of educational productivity research. *International Journal of Educational Research, 11*, 145–252.

Freeman, K. A., & Walberg, H. J. (1999). Childhood traits and conditions of eminent African American women. *Journal for the Education of the Gifted, 22*(4), 402–419.

Friedrich, A., Flunger, B., Nagengast, B., Jonkmann, K., & Trautwein, U. (2015). Pygmalion effects in the classroom: Teacher expectancy effects on students' math achievement. *Contemporary Educational Psychology, 41*, 1–12. Retrieved from: https://doi.org/10.1016/j.cedpsych.2014.10.006

Goertzel, V., Goertzel, M. G., Goertzel, T. G., & Hansen, A. (2004). *Cradles of eminence: Childhoods of more than 700 famous men and women* (2nd ed.). Scottsdale, AZ: Gifted Psychology Press.

Hong, E., & Milgram, R. M. (2011). Preventing talent loss: A major challenge facing educators and parents. In *Preventing talent loss* (pp. 3–10). New York, NY: Routledge.

Kaufman, S. B., & Kaufman, J. C. (2007). Ten years to expertise, many more to greatness: An investigation to writers. *Journal of Creative Behavior, 41*, 114–124.

Kiewra, K. (2014). Seven ways parents help children unleash their talents. *Parenting for High Potential, 3*(5), 4–6, 18–19.

Kitano, M. K. (1998). Gifted Latina women. *Journal for the Education of the Gifted, 21*(2), 131–159. Retrieved from: https://doi.org/10.1177/016235329802100202

Merton, R. K. (1968). The Matthew effect in science. *Science, 159*, 56–63.

Okagaki, L., & Sternberg, R. J. (1993). Parental beliefs and children's school performance. *Child Development, 64*, 36–56.

Olszewski-Kublius, P. (2010). *Psychological factors in the development of adulthood giftedness from childhood talent.* Retrieved from: http://www.ctd.northwestern.edu/resources/displayArticle/?id=125

Olszewski-Kublius, P., Subotnik, R. F., & Worrell, F. C. (2018). *Talent development as framework for gifted education: Implications for best practices and applications in schools.* Waco, TX: Prufrock Press Inc.

Paik, S. J. (2008). Altering the curriculum of the home: Learning environments for Korean and U.S. students. *Marriage and Family Review, 43*, 289–307.

Paik, S. J. (2012). From dogmatic mastery to creative productivity. In D. Ambrose & R. Sternberg (Eds.) *How dogmatic beliefs harm creativity and higher-level thinking.* New York, NY: Routledge.

Paik, S. J. (2013). Nurturing talent, creativity, and productive giftedness: A new mastery model. In K. H. Kim, J. C. Kaufman, J. Baer, & B. Sriraman (Eds.), *Creatively gifted students are not like other gifted students: Research, theory, and practice* (pp. 101–119). Boston, MA: SensePublishers.

Paik, S. J. (2015). Educational productivity. In *International encyclopedia of the social & behavioral sciences* (pp. 272–278). Elsevier. Retrieved from: http://linkinghub.elsevier.com/retrieve/pii/B9780080970868920762

Paik, S. J., Choe, S. M., Otto, W. J., & Rahman, R. (2018). Learning about the lives and early experiences of notable Asian American women: Productive giftedness, childhood traits, and supportive conditions. *Journal for the Education of the Gifted, 41*(2), 160–192.

Paik, S. J., Gozali, C., & Marshall-Harper, K. R. (2019). Productive giftedness: A new mastery approach to understanding talent development. In R. F. Subotnik, S. G. Assouline, P. Olszewski-Kubilius, H. Stoeger, & A. Ziegler (Eds.), *The future of research in talent development: Promising trends, evidence, and implications of innovative scholarship for policy and practice. New Directions for Child and Adolescent Development, 168,* 131–159.

Paik, S. J., & Walberg, H. J. (2007). *Narrowing the achievement gap: Strategies for educating Latino, Black, and Asian students.* New York, NY: Springer.

Redding, S. (2003). Parents and learning. In *Educational practices series-2.* Lausanne, Switzerland: International Academy of Education.

Roberts, B. (2002). *Biographical research.* Philadelphia, PA: Open University Press.

Sacerdote, B. (2011). Peer effects in education: How might they work, how big are they and how much do we know thus far? In E. A. Hanushek, S. Machin, & L. Woessman (Eds.), *Handbook of the economics of education* (Vol. 3, pp. 249–277). San Diego, CA: Elsevier. Retrieved from: http://www.sciencedirect.com/science/article/pii/B9780444534293000041

Scandura, T. A. (1992). Mentorship and career mobility: An empirical investigation. *Journal of Organizational Behavior, 13*(2), 169–174.

Sternberg, R. J. (1999). The theory of successful intelligence. *Review of General Psychology, 3*(4), 292.

Subotnik, R., Edmiston, A. M., Cook, L., & Ross, M.D. (2010). Mentoring for talent development, creativity, social skills, and insider knowledge: The APA Catalyst Program. *Journal of Advanced Academics, 21*(4), 714–739.

Tableman, B. (2004). *Best practice briefs: School climate and learning* (No. 31, pp. 1–10). Lansing, MI: University-Community Partnerships: Michigan State University.

Vardardottir, A. (2013). Peer effects and academic achievement: a regression discontinuity approach. *Economics of Education Review, 36*, 108–121. Retrieved from: https://doi.org/10.1016/j.econedurev.2013.06.011

Walberg, H. J. (1982). Childhood traits and environmental conditions of highly eminent adults. *Gifted Child Quarterly, 25*, 103–107.

Walberg, H. J. (1984). Improving the productivity of America's schools. *Educational Leadership, 41*, 19–27.

Walberg, H. J., & Paik, S. J. (1997). Home environments for learning. In H. J. Walberg & G. D. Haertel (Eds.), *Psychology and educational practice* (pp. 356–368). Berkeley, CA: McCutchan Publishing.

Walberg, H. J., & Paik, S. J. (2005). Making giftedness productive. In Sternberg, R. J. & Davidson, J. E. (Eds), *Conceptions of giftedness* (Vol. 2, pp. 395–410). New York, NY: Cambridge University Press.

Walberg, H. J., & Stariha, W. E. (1992). Productive human capital: Learning, creativity, and eminence. *Creativity Research Journal, 5*, 323–340.

Wallace, T., & Walberg, H. J. (1987). Personality traits and childhood environments of eminent essayists. *Gifted Child Quarterly, 31*(2), 65–69.

Toward a New Philosophy of Legality and Social Movements

You should now begin thinking about larger social movements might begin to construct alternatives to liberal or Western legal stories. In the reading that follows you will consider a theoretical framework that begins to imagine an alternative social order. Finally, it is important to think about the future. How might social movements now use similar tactics and beliefs from the past? In what ways will those movements be different?

FUTURES OF SOCIAL MOVEMENTS

Charles Tilly and Lesley Wood[1]

Phoenix, Arizona, is located in the Sonoran Desert, where temperatures can rise to 120 Fahrenheit (49 degrees Celsius). According to the U.S. census, the city is home to more than 1 million people, 41 percent of the population identifying themselves as Hispanic. Arizona borders Mexico, and there are ongoing tensions about immigration and the rights of non-citizens. In 2004, the state of Arizona passed Proposition 200, a law that limited the availability of certain benefits to residents without current immigration documentation. The following year, the Minuteman Project was launched as "concerned citizens" formed armed patrols to monitor the United States/Mexico border to stop those trying to cross into the United States (Castañeda 2006, 2019; Shapira 2013). In 2006, members of Congress proposed bills that would limit the rights of undocumented immigrants to receive social services and support. These bills also included stipulations that made defending and supporting undocumented immigrants a crime. In response, there were massive immigrant rights marches across the country (Voss and Bloemraad 2011; Zepeda-Millán 2017).

Phoenix was one of the fastest growing cities in the United States growing from 983,403 people in 1990 to 1,552,259 in 2007, when the economic recession happened. Between 2007 and 2008, housing values in the area registered the largest decline in the country, over 30 percent of their previous value (Florida 2009). Unemployment increased, population growth declined, and tensions around immigration intensified. Democratic governor Janet Napolitano passed the State Employer Sanctions law, which levied penalties against businesses that hired undocumented immigrants. The law went into effect in 2008, at the same time that local sheriff, Joe Arpaio, increased his raids into Latino communities, detaining and deporting, at the police's discretion, anyone found without documentation. To add to the tension, on March 27, 2010, a rancher was killed near the border, and although suspects were not identified, the murder was blamed on undocumented immigrants or drug smugglers.

---

[1]   Ernesto Castañeda revised this [reading].

At the Federal level, Republicans framed the Obama administration as being "soft" on immigration enforcement. Arguing this, the new Republican governor, Jan Brewer (2009 to 2015), signed bill SB1070 in 2010. The law required police to question people about their immigration status if the police suspected them to be undocumented. Therefore, police could arrest day laborers while soliciting work if they were in the United States illegally, and police departments could have been sued if they did not actively enforce immigration laws.

From the date the bill was announced in early April, until it went into effect in July 2010, supporters and opponents of the bill rallied at the State Capitol building in Phoenix and marched through the city's streets. Sometimes they faced off against one another, chanting at each other across a line of caution tape. "We have rights!" shouted anti-SB1070 demonstrators. "No, you don't!" the pro-SB1070 group would shout in response (Daly 2010). Opponents of the bill chanted "Si, se puede," a phrase coined by Chicano civil rights leaders Dolores Huerta and Hugo Chavez that means, "Yes, we can." The use of a slogan in Spanish is especially significant in this context as demonstrators demanded a more inclusive society. The use of Spanish and the historical connection to the chant is also a continuation of a longstanding movement for Latino and immigrant rights in America. Others locked themselves to the doors of the Capitol building and were arrested for civil disobedience (Lemons 2010). The Phoenix Suns basketball team wore shirts that read "Los Suns" and explained that they were doing this "to honor [the] Latino community and the diversity of our league, the state of Arizona, and our nation" (Kerby 2010). Other opponents called for a boycott of the state, refusing to buy goods or services from Arizona or to visit the state. This boycott was endorsed by municipalities, individuals, and organizations across the country (AZ Central.com 2010). In response, a "buycott" was organized by the bill's supporters who encouraged spending at local stores and Arizona-based businesses (*Freedom's Wings* 2010).

A month after the bill was signed; more than 100,000 people marched in opposition to it (Flaherty 2010). The *Arizona Republic* reported: "Banging drums, chanting, singing, and waving American flags, the throng made its way toward the Capitol. Organizers, scattered throughout the crowds, picked up trash and provided water to the marchers." The following week, the Arizona Tea Party organized the "Phoenix Rising" rally inside a baseball stadium in support of the bill. Among the speakers was Sheriff Arpaio, known for his controversial raids of immigrant communities. He spoke to the crowd, and called July 29—the day SB 1070 was set to go into effect—the "magic day." He explained, "That's the day that—barring any legal holds—the law goes into effect. That's when I'm going to start enforcing that law." The crowd began to chant, "Joe, Joe, Joe!" enthusiastically. Rally organizer Daniel Smeriglio, head of the Pennsylvania-based Voice of the People USA, thanked the crowd for taking a stand. In a WUNC display, he said, "I know the heat is a deterrent, [but] we are here to say somebody did something and we stand with you. You represent the very best of America. That is why we are here" (Sexton, Madrid, and Gardiner 2010).

Randy Leever described an anti-immigrant rally in the small town of Palominas, Arizona, located right by the U.S.–Mexico border, a few months later. A crowd of between 500 and 800 conservative Americans gathered beside the 15-foot-tall border fence. Hundreds of small U.S. flags and nationalist messages were attached to the fence posts (Cooper 2010; Leever in Chron.com 2010). The rally was held on the land of Glenn Spencer, president of the border watch group American Border Patrol, whose property ends at the border fence. The United Border Coalition/United We Stand for Americans and Tea Party Nation organizations planned and sponsored the event. The rally attracted some big names: Arizona state senator Russell Pearce, who co-authored the state's immigration law, U.S. Senate hopeful J. D. Hayworth, and—the favorite among many attendees—Sheriff Arpaio. Leever reports,

> Some of the most salient points presented by a few of the speakers were greeted with loud applause and cheering. At one point, many of the crowd lined up at the fence and were chanting "USA, USA, USA," while waving American flags.
>
> (Leever in Chron.com 2010)

Down the highway from the rally was a group of 30 counterprotesters, who claimed that Arizona's immigration policies were racist and inhumane. Three of these protesters were able to get into the event and turned their backs to the stage as Arpaio began to speak.

Although the rally at the border attracted a great deal of attention, most of the marches and rallies about Arizona's immigration law took place at the state capitol buildings, the site of state power. Even a year after the bill was passed, supporters and opponents of the bill continued to march and rally there, sometimes at the same time. On April 22, 2011, hundreds of opponents and a few dozen supporters of the legislation rallied there, trying to out-chant one another and promote their position to authorities and the public (Cone Sexton 2011).

No one attuned to national and international news during the spring and summer of 2010 should have any trouble decoding these Arizona protests or their spin-offs in Alabama and elsewhere. North Americans and people across the world can easily recognize them as street demonstrations, a standard means of broadcasting support or opposition regarding political issues. In this case, demonstration and counterdemonstration represented opposition to, and support for, a law that will make migration from Mexico to the United States more difficult. While the people of Arizona took to the streets or gathered in baseball stadiums and plazas, hundreds of street demonstrations were occurring elsewhere in the world. Some of them were concerned with immigration and human rights, but most of them took up other locally urgent questions. In the early twenty-first century, the street demonstration looks like an all-purpose political tool–perhaps less effective in the short run than buying a legislator or mounting a military coup. Within democratic and semidemocratic regimes, demonstrations are an effective alternative to elections, opinion polls, and letter writing as a way of voicing public positions.

As the case of Arizona shows, the twenty-first-century demonstration has two major variants. In the first variant, outside the capitol buildings, participants gather, or rally, in a symbolically potent public location, where through speech and action they display their collective attachment to a well-defined cause. In the second, they proceed through public thoroughfares offering similar displays of commitment. Often, the two combine, as activists march to a rallying place, or as multiple columns converge from different places on a single symbolically powerful destination and/or then march again (such destinations include the Washington Mall, Trafalgar Square, and Tahrir Square). Increasingly, counterdemonstrators show up to advocate a contrary view and to challenge the demonstrators' claim to the spaces in question. Police or troops may station themselves along the line of march or around the place of assembly, and deliberately separate demonstrators from counterdemonstrators. Sometimes police or troops bar demonstrators' access to important spaces, buildings, monuments, or people. Passersby or spectators often signal their approval or disapproval of the cause that the demonstrators are supporting. Later, they may join the discussion in lunchtime arguments or online debates.

Hundreds of comments were posted online in response to coverage about the protests on May 29 on ArizonaCentral.com. Someone whose username was "Mr. Cynic" wrote:

> Regardless of the number of protesters that marched, the fact remains that 60 percent of the general public is in favor of the law. Vocal minorities are just that, and their cause is not helped when they have to import marchers from California and other states. Obama can fire up Eric Holder and send

him to court and Al Sharpton can blather on all he wants. It will not matter in the long run because in this country, the majority still rules.

Despite his dismissal of the protesters, "Mr. Cynic" clearly understands that the demonstrators are trying to display the worthiness, unity, numbers, and commitment of their cause and themselves. His comments try to undermine such displays by arguing that the group is not worthy, nor united or committed. The contest for legitimacy that surrounds social movements is one that has serious consequences for public life.

Thanks to legal challenges by anti-SB1020, on June 25, 2012, the U.S. Supreme Court struck down three of the four provisions of S.B. 1070. Those that required legal immigrants to carry registration documents at all times; allowed state police to arrest any individual for suspicion of being an illegal immigrant; and made it a crime for an illegal immigrant to search for a job (or to hold one) in the state.

U.S. District Judge Susan Ritchie Bolton found Judge Arpaio to be in contempt of the law on July 31, 2017 (Cassidy 2017) with sentencing scheduled on October 5, 2017. This was a victory for immigrant rights' groups until 2017, when President Trump offered a presidential pardon to Arpaio (Hirschfeld Davis, and Haberman 2017). This episode reveals the tensions between state and local laws and the federal government in the United States. It also shows how mobilization may be able to create change at one level, but fail at another.

Conclusions

[...] Street demonstrations also have some identifiable kin: municipal parades, party conventions, mass meetings, inaugurals, commencements, religious revivals, and electoral rallies. Most citizens of democracies know the difference. Participants in such events sometimes bend them toward the forms and programs of demonstrations, for example by wearing ostentatious symbols or shouting slogans in support of a cause at a college commencement. Many of the same principles apply: the separation of participants from spectators, the presence of guards to contain the crowd, and so on. Considered as a whole, this array of gatherings exhibits (1) remarkable coherence, (2) systematic internal variation, and (3) type by type, impressive uniformity across places, programs, and participants.

[...] They documented the distinctive combination of campaigns, repertoire, and WUNC displays in a form of politics that were almost non-existent before the mid-eighteenth century, yet became available for popular making of claims across much of the world during the next two centuries. Successful movements helped to spread the ideas and tactics internationally. They also documented the marvelous duality of social movements: quite general and recognizable in their broad outlines, yet impressively adaptable to local circumstances and idioms. That duality comes across in the news from Arizona.

HISTORICAL CONTINUITIES AND INNOVATIONS

Residents of Arizona might have been surprised to learn that their protests owe something to the violent victories of a dissolute demagogue in London during the 1760s, and to the anti-British agitation of a failed brewer in Boston at about the same time. But we now know that John Wilkes, Samuel Adams, and their collaborators really started something that would influence social groups across the world for many years. The people of Arizona are still using a twenty-first-century version of that innovation of the eighteenth and nineteenth centuries.

Let us indulge a historical fantasy: Suppose that John Wilkes and Samuel Adams time traveled intact from the 1760s to Arizona in May 2010 and watched the immigrant rights demonstrators. Conversing to see if they could figure out what these twenty-first-century people were doing and why they could say:

> Wilkes: I've never seen anything like it.
> Adams: You can say that again.
> Wilkes: But it's something like a church service ...
> Adams: Or a workmen's parade.
> Wilkes: Where is the audience? Who are they talking to?
> Adams: And where are the troops or constables?
> Wilkes: Still one thing's familiar: they're arguing about a people's liberty.
> Adams: You know, it reminds me of an election campaign, with people wearing candidates' colors, holding flags, chanting slogans, gathering in central squares, and marching along major thoroughfares.
> Wilkes: Except that it's so *civilized*. How do these people expect to make any difference?
> Adams: Maybe we should ask them.

The fantastic encounter does not show Wilkes and Adams the full apparatus of social movements at work: the combination of multiple performances and WUNC displays in sustained, coordinated making of program, identity, and/or standing claims. Nor does it tell them about the many other activists outside of Arizona who are likewise joining social movements for and against the immigrant rights, often employing news releases, petitions, and public meetings in addition to street demonstrations. But this imaginary conversation does raise crucial questions about the present and future of social movements. Has the social movement lost its political effectiveness? Is the internationalization of power, politics, and social movement organization rendering amateur local, regional, or even national efforts obsolete? If the forms of social movements have changed so much over the last two centuries, what further changes might we expect to see during the rest of the twenty-first century?

How Can We Predict the Future?

Most likely the right answer to all these questions is: it depends. No doubt, it depends on which countries, which issues, which claimants, and which objects of claims we have in mind; for the moment, the futures of all social movements in Kazakhstan, for example, look dim, while social movements still seem to be enjoying active lives in Canada and Spain. Currently, movements protesting climate change are making little headway, while movements against police brutality are at least attracting energetic international support. More generally, we must distinguish among possible future trajectories for social movements on one side, and a number of different social movement scales on the other. Figure 2.1 schematizes the distinctions.

The figure builds in two main dimensions: one, directions of change from growth to decline; the other, scales from local to global. The diagram's "global" scale represents the possibility voiced by today's advocates of transnational activism, not merely that international actors and international targets will become routine in future social movements but that social movements will regularly coordinate popular claim making across the entire globe. [...]

Figure 2.1 flattens into two dimensions a series of likely further changes in social movements we have seen occurring from their earliest days: changes in campaigns, repertoires, and WUNC displays. Surely the twenty-first century will bring a new program, identity, and standing claims—new issues for campaigns—that the century's first few years leave almost unimaginable; suppose, for example, that animal rights activists mounted campaigns to gain citizenship rights for the great apes. Someone will almost certainly invent new social movement performances and thereby alter the general social movement repertoire. WUNC displays will evolve as well, perhaps by adopting technologies that will broadcast instantly how many people are voicing support or opposition for a given social movement claim—thus giving new expression to the **Numbers** in WUNC. If social movements survive the twenty-first

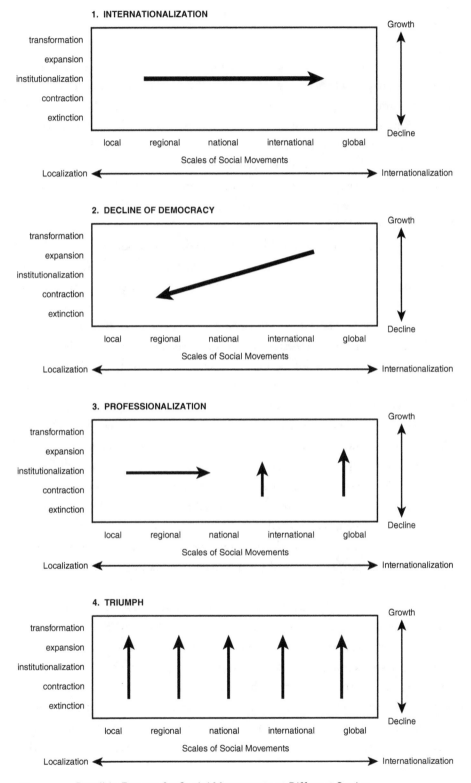

Figure 2.1   Possible Futures for Social Movements at Different Scales

century, they will surely leave it much transformed with regard to campaigns, repertoires, and WUNC displays.

Despite neglecting such changes in social movements, the diagram implies a wide range of hypothetical possibilities. We might, for example, imagine a future combination of extinction of social movements at the local level, institutionalization at the national level, and expansion plus dramatic transformation at the global level. Or we could imagine that massive declines in state power will simultaneously activate linked regional and international movements, on the model of demands for indigenous rights or regional autonomy that seize power from states but also receive backing and guarantees from international organizations.

An overall shift to the right side within the diagram would mean that local, regional, and perhaps even national social movements gave way to international and global movements: extensive internationalization. A general shift to the left of the diagram—not much expected these days—would mean a decline of larger-scale movements in favor of a new localism. A net shift upward would signify general expansion and transformation of social movement activity. Vertical moves toward the middle would signal widespread institutionalization: the whole world involved in social movements at multiple scales, but with nongovernmental organizations, professional social movement entrepreneurs, and close relations to political authorities dominating the action. Below the midpoint, a general shift downward would represent decline or disappearance of social movements, likewise across the board. More plausible predictions would feature separate trajectories for social movements at different scales, for example, expansion and transformation of international social movements at the same time as local social movements contracted and institutionalized.

We must ground any predictions on the knowledge we have gleaned from examining two centuries of social movement history and the [reading]'s main arguments:

From their eighteenth-century origins onward, social movements have proceeded not as solo performances but as interactive campaigns. By now, this observation should be self-evident. Thus, to predict future social movements involves thinking about changing relations among claimants, objects of claims, audiences, and authorities rather than simply extrapolating the most visible features of social movement performances. Think of, for example, the intricate interplay of movements, counter-movements, authorities, publics, and external powers across the fast-changing world in 1989 with the fall of the Soviet Union.

Social movements combine three kinds of claims: program, identity, and standing. Program claims involve stated support for or opposition to actual or proposed actions by the objects of movement claims. Identity claims consist of assertions that "we"—the claimants—constitute a unified force to be reckoned with. WUNC (worthiness, unity, numbers, and commitment) performances back up identity claims. Standing claims assert ties and similarities to other political actors, for example as excluded minorities, properly constituted citizens' groups, or loyal supporters of the regime. They sometimes concern the standing of *other* political actors, for example in calls for expulsion of immigrants or their exclusion from citizenship. The nineteenth-century United States showed us a dazzling (and sometimes depressing) array of program, identity, and standing claims with regard to which racial, ethnic, and gender categories deserved citizenship rights. Clearly, program, identity, and standing claims can evolve in partial independence from each other; standing claims, for example, depend sensitively on which political actors already have full standing, and which political procedures change an actor's standing. They thus depend on the rise or fall of democracy.

The relative salience of program, identity, and standing claims varies significantly among social movements, among claimants within movements, and among phases of movements. If institutionalization eclipsed identity and standing claims in favor of programs advocated or opposed by established specialists in social movement claim making, that eclipse would constitute a major change in twenty-first-century social movements. Professionalization of social movement organizations and entrepreneurs sometimes leads to new identity and standing claims. Yet, professionalization tips the balance away from identity and standing toward programs.

Democratization promotes the formation of social movements. [...] To single out the effects of democratization on social movements, we must separate them from common causes of democratization and social movements as well as from reciprocal influences of social movements on democratization. Once this is done, however, we see that predicting the future of twenty-first-century social movements depends heavily on expectations concerning future democratization or dedemocratization. In China and Egypt, we have to decide whether pro-democracy movements or ongoing state repression are more likely in the future.

Social movements assert popular sovereignty. Over our two centuries of history, the argument holds up well. The rise and fall of social movements in France, for instance, neatly chart fluctuations in claims of popular sovereignty, so much so that France's authoritarian regimes took great care to suppress social movement campaigns, performances, and WUNC displays. Nevertheless, we have encountered two important qualifications to the general principle. First, professional social movement entrepreneurs and nongovernmental organizations sometimes represent themselves as speaking for "the people" without creating either deep grass roots or means for ordinary people to speak through them. Second, social movements have supported programs that, when realized, actually diminished popular sovereignty by implanting authoritarian leaders, charismatic cults, or programs of widespread exclusion. Any predictions concerning future social movements and their consequences will have to consider the possibility of reactive, exclusionary, nationalistic social movements and dedemocratization.

As compared with locally grounded forms of popular politics, social movements depend heavily on political entrepreneurs for their scale, durability, and effectiveness. We have certainly seen political entrepreneurs repeatedly in the midst of social movements. From Great Britain's Reform mobilization of the 1830s to recent mobilizations like Occupy Wall Street, entrepreneurs and their nongovernmental organizations have figured prominently in campaign after campaign. Indeed, the overall trend has increased the salience and influence of political entrepreneurs from opportunists to life-long core activists (Díaz Cepeda and Castañeda 2019). The future depends in part on whether that trend will continue, and which sorts of entrepreneurs will flourish in social movements.

Once social movements establish themselves in one political setting, modeling, communication, and collaboration facilitate their adoption in other connected settings. This observation has taken on new meaning as our analysis has developed, for connections of existing social movement settings with potential new settings are always only a fraction of all the new settings with which connections could, in principle, form. We have seen that selectivity most clearly in the connections facilitated by new communications media: generally lowering the cost of communications for people who have access to the system, but excluding others who lack that access. The same holds for interpersonal networks: expansion of social movement activity along existing networks excludes those who do not belong. Despite the engaging image of so-called Facebook revolutions, that play of inclusion and exclusion is likely to continue through the twenty-first century. As a consequence, some of our predictions will rest on estimates of who will connect with whom, and who will not.

The forms, personnel, and claims of social movements vary and evolve historically. As our whimsical vignette of Wilkes and Adams in Arizona suggests, social movement forms have undergone continuous mutation since the later eighteenth century and are still mutating. We have observed three distinguishable but inter-acting sources of change and variation in social movements: overall political and economic environments; incremental change in campaigns, repertoires, and WUNC displays within social movements; and diffusion of social movement models among sites of activism. To anticipate the future, we must specify how each of the three will change, not to mention how they will interact. For clues, we should pay particular attention to new sites of social movement action such as the 99 percent (Occupy Everywhere [...]) protests, asking who does what on behalf of which claims.

The social movement, as an invented institution, could disappear or mutate into some quite different form of politics. We still have no guarantee that the social movement as it has prevailed for two centuries will continue forever. We must take seriously the possibility that the twenty-first century will destroy social movements as vehicles of popular claim making because the conditions for their survival have dissolved or because new forms of claim making have supplanted them. One dream of digital democracy proposes continuous, electronically medi-ated opinion polling and voting as a cheap, efficient substitute for associating, meeting, marching, petitioning, addressing mass media, and the rest of the social movement repertoire—a frightening prospect for lovers of social movements in something like their recognizable historical form. A case in hand, is that of Anonymous [...].

Possible Futures

How can we apply these principles to the future? Figure 2.1 uses ideas and evidence [...] to speculate about what could happen to social movements during the rest of the twenty-first century. It combines some of the more likely possibilities into four scenarios: internationalization, democratic decline, professionalization, and triumph.

  –*Internationalization* entails a net shift away from local, regional, and national social movements toward international and global social movement activity.
  –*Decline of democracy* would depress all sorts of social movements, especially at the large scale, but could leave pockets of local or regional social move-ment activity where some democratic institutions survived.

–*Professionalization* would most likely diminish the relative importance of local and regional social movements while shifting the energies of activists and organizers to national, international, and global scales.

–*Triumph*, finally, describes the glorious dream of social movements everywhere, serving at all scales from local to global as a means for advancing popular claims. Let us draw on implications [...] to identify circumstances that would cause each of the four scenarios as well as reflect on likely consequences of each scenario for popular politics.

Internationalization. Many observers and activists of early twenty-first-century social movements assume that internationalization is already sweeping the field and will continue to a point at which most social movements will operate internationally or even globally. They project that environmentalists, feminists, human rights advocates, and opponents of global capital will increasingly join forces across countries and continents. Under what conditions might we now expect internationalization to dominate the futures of social movements? Considering the evidence [...] (such as the Via Campesina movement [...]), these are the most likely candidates:

- continued growth and impact by international networks of power and of organizations implementing them—financial networks, trade connections, multinational corporations, international governmental and regulatory institutions, intercontinental criminal enterprises;
- vulnerability of those networks to shaming, subversion, boycotts, or governmental regulation;
- expansion of connections among widely dispersed populations whose welfare those international networks affect, especially adversely;
- proliferation of organizations, brokers, and political entrepreneurs specialized in connecting those populations and coordinating their action; and
- formation of at least a modicum of democracy at an international scale—relatively broad, equal, consultative, and protective relations between citizens and agents of international governmental institutions.

Predicting that extensive internationalization of social movements will occur during the twenty-first century depends on implicit predictions that most or all of these conditions will apply. But Brexit, the Trump election, and growing nationalist movements point to a return to the nation-state as the site of protest.

If the scenario of internationalization prevailed, we might reasonably expect some further consequences for popular politics in the short and medium terms.

First, given the minimum requirements of large-scale social movements for information, time, contacts, and resources, the existing elite bias of social movement participation would increase; the lowering of communication costs through the internet and cellphones surely would not override the increased coordination costs for a very long time. Second, for this reason and because of uneven access to communication channels, inequality between sites of active movement participation and all others would sharpen; relatively speaking, excluded people would suffer even more acutely than today from lack of means to mount effective campaigns, performances, and WUNC displays. Third, brokers, entrepreneurs, and international organizations would become even more crucial to the effective voicing of claims by means of social movements. All these changes point to declines in democratic participation; they would both narrow the range of participants in social movements and make participation more unequal.

Democratic decline. What if democracy declined as a result of causes outside of the social movement sphere: weakening of barriers between categorical inequality and public politics, segregation of new or existing trust networks from public politics, and so on? Because democracy always operates in connection with particular centers of power, a lot would depend on whether the decline occurred at all scales or only, for example, at the national scale. A plausible version of this scenario would have democracy suffering at the local or national level because it would take a political catastrophe to produce simultaneous dedemocratization across the world's thousands of local, regional, and national regimes. (Imagine rogue networks of bankers, soldiers, communications providers, or medical researchers, for example, who could decide which segments of the world population would—and would not—have access to their services.) The case of San Francisco shutting down cellphone use in the BART systems after protests from the killing of Charles Hill reveal such temporary loss of civil rights [...]. In recent years, we have witnessed the election of people with anti-democratic dictatorial tendencies in Philippines, Eastern Europe, and beyond. Under most circumstances, democratic collapse at the large scale would still leave surviving democratic enclaves scattered across the world. We then might expect to find increasing differentiation of social movement practices across those surviving enclaves, as communication and collaboration among the world's social movement activists diminished and as local or regional activists adapted increasingly to their particular conditions.

Professionalization. In this scenario, professionalization leads to institutionalization, NGOization, and hence to declining innovation and radicalism of social movements. Committed populists often worry that social movement activists, already drawn disproportionately from prosperous, well-educated, well-connected segments of the population, will sell out the interests of truly disadvantaged people, establish comfortable relations with authorities, rely increasingly on support from the rich and powerful, and/or become social movement bureaucrats, more interested in forwarding their own organizations and careers than in the welfare of their supposed constituencies.

As compared with the early nineteenth century, some professionalization and institutionalization of social movements have unquestionably occurred in relatively democratic regimes: creation of protective legal codes, formation of police forces specializing in contained protection of social movement activity, establishment of negotiated routines for police–demonstrator interactions, creation of conventions for reporting on social movements in mass media, and multiplication of organizations specializing in social movement campaigns, performances, and WUNC displays. These changes have opened up full-time careers in social movement activism. Professionalization and institutionalization have proceeded hand in hand.

Up to the early twenty-first century, however, new issues, groups, tactics, and targets have repeatedly arisen at the edge of the established social movement sector. Many peripheral claimants failed, some quickly shifted to standard social movement practices, but a few brought their own innovations—sit-ins, occupations of public buildings and squares, teach-ins, giant puppet shows, cartoonlike costumes, new uses of media—onto the public scene. Predicting general professionalization and institutionalization of social movements, then, implies that opportunities for genuinely new issues, groups, tactics, and targets will diminish significantly. That could occur, in principle, either through declining incentives for popular claim making or through closing out of claimants who are not already part of the social movement establishment. But by definition social movements are truly disruptive and antiestablishment.

Triumph. What about across-the-board expansion of social movements at all scales, from local to global? Such a surprising future would require democratization of the many world regions currently living under authoritarian regimes, warlords, or petty tyrannies. It would also require a more general division of government and power such that local authorities still had the capacity to affect local lives and respond to local demands, even if international authorities gained power within their own spheres. It would, finally, mean that local, regional, and national activist networks, organizations, and entrepreneurs continued to act in partial independence at their own scales instead of subordinating their programs to those of international or global scope. Conversely, if widespread de-democratization occurred at all scales across the world, if centers of power increased their own protections against popular pressure, and if linking networks, organizations, and brokers either disintegrated or fell under authorities' control, a general decline of social movements would follow.

In the domain of social movements, we should be suspicious of *if–then* statements—if democratization, then social movement expansion; if internationalization, then sharpening inequality; and so on. Despite the ample documentation [...] and generations of scholarly work, we have nothing like an *if–then* causal science of social movements. Flat predictions for the remainder of the twenty-first century involve even greater uncertainties. After all, they depend on a combination of three sorts of reasoning: (1) extrapolation of existing trends into the future, (2) *if–then* statements about the proximate causes of change in social movements, and (3) speculations about changes in the causes of those causes. To predict that the modest internationalization of social movements since 1990 or so will swell into a great wave, for example, we must assume that we have actually read that trend correctly; that the expansion of connections among dispersed populations affected by international power networks does, indeed, promote coordination of social movement activity among those dispersed populations; and that whatever causes the expansion of connections to occur will continue to operate through the century's many remaining years.

In the face of all this uncertainty, can we place any bets on the likely prevalence of one scenario or another? What combinations of internationalization, democratic decline, professionalization, and/or triumph are more probable? Throwing all if-then prudence to the winds, let us state a few guesses about the twenty-first century.

> *Internationalization*: slower, less extensive, and less complete than technology enthusiasts say, but likely to continue for decades.
>
> *Decline of democracy*: a split decision, with some democratic decline (and therefore some diminution in the prevalence and efficacy of social movements) in major existing democracies but substantial democratization (hence social movement expansion) in such currently undemocratic countries as China.
>
> *Professionalization*: another split decision, with professional social movement entrepreneurs, nongovernmental organizations, and accommodations with authorities increasingly dominant in large-scale social movements

but consequently abandoning those portions of local and regional claim making they cannot co-opt into international activism.

Triumph: alas, exceedingly unlikely.

"Alas" because, for all the reasons laid out in previous chapters, the triumph of social movements at all scales would benefit humanity, despite all the dangers of movements that many of us would oppose. The broad availability of social movements signals the presence of democratic institutions and usually promotes their functioning. It provides a crucial channel for groups, categories of people, and issues that currently have no voice in a regime's routine politics to acquire visible places in public politics. We should scan contemporary and future contentious performances and social movements carefully, in hope of refuting this pessimistic forecast [...].

SUMMARY

1. Different philosophies about what constitutes reality influence how people tell stories about law.
2. One philosophy argues that one can read legal cases that outline general moral principles and compare those principles to logical propositions about right and wrong. Such a belief is built upon the major premise that human law can contain a set of consistent and objective moral truths.
3. However, other theories argue that everyday people in the United States tend to tell three types of stories people tell about law: before the law, with the law, and up against the law.
4. The first type, before the law, imagined and treated legality as an objective realm of disinterested action: formerly ordered, rational, and hierarchical system of rules and procedures.
5. The second, with the law, described legality as a game to be played, where rules can be bent or invented by self-interested actors set out to win.
6. The third narrative, up against the law, where law is seen as the product of unequal power and is used arbitrarily and capriciously against the interests of the most vulnerable.
7. Lawyers have pursued a strategy for legal sovereignty for American Indians: the ability to look and act like a government with other state and federal government agencies. The assumption that the lawyers in this study made is that power can be earned by giving up nonlegal cultural practices and behaviors.

8. This was akin to a second colonization from the point of view of American Indians and frames all three stories about law as a contest between law as an ideal and as something to be resisted.

9. Patricia-Hill Collins argued that by insisting on self-definition, Black women have reclaimed the power to tell one's narrative and question the power of others to limit their definitions.

10. Dr. Martin Luther King Jr. defined an unjust law as a code that a numerical or power majority group compels a minority group to obey but does not make binding on itself. He continued that this reality is difference made legal.

11. Justice Sotomayor said she had to work harder given her marginalized identities of race, gender, and class.

12. There are also structural elements one must consider when confronting unequal power relationships, including social institutions like family, education, and social groups.

13. Social movements in the future are likely to constitute new stories about law that are more diverse, global, and based on different experiences from those in the United States.

REFERENCES

Dworkin, R. 2006. *Justice in Robes*. Cambridge, MA: Belknap Press. 155, 246.

Ewick, P., and S. S. Silbey 1998. *The Common Place of Law: Stories from Everyday Life*. Chicago: University of Chicago Press. 28

Medcalf, L. 1978. *Law and Identity: Lawyers, Native Americans and Legal Practice*. 123–4.

UNIT III

Cases and Controversies

LEARNING OUTCOMES

1. Students will be able to read cases and apply a contextual framework focused on lived experience.
2. Students will be able to describe how judges interpret constitutional text within historical-structural controversies, including racism, criminal justice, intersectionality, and modern challenges of state administration.
3. Students will be able to contrast law as universal idea from law as lived injustice.
4. Students will be able to better evaluate how historical injustices persist throughout the system.
5. Students will be able to describe the tension between law as social control and law as rights.

Thus far you have read cases within a context curated for you. In the introduction, you examined several cases within a sociolegal context that helped you see beyond law as merely a set of formal rules based on an ideal. You also learned how interpretation and close reading influence how judges ultimately make decisions that affect all of our lives. In the second section, you were introduced to intersectional readings from the humanities. These readings were intended to help you bring different perspectives focused on the lived experiences of those who are most often excluded from traditional stories about law. These stories also highlighted the intersections of race, gender, and class in cases of systemic injustice. In the third section, you examined social theories that challenged traditional justifications for law. You were also introduced to how stories of law tend to follow three patterns: before the law, with the law, and up against the law. These stories are important when thinking about how social movements of the future might mobilize with legal institutions and under what conditions they resist.

In this section, you will now read case excerpts organized around four controversies: systemic racism, criminal justice, intersectional injustice, and modern challenges to state administration. You are encouraged to draw upon the contextual framework provided thus far to decenter formal law and law as an ideal. Instead, engage with the readings in a way to spot issues as they arise based on the lived experience of those involved. You should also pay attention to how judges write about these cases. Do they look for a universal moral basis? Are they attempting to balance interests? What concepts are they using to support their reasoning? How does their interpretation depend on the constraints and opportunities of being a judge in a complicated system of unequal power?

Race and Participatory Politics

UNITED STATES V. THE AMISTAD (1841)

MR. JUSTICE STORY delivered the opinion of the Court.

This is the case of an appeal from the decree of the Circuit Court of the district of Connecticut, sitting in admiralty. The leading facts, as they appear upon the transcript of the proceedings, are as follows: on the 27th of June, 1839, the schooner L'Amistad, being the property of Spanish subjects, cleared out from the port of Havana, in the island of Cuba, for Puerto Principe, in the same island. On board of the schooner were the master, Ramon Ferrer, and Jose Ruiz and Pedro Montez, all Spanish subjects. The former had with him a negro boy named Antonio, claimed to be his slave. Jose Ruiz had with him forty-nine negroes claimed by him as his slaves, and stated to be his property in a certain pass or document signed by the Governor General of Cuba. Pedro Montez had with him four other negroes, also claimed by him as his slaves and stated to be his property in a similar pass or document, also signed by the Governor General of Cuba. On the voyage, and before the arrival of the vessel at her port of destination, the negroes rose, killed the master, and took possession of her. On the 26th of August, the vessel was discovered by Lieutenant Gedney, of the United States brig Washington, at anchor on the high seas at the distance of half a mile from the shore of

U.S. Supreme Court, "United States v. The Amistad," 1841.

Long Island. A part of the negroes were then on shore, at Culloden Point, Long Island, who were seized by Lieutenant Gedney and brought on board.

The vessel, with the negroes and other persons on board, was brought by Lieutenant Gedney into the district of Connecticut, and there libelled for salvage in the District Court of the United States. A libel for salvage was also filed by Henry Green and Pelatiah Fordham, of Sag Harbor, Long Island. On the 18th of September, Ruiz and Montez filed claims and libels, in which they asserted their ownership of the negroes as their slaves, and of certain parts of the cargo, and prayed that the same might be "delivered to them, or to the representatives of her Catholic Majesty, as might be most proper." On the 19th of September, the attorney of the United States for the district of Connecticut filed an information or libel setting forth that the Spanish minister had officially presented to the proper department of the Government of the United States a claim for the restoration of the vessel, cargo, and slaves as the property of Spanish subjects which had arrived within the jurisdictional limits of the United States and were taken possession of by the said public armed brig of the United States under such circumstances as made it the duty of the United States to cause the same to be restored to the true proprietors pursuant to the treaty between the United States and Spain, and praying the Court, on its being made legally to appear that the claim of the Spanish minister was well founded, to make such order for the disposal of the vessel, cargo, and slaves as would best enable the United States to comply with their treaty stipulations. But if it should appear that the negroes were persons transported from Africa in violation of the laws of the United States, and brought within the United States contrary to the same laws, he then prayed the Court to make such order for their removal to the cost of Africa, pursuant to the laws of the United States, as it should deem fit.

On the 19th of November, the Attorney of the United States filed a second information or libel, similar to the first, with the exception of the second prayer above set forth in his former one. On the same day, Antonio G. Vega, the vice-consul of Spain for the State of Connecticut, filed his libel alleging that Antonio was a slave, the property of the representatives of Ramon Ferrer, and praying the Court to cause him to be delivered to the said vice-consul that he might be returned by him to his lawful owner in the island of Cuba.

On the 7th of January, 1840, the negroes, Cinque and others, with the exception of Antonio, by their counsel, filed an answer denying that they were slaves or the property of Ruiz and Montez, or that the Court could, under the Constitution or laws of the United States or under any treaty, exercise any jurisdiction over their persons by reason of the premises, and praying that they might be dismissed. They specially set forth and insisted in this answer that they were native-born Africans, born free, and still, of right, ought to be free, and not slaves; that they were, on or about the 15th of April, 1839, unlawfully kidnapped and forcibly and wrongfully carried on board a certain vessel on the coast of Africa which was unlawfully engaged in the slave trade, and were unlawfully transported in the same vessel to the island of Cuba for the purpose of being there unlawfully sold as slaves; that Ruiz and Montez, well knowing the premises, made a pretended purchase of them; that afterwards, on or about the 28th of June, 1839, Ruiz and Montez, confederating with Ferrer (master of the Amistad), caused them, without law or right, to be placed on board of the Amistad, to be transported to some place unknown to them, and there to be enslaved for life; that, on the voyage, they rose on the master and took possession of the vessel, intending to return therewith to their native country, or to seek an asylum in some free State, and the vessel arrived, about the 26th of August, 1839, off Montauk Point, near Long Island; a part of them were sent on shore, and were seized by Lieutenant Gedney, and carried on board; and all of them were afterwards brought by him into the district of Connecticut.

On the 7th of January, 1840, Jose Antonio Tellincas and Messrs. Aspe and Laca, all Spanish subjects residing in Cuba, filed their 40 U.S. 590 claims, as owners, to certain portions of the goods found on board of the schooner L'Amistad. On the same day, all the libelants and claimants, by their counsel, except Jose Ruiz and Pedro Montez (whose libels and claims, as stated of record, respectively, were pursued by the Spanish minister, the same being merged in his claims), appeared, and the negroes also appeared by their counsel, and the case was heard on the libels, claims, answers and testimony of witnesses.

On the 23d day of January, 1840, the District Court made a decree. By that decree, the Court rejected the claim of Green and Fordham for salvage, but allowed salvage to Lieutenant Gedney and others on the vessel and cargo of one-third of the value thereof, but not on the negroes, Cinque and others; it allowed the claim of Tellincas and Aspe and Laca, with the exception of the above-mentioned salvage; it dismissed the libels and claims of Ruiz and Montez, with costs, as being included under the claim of the Spanish minister; it allowed the claim of the Spanish vice-consul, for Antonio, on behalf of Ferrer's representatives; it rejected the claims of Ruiz and Montez for the delivery of the negroes, but admitted them for the cargo, with the exception of the above-mentioned salvage; it rejected the claim made by the attorney of the United States on behalf of the Spanish minister for the restoration of the negroes under the treaty, but it decreed that they should be delivered to the president of the United States, to be transported to Africa pursuant to the act of 3d March, 1819.

From this decree, the district attorney, on behalf of the United States, appealed to the Circuit Court, except so far as related to the restoration of the slave Antonio. The claimants, Tellincas, and Aspe and Laca, also appealed from that part of the decree which awarded salvage on the property respectively claimed by them. No appeal was interposed by Ruiz or Montez, nor on behalf of the representatives of the owners of the Amistad. The Circuit Court by a mere pro form a decree, affirmed the decree of the District Court, reserving the question of salvage upon the claims of Tellincas, and Aspe and Laca. And from that decree, the present appeal has been brought to this Court.

The cause has been very elaborately argued as well upon the merits as upon a motion of behalf of the appellees to dismiss the appeal. On the part of the United States, it has been contended: 1. That due and sufficient proof concerning the property has been made to authorize the restitution of the vessel, cargo, and negroes to the Spanish subjects on whose behalf they are claimed pursuant to the treaty with Spain, of the 27th of October, 1795. 2. That the United States had a right to intervene in the manner in which they have done to obtain a decree for the restitution of the property upon the application of the Spanish minister. These propositions have been strenuously denied on the other side. Other collateral and incidental points have been stated upon which it is not necessary at this moment to dwell.

Before entering upon the discussion of the main points involved in this interesting and important controversy, it may be necessary to say a few words as to the actual posture of the case as it now stands before us. In the first place, then, the only parties now before the Court, on one side, are the United States, intervening for the sole purpose of procuring restitution of the property, as Spanish property, pursuant to the treaty, upon the grounds stated by the other parties claiming the property in their respective libels. The United States do not assert any property in themselves, nor any violation of their own rights, or sovereignty or laws, by the acts complained of. They do not insist that these negroes have been imported into the United States, in contravention of our own slave trade acts. They do not seek to have these negroes delivered up for the purpose of being transferred to Cuba, as pirates or robbers or as fugitive criminals found within our territories who have been guilty of offences against the laws of Spain. They do not assert that the seizure and bringing the vessel and cargo and negroes into port by Lieutenant Gedney for the purpose of adjudication is a tortious act. They simply confine themselves to the right of the Spanish claimants to the restitution of their property upon the facts asserted in their respective allegations.

In the next place, the parties before the Court on the other side, as appellees, are Lieutenant Gedney, on his libel for salvage, and the negroes (Cinque and others), asserting themselves, in their answer, not to be slaves, but free native Africans, kidnapped in their own country and illegally transported by force from that country, and now entitled to maintain their freedom.

No question has been here made as to the proprietary interests in the vessel and cargo. It is admitted that they belong to Spanish subjects, and that they ought to be restored. The only point on this head is whether the restitution ought to be upon the payment of salvage, or not? The main controversy is whether these negroes are the property of Ruiz and Montez, and ought to be delivered up; and to this, accordingly, we shall first direct our attention.

It has been argued on behalf of the United States that the Court are bound to deliver them up according to the treaty of 1795 with Spain, which has in this particular been continued in full force by the treaty of 1819, ratified in 1821. The sixth article of that treaty seems to have had principally in view cases where the property of the subjects of either State had been taken possession of within the territorial jurisdiction of the other during war. The eighth article provides for cases where the shipping of the inhabitants of either State are forced, through stress of weather, pursuit of pirates or enemies, or any other urgent necessity, to seek shelter in the ports of the other. There may well be some doubt entertained whether the present case, in its actual circumstances, falls within the purview of this article. But it does not seem necessary, for reasons hereafter stated, absolutely to decide it. The ninth article provides,

> "that all ships and merchandise, of what nature soever, which shall be rescued out of the hands of any pirates or robbers on the high seas shall be brought into some port of either State and shall be delivered to the custody of the officers of that port in order to be taken care of and restored, entire, to the true proprietor as soon as due and sufficient proof shall be made concerning the property thereof."

This is the article on which the main reliance is placed on behalf of the United States for the restitution of these negroes. To bring the case within the article, it is essential to establish: 1st, That these negroes, under all the circumstances, fall within the description of merchandise, in the sense of the treaty. 2d, That there has been a rescue of them on the high seas, out of the hands of the pirates and robbers, which, in the present case, can only be by showing that they themselves are pirates and robbers; and 3d, That Ruiz and Montez, the asserted proprietors, are the true proprietors, and have established their title by competent proof.

If these negroes were, at the time, lawfully held as slaves under the laws of Spain and recognised by those laws as property capable of being lawfully bought and sold, we see no reason why they may not justly be deemed, within the intent of the treaty, to be included under the denomination of merchandise, and, as such, ought to be restored to the claimants, for, upon that point, the laws of Spain would seem to furnish the proper rule of interpretation. But, admitting this, it is clear, in our opinion that neither of the other essential facts and requisites has been established in proof, and the onus probandi of both lies upon the claimants to give rise to the casus foederis. It is plain beyond controversy, if we examine the evidence, that these negroes never were the lawful slaves of Ruiz or Montez or of any other Spanish subjects.

They are natives of Africa, and were kidnapped there, and were unlawfully transported to Cuba in violation of the laws and treaties of Spain and the most solemn edicts and declarations of that government. By those laws and treaties and edicts, the African slave trade is utterly abolished; the dealing in that trade is deemed a heinous crime; and the negroes thereby introduced into the dominions of Spain are declared to be free. Ruiz and Montez are proved to have made the pretended purchase of these negroes with a full knowledge of all the circumstances. And so cogent and irresistible is the evidence in this respect that the district attorney has admitted in open Court, upon the record, that these negroes were native Africans, and recently imported into Cuba, as alleged in their answers to the libels in the case. The supposed proprietary interest of Ruiz and Montez is completely displaced if we are at liberty to look at the evidence or the admissions of the district attorney.

If then, these negroes are not slaves, but are kidnapped Africans who, by the laws of Spain itself, are entitled to their freedom, and were kidnapped and illegally carried to Cuba, and illegally detained and restrained on board the Amistad, there is no pretence to say that they are pirates or robbers. We may lament the dreadful acts by which they asserted their liberty and took possession of the Amistad and endeavored to regain their native country, but they cannot be deemed pirates or robbers in the sense of the law of nations or the treaty with Spain or the laws of Spain itself, at least, so far as those laws have been brought to our knowledge. Nor do the libels of Ruiz or Montez assert them to be such.

This posture of the facts would seem, of itself, to put an end to the whole inquiry upon the merits. But it is argued on behalf of the United States that the ship and cargo and negroes were duly documented as belonging to Spanish subjects, and this Court have no right to look behind these documents; that full faith and credit is to be given to them; and that they are to be held conclusive evidence in this cause even although it should be established by the most satisfactory proofs that they have been obtained by the grossest frauds and impositions upon the constituted authorities of Spain. To this argument we can in no wise assent. There is nothing in the treaty which justifies or sustains the argument. We do not here meddle with the point whether there has been any connivance in this illegal traffic on the part of any of the colonial authorities or subordinate officers of Cuba because, in our view, such an examination is unnecessary, and ought not to be pursued unless it were indispensable to public justice, although it has been strongly pressed at the bar.

What we proceed upon is this—that, although public documents of the government accompanying property found on board of the private ships of a foreign nation certainly are to be deemed prima facie evidence of the facts which they purport to State, yet they are always open to be impugned for fraud, and whether that fraud be in the original obtaining of these documents or in the subsequent fraudulent and illegal use of them, when once it is satisfactorily established, it overthrows all their sanctity and destroys them as proof. Fraud will vitiate any—even the most solemn—transactions, and an asserted title to property founded upon it is utterly void. The very language of the ninth article of the treaty of 1795 requires the proprietor to make due and sufficient proof of his property. And how can that proof be deemed either due or sufficient which is but a connected and stained tissue of fraud? This is not a mere rule of municipal jurisprudence. Nothing is more clear in the law of nations, as an established rule to regulate their rights and duties and intercourse, than the doctrine that the ship's papers are but prima facie evidence, and that, if they are shown to be fraudulent, they are not to be held proof of any valid title. This rule is familiarly applied, and, indeed, is of everyday's occurrence in cases of prize, in the contests between belligerents and neutrals, as is apparent from numerous cases to be found in the reports of this Court, and it is just as applicable to the transactions of civil intercourse between nations in times of peace.

If a private ship, clothed with Spanish papers, should enter the ports of the United States claiming the privileges and immunities and rights belonging to the bona fide subjects of Spain under our treaties or laws, and she should, in reality, belong to the subjects of another nation which was not entitled to any such privileges, immunities, or rights, and the proprietors were seeking, by fraud, to cover their own illegal acts under the flag of Spain, there can be no doubt that it would be the duty of our Courts to strip off the disguise and to look at the case according to its naked realities. In the solemn treaties between nations, it can never be presumed that either State intends to provide the means of perpetrating or protecting frauds, but all the provisions are to be construed intended to be applied to bona fide transactions. The 17th article of the treaty with Spain, which provides for certain passports and certificates as evidence of property on board of the ships of both States, is, in its terms, applicable only to cases where either of the parties is engaged in a war.

This article required a certain form of passport to be agreed upon by the parties and annexed to the treaty; it never was annexed, and therefore, in the case of The Amiable Isabella, 6 Wheat. 1, it was held inoperative.

It is also a most important consideration in the present case, which ought not to be lost sight of, that, supposing these African negroes not to be slaves, but kidnapped and free negroes, the treaty with Spain cannot be obligatory upon them, and the United States are bound to respect their rights as much as those of Spanish subjects. The conflict of rights between the parties under such circumstances becomes positive and inevitable, and must be decided upon the eternal principles of justice and international law. If the contest were about any goods on board of this ship, to which American citizens asserted a title which was denied by the Spanish claimants, there could be no doubt of the right to such American citizens to litigate their claims before any competent American tribunal, notwithstanding the treaty with Spain. A fortiori, the doctrine must apply where human life and human liberty are in issue, and constitute the very essence of the controversy. The treaty with Spain never could have intended to take away the equal rights of all foreigners who should contest their claims before any of our Courts to equal justice, or to deprive such foreigners of the protection given them by other treaties or by the general law of nations. Upon the merits of the case, then, there does not seem to us to be any ground for doubt that these negroes ought to be deemed free, and that the Spanish treaty interposes no obstacle to the just assertion of their rights.

There is another consideration growing out of this part of the case which necessarily rises in judgment. It is observable that the United States, in their original claim, filed it in the alternative to have the negroes, if slaves and Spanish property, restored to the proprietors, or, if not slaves, but negroes who had been transported from Africa in violation of the laws of the United States and brought into the United States contrary to the same laws, then the Court to pass an order to enable the United States to remove such persons to the coast of Africa, to be delivered there to such agent as may be authorized to receive and provide for them. At a subsequent period, this last alternative claim was not insisted on, and another claim was interposed omitting it, from which the conclusion naturally arises that it was abandoned. The decree of the District Court, however, contained an order for the delivery of the negroes to the United States, to be transported to the coast of Africa under the Act of the 3d of March, 1819, ch. 224. The United States do not now insist upon any affirmance of this part of the decree, and, in our judgment, upon the admitted facts, there is no ground to assert that the case comes within the purview of the act of 1819, or of any other of our prohibitory slave trade acts. These negroes were never taken from Africa, or brought to the United States, in contravention of those acts. When the Amistad arrived, she was in possession of the negroes, asserting their freedom, and in no sense could they possibly intend to import themselves here, as slaves or for sale as slaves. In this view of the matter, that part of the decree of the District Court is unmaintainable, and must be reversed.

The view which has been thus taken of this case upon the merits under the first point renders it wholly unnecessary for us to give any opinion upon the other point, as to the right of the United States to intervene in this case in the manner already stated. We dismiss this, therefore, as well as several minor points made at the argument.

Upon the whole, our opinion is that the decree of the Circuit Court, affirming that of the District Court, ought to be affirmed except so far as it directs the negroes to be delivered to the President, to be transported to Africa in pursuance of the Act of the 3d of March 1819, and, as to this, it ought to be reversed, and that the said negroes be declared to be free, and be dismissed from the custody of the Court, and go without delay.

From

SCOTT V. SANDFORD

60 U.S. 393 (1857).

Upon the whole, therefore, it is the judgment of this court that it appears by the record before us that the plaintiff in error is not a citizen of Missouri in the sense in which that word is used in the Constitution, and that the Circuit

Chief Justice Taney, Selection from "Scott v. Sandford, 60 U.S. 393," Legal Information Institute, pp. 403–410, 454.

Court of the United States, for that reason, had no jurisdiction in the case, and could give no judgment in it. Its judgment for the defendant must, consequently, be reversed, and a mandate issued directing the suit to be dismissed for want of jurisdiction.

The question is simply this: can a negro whose ancestors were imported into this country and sold as slaves become a member of the political community formed and brought into existence by the Constitution of the United States, and as such become entitled to all the rights, and privileges, and immunities, guaranteed by that instrument to the citizen, one of which rights is the privilege of suing in a court of the United States in the cases specified in the Constitution?

It will be observed that the plea applies to that class of persons only whose ancestors were negroes of the African race, and imported into this country and sold and held as slaves. The only matter in issue before the court, therefore, is, whether the descendants of such slaves, when they shall be emancipated, or who are born of parents who had become free before their birth, are citizens of a State in the sense in which the word "citizen" is used in the Constitution of the United States. And this being the only matter in dispute on the pleadings, the court must be understood as speaking in this opinion of that class only, that is, of those persons who are the descendants of Africans who were imported into this country and sold as slaves.

The situation of this population was altogether unlike that of the Indian race. The latter, it is true, formed no part of the colonial communities, and never amalgamated with them in social connections or in government. But although they were uncivilized, they were yet a free and independent people, associated together in nations or tribes and governed by their own laws. Many of these political communities were situated in territories to which the white race claimed the ultimate right of dominion. But that claim was acknowledged to be subject to the right of the Indians to occupy it as long as they thought proper, and neither the English nor colonial Governments claimed or exercised any dominion over the tribe or nation by whom it was occupied, nor claimed the right to the possession of the territory, until the tribe or nation consented to cede it. These Indian Governments were regarded and treated as foreign Governments as much so as if an ocean had separated the red man from the white, and their freedom has constantly been acknowledged, from the time of the first emigration to the English colonies to the present day, by the different Governments which succeeded each other. Treaties have been negotiated with them, and their alliance sought for in war, and the people who compose these Indian political communities have always been treated as foreigners not living under our Government. It is true that the course of events has brought the Indian tribes within the limits of the United States under subjection to the white race, and it has been found necessary, for their sake as well as our own, to regard them as in a state of pupilage, and to legislate to a certain extent over them and the territory they occupy. But they may, without doubt, like the subjects of any other foreign Government, be naturalized by the authority of Congress, and become citizens of a State, and of the United States, and if an individual should leave his nation or tribe and take up his abode among the white population, he would be entitled to all the rights and privileges which would belong to an emigrant from any other foreign people.

The words "people of the United States" and "citizens" are synonymous terms, and mean the same thing. They both describe the political body who, according to our republican institutions, form the sovereignty and who hold the power and conduct the Government through their representatives. They are what we familiarly call the "sovereign people," and every citizen is one of this people, and a constituent member of this sovereignty. The question before us is whether the class of persons described in the plea in abatement compose a portion of this people, and are considered as a subordinate [p405] and inferior class of beings who had been subjugated by the dominant race, and, whether emancipated or not, yet remained subject to their authority, and had no rights or privileges but such as those who held the power and the Government might choose to grant them.

It is not the province of the court to decide upon the justice or injustice, the policy or impolicy, of these laws. The decision of that question belonged to the political or lawmaking power, to those who formed the sovereignty and framed the Constitution. The duty of the court is to interpret the instrument they have framed with the best lights we can obtain on the subject, and to administer it as we find it, according to its true intent and meaning when it was adopted.

It is very clear, therefore, that no State can, by any act or law of its own, passed since the adoption of the Constitution, introduce a new member into the political community created by the Constitution of the United States. It cannot make him a member of this community by making him a member of its own. And, for the same reason, it cannot introduce any person or description of persons who were not intended to be embraced in this new political family which the Constitution brought into existence, but were intended to be excluded from it.

It is difficult at this day to realize the state of public opinion in relation to that unfortunate race which prevailed in the civilized and enlightened portions of the world at the time of the Declaration of Independence and when the Constitution of the United States was framed and adopted. But the public history of every European nation displays it in a manner too plain to be mistaken.

They had for more than a century before been regarded as beings of an inferior order, and altogether unfit to associate with the white race either in social or political relations, and so far inferior that they had no rights which the white man was bound to respect, and that the negro might justly and lawfully be reduced to slavery for his benefit. He was bought and sold, and treated as an ordinary article of merchandise and traffic whenever a profit could be made by it.

This opinion was at that time fixed and universal in the civilized portion of the white race. It was regarded as an axiom in morals as well as in politics which no one thought of disputing or supposed to be open to dispute, and men in every grade and position in society daily and habitually acted upon it in their private pursuits, as well as in matters of public concern, without doubting for a moment the correctness of this opinion.

And in no nation was this opinion more firmly fixed or more uniformly acted upon than by the English Government and English people. They not only seized them on the coast of Africa and sold them or held them in slavery for their own use, but they took them as ordinary articles of merchandise to every country where they could make a profit on them, and were far more extensively engaged in this commerce than any other nation in the world.

The opinion thus entertained and acted upon in England was naturally impressed upon the colonies they founded on this side of the Atlantic. And, accordingly, a negro of the African race was regarded by them as an article of property, and held, and bought and sold as such, in every one of the thirteen colonies which united in the Declaration of Independence and afterwards formed the Constitution of the United States. The slaves were more or less numerous in the different colonies as slave labor was found more or less profitable. But no one seems to have doubted the correctness of the prevailing opinion of the time.

The legislation of the different colonies furnishes positive and indisputable proof of this fact.

It begins by declaring that,

[w]hen in the course of human events it becomes necessary for one people to dissolve the political bands which have connected them with another, and to assume among the powers of the earth the separate and equal station to which the laws of nature and nature's God entitle them, a decent respect for the opinions of mankind requires that they should declare the causes which impel them to the separation.

It then proceeds to say:

We hold these truths to be self-evident: that all men are created equal; that they are endowed by their Creator with certain unalienable rights; that among them is life, liberty, and the pursuit of happiness; that to secure these rights, Governments are instituted, deriving their just powers from the consent of the governed.

The general words above quoted would seem to embrace the whole human family, and if they were used in a similar instrument at this day would be so understood. But it is too clear for dispute that the enslaved African race were not intended to be included, and formed no part of the people who framed and adopted this declaration, for if the language, as understood in that day, would embrace them, the conduct of the distinguished men who framed the Declaration of Independence would have been utterly and flagrantly inconsistent with the principles they asserted, and instead of the sympathy of mankind to which they so confidently appealed, they would have deserved and received universal rebuke and reprobation.

Yet the men who framed this declaration were great men—high in literary acquirements, high in their sense of honor, and incapable of asserting principles inconsistent with those on which they were acting. They perfectly understood the meaning of the language they used, and how it would be understood by others, and they knew that it would not in any part of the civilized world be supposed to embrace the negro race, which, by common consent, had been excluded from civilized Governments and the family of nations, and doomed to slavery. They spoke and acted according to the then established doctrines and principles, and in the ordinary language of the day, and no one misunderstood them. The unhappy black race were separated from the white by indelible marks, and laws long before established, and were never thought of or spoken of except as property, and when the claims of the owner or the profit of the trader were supposed to need protection.

From

PLESSY V. FERGUSON (NO. 210)

Argued: April 18, 1896; Decided: May 18, 1896

163 U.S. 537

Legislation is powerless to eradicate racial instincts or to abolish distinctions based upon physical differences, and the attempt to do so can only result in accentuating the difficulties of the present situation. If the civil and political rights of both races be equal, one cannot be inferior to the other civilly [p552] or politically. If one race be inferior to the other socially, the Constitution of the United States cannot put them upon the same plane (551–552).

By the Fourteenth Amendment, all persons born or naturalized in the United States and subject to the jurisdiction thereof are made citizens of the United States and of the State wherein they reside, and the States are forbidden from making or enforcing any law which shall abridge the privileges or immunities of citizens of the United States, or shall deprive any person of life, liberty, or property without due process of law, or deny to any person within their jurisdiction the equal protection of the laws.

The proper construction of this amendment was first called to the attention of this court in the Slaughterhouse Cases, 16 Wall. 36, which involved, however, not a question of race, but one of exclusive privileges. The case did not call for any expression of opinion as to the exact rights it was intended to secure to the colored race, but it was said generally that its main purpose was to establish the citizenship of the negro, to give definitions of citizenship of the United States and of the States, and to protect from the hostile legislation of the States the privileges and immunities of citizens of the United States, as distinguished from those of citizens of the States [p544].

The object of the amendment was undoubtedly to enforce the absolute equality of the two races before the law, but, in the nature of things, it could not have been intended to abolish distinctions based upon color, or to enforce social, as distinguished from political, equality, or a commingling of the two races upon terms unsatisfactory to either. Laws permitting, and even requiring, their separation in places where they are liable to be brought into contact do not necessarily

Justice Brown, "Plessy v. Ferguson," Legal Information Institute, pp. 543–547, 551–552.

imply the inferiority of either race to the other, and have been generally, if not universally, recognized as within the competency of the state legislatures in the exercise of their police power. The most common instance of this is connected with the establishment of separate schools for white and colored children, which has been held to be a valid exercise of the legislative power even by courts of States where the political rights of the colored race have been longest and most earnestly enforced.

One of the earliest of these cases is that of Roberts v. City of Boston, 5 Cush. 19, in which the Supreme Judicial Court of Massachusetts held that the general school committee of Boston had power to make provision for the instruction of colored children in separate schools established exclusively for them, and to prohibit their attendance upon the other schools. "The great principle," said Chief Justice Shaw, p. 206, "advanced by the learned and eloquent advocate for the plaintiff" (Mr. Charles Sumner), is that, by the constitution and laws of Massachusetts, all persons without distinction of age or sex, birth or color, origin or condition, are equal before the law. ... But when this great principle comes to be applied to the actual and various conditions of persons in society, it will not warrant the assertion that men and women are legally clothed with the same civil and political powers, and that children and adults are legally to have the same functions and be subject to the same treatment, but only that the rights of all, as they are settled and regulated by law, are equally entitled to the paternal consideration and protection of the law for their maintenance and security.

Mr. Justice Bradley observed that the Fourteenth Amendment does not invest Congress with power to legislate upon subjects that are within the [p547] domain of state legislation, but to provide modes of relief against state legislation or state action of the kind referred to. It does not authorize Congress to create a code of municipal law for the regulation of private rights, but to provide modes of redress against the operation of state laws and the action of state officers, executive or judicial, when these are subversive of the fundamental rights specified in the amendment. Positive rights and privileges are undoubtedly secured by the Fourteenth Amendment, but they are secured by way of prohibition against state laws and state proceedings affecting those rights and privileges, and by power given to Congress to legislate for the purpose of carrying such prohibition into effect, and such legislation must necessarily be predicated upon such supposed state laws or state proceedings, and be directed to the correction of their operation and effect.

BROWN V. BOARD OF EDUCATION (1954)

MR. CHIEF JUSTICE WARREN delivered the opinion of the Court.

These cases come to us from the States of Kansas, South Carolina, Virginia, and Delaware. They are premised on different facts and different local conditions, but a common legal question justifies their consideration together in this consolidated opinion.

In each of the cases, minors of the Negro race, through their legal representatives, seek the aid of the courts in obtaining admission to the public schools of their community on a nonsegregated basis. In each instance, they had been denied admission to schools attended by white children under laws requiring or permitting segregation according to race. This segregation was alleged to deprive the plaintiffs of the equal protection of the laws under the Fourteenth Amendment. In each of the cases other than the Delaware case, a three-judge federal district court denied relief to the plaintiffs on the so-called "separate but equal" doctrine announced by this Court in Plessy v. Ferguson, 163 U. S. 537. Under that doctrine, equality of treatment is accorded when the races are provided substantially equal facilities, even though these facilities be separate. In the Delaware case, the Supreme Court of Delaware adhered to that doctrine, but ordered that the plaintiffs be admitted to the white schools because of their superiority to the Negro schools.

The plaintiffs contend that segregated public schools are not "equal" and cannot be made "equal," and that hence they are deprived of the equal protection of the laws. Because of the obvious importance of the question presented, the Court took jurisdiction.

Today, education is perhaps the most important function of state and local governments. Compulsory school attendance laws and the great expenditures for education both demonstrate our recognition of the importance of education to our democratic society. It is required in the performance of our most basic public responsibilities, even service in the armed forces. It is the very foundation of good citizenship. Today it is a principal instrument in awakening the child to cultural values, in preparing him for later professional training, and in helping him to adjust normally to his environment. In these days, it is doubtful that any child may reasonably be expected to succeed in life if he is denied the opportunity of

U.S. Supreme Court, "Brown v. Board of Education of Topeka," 1954.

an education. Such an opportunity, where the state has undertaken to provide it, is a right which must be made available to all on equal terms.

We come then to the question presented: does segregation of children in public schools solely on the basis of race, even though the physical facilities and other "tangible" factors may be equal, deprive the children of the minority group of equal educational opportunities? We believe that it does.

"Segregation of white and colored children in public schools has a detrimental effect upon the colored children. The impact is greater when it has the sanction of the law, for the policy of separating the races is usually interpreted as denoting the inferiority of the negro group. A sense of inferiority affects the motivation of a child to learn. Segregation with the sanction of law, therefore, has a tendency to [retard] the educational and mental development of negro children and to deprive them of some of the benefits they would receive in a racial[ly] integrated school system."

Whatever may have been the extent of psychological knowledge at the time of Plessy v. Ferguson, this finding is amply supported by modern authority. Any language in Plessy v. Ferguson contrary to this finding is rejected.

We conclude that, in the field of public education, the doctrine of "separate but equal" has no place. Separate educational facilities are inherently unequal. Therefore, we hold that the plaintiffs and others similarly situated for whom the actions have been brought are, by reason of the segregation complained of, deprived of the equal protection of the laws guaranteed by the Fourteenth Amendment. This disposition makes unnecessary any discussion whether such segregation also violates the Due Process Clause of the Fourteenth Amendment.

BAKER V. CARR (1962)

MR. JUSTICE BRENNAN delivered the opinion of the Court.

This civil action was brought under 42 U.S.C. §§ 1983 and 1988 to redress the alleged deprivation of federal constitutional rights. The complaint, alleging that, by means of a 1901 statute of Tennessee apportioning the members of the General Assembly among the State's 95 counties, "these plaintiffs and others similarly situated, are denied the equal protection of the laws accorded them by the Fourteenth Amendment to the Constitution of the United States by virtue

U.S. Supreme Court, "Baker v. Carr," 1962.

of the debasement of their votes," was dismissed by a three-judge court convened under 28 U.S.C. § 2281 in the Middle District of Tennessee. The court held that it lacked jurisdiction of the subject matter and also that no claim was stated upon which relief could be granted. 179 F. Supp. 824. We noted probable jurisdiction of the appeal. 364 U.S. 898. We hold that the dismissal was error, and remand the cause to the District Court for trial and further proceedings consistent with this opinion.

We hold that the claim pleaded here neither rests upon nor implicates the Guaranty Clause, and that its justiciability is therefore not foreclosed by our decisions of cases involving that clause. The District Court misinterpreted Colegrove v. Green and other decisions of this Court on which it relied. Appellants' claim that they are being denied equal protection is justiciable, and if "discrimination is sufficiently shown, the right to relief under the equal protection clause is not diminished by the fact that the discrimination relates to political rights."

But it is argued that this case shares the characteristics of decisions that constitute a category not yet considered, cases concerning the Constitution's guaranty, in Art. IV, § 4, of a republican form of government. A conclusion as to whether the case at bar does present a political question cannot be confidently reached until we have considered those cases with special care. We shall discover that Guaranty Clause claims involve those elements which define a "political question," and, for that reason and no other, they are nonjusticiable. In particular, we shall discover that the nonjusticiability of such claims has nothing to do with their touching upon matters of state governmental organization.

The due process and equal protection claims were held nonjusticiable in Pacific States not because they happened to be joined with a Guaranty Clause claim, or because they sought to place before the Court a subject matter which might conceivably have been dealt with through the Guaranty Clause, but because the Court believed that they were invoked merely in verbal aid of the resolution of issues which, in its view, entailed political questions. Pacific States may be compared with cases such as Mountain Timber Co. v. Washington, 243 U. S. 219, wherein the Court refused to consider whether a workmen's compensation act violated the Guaranty Clause but considered at length, and rejected, due process and equal protection arguments advanced against it, and O'Neill v. Leamer, 239 U. S. 244, wherein the Court refused to consider whether Nebraska's delegation of power to form drainage districts violated the Guaranty Clause, but went on to consider and reject the contention that the action against which an injunction was sought was not a taking for a public purpose.

We conclude, then, that the nonjusticiability of claims resting on the Guaranty Clause, which arises from their embodiment of questions that were thought "political," can have no bearing upon the justiciability of the equal protection claim presented in this case

When challenges to state action respecting matters of "the administration of the affairs of the State and the officers through whom they are conducted" have rested on claims of constitutional deprivation which are amenable to judicial correction, this Court has acted upon its view of the merits of the claim.

In Gomillion v. Lightfoot, 364 U. S. 339, we applied the Fifteenth Amendment to strike down a redrafting of municipal boundaries which effected a discriminatory impairment of voting rights, in the face of what a majority of the Court of Appeals thought to be a sweeping commitment to state legislatures of the power to draw and redraw such boundaries. Gomillion was brought by a Negro who had been a resident of the City of Tuskegee, Alabama, until the municipal boundaries were so recast by the State Legislature as to exclude practically all Negroes. The plaintiff claimed deprivation of the right to vote in municipal elections. The District Court's dismissal for want of jurisdiction and failure to state a claim upon which relief could be granted was affirmed by the Court of Appeals. This Court unanimously reversed. This Court's answer to the argument that States enjoyed unrestricted control over municipal boundaries was:

> "Legislative control of municipalities, no less than other state power, lies within the scope of relevant limitations imposed by the United States Constitution. ... The opposite conclusion, urged upon us by respondents, would sanction the achievement by a State of any impairment of voting rights whatever so long as it was cloaked in the garb of the realignment of political subdivisions. 'It is inconceivable that guaranties embedded in the Constitution of the United States may thus be manipulated out of existence.'" 364 U.S. at 364 U. S. 344–345.

We conclude that the complaint's allegations of a denial of equal protection present a justiciable constitutional cause of action upon which appellants are entitled to a trial and a decision. The right asserted is within the reach of judicial protection under the Fourteenth Amendment.

The judgment of the District Court is reversed, and the cause is remanded for further proceedings consistent with this opinion.

Reversed and remanded.

Criminal Justice: Balancing Interests

GITLOW V. NEW YORK (1925)

MR. JUSTICE SANFORD delivered the opinion of the Court.

Benjamin Gitlow was indicted in the Supreme Court of New York, with three others, for the statutory crime of criminal anarchy. New York Penal Laws, §§ 160, 161. [Footnote 1] He was separately tried, convicted, and sentenced to imprisonment. The judgment was affirmed by the Appellate Division and by the Court of Appeals. 195 App.Div. 773; 234 N.Y. 132 and 539. The case is here on writ of error to the Supreme Court, to which the record was remitted. 260 U.S. 703.

The contention here is that the statute, by its terms and as applied in this case, is repugnant to the due process clause of the Fourteenth Amendment. Its material provisions are:

> "§ 160. Criminal anarchy defined. Criminal anarchy is the doctrine that organized government should be overthrown by force or violence, or by assassination of the executive head or of any of the executive officials of government, or by any unlawful means. The advocacy of such doctrine either by word of mouth or writing is a felony."

"§ 161. Advocacy of criminal anarchy. Any person who:"

> "1. By word of mouth or writing advocates, advises or teaches the duty, necessity or propriety of overthrowing or overturning organized government by force or violence, or by assassination of the executive head or of any of the executive officials of government, or by any unlawful means; or,"
>
> "2. Prints, publishes, edits, issues or knowingly circulates, sells, distributes or publicly displays any book, paper, document, or written or printed matter in any form, containing or advocating, advising or teaching the doctrine that organized government should be overthrown by force, violence or any unlawful means"
>
> "Is guilty of a felony and punishable" by imprisonment or fine, or both.

U.S. Supreme Court, "Gitlow v. New York," 1925.

The indictment was in two counts. The first charged that the defendant had advocated, advised and taught the duty, necessity and propriety of overthrowing and overturning organized government by force, violence and unlawful means, by certain writings therein set forth entitled "The Left Wing Manifesto"; the second, that he had printed, published and knowingly circulated and distributed a certain paper called "The Revolutionary Age," containing the writings set forth in the first count advocating, advising and teaching the doctrine that organized government should be overthrown by force, violence and unlawful means.

There was no evidence of any effect resulting from the publication and circulation of the Manifesto. No witnesses were offered in behalf of the defendant. The sole contention here is, essentially, that as there was no evidence of any concrete result flowing from the publication of the Manifesto or of circumstances showing the likelihood of such result, the statute as construed and applied by the trial court penalizes the mere utterance, as such, of "doctrine" having no quality of incitement, without regard either to the circumstances of its utterance or to the likelihood of unlawful sequences, and that, as the exercise of the right of free expression with relation to government is only punishable "in circumstances involving likelihood of substantive evil," the statute contravenes the due process clause of the Fourteenth Amendment.

The argument in support of this contention rests primarily upon the following propositions: 1st, that the "liberty" protected by the Fourteenth Amendment includes the liberty of speech and of the press, and 2nd, that while liberty of expression "is not absolute," it may be restrained "only in circumstances where its exercise bears a causal relation with some substantive evil, consummated, attempted or likely," and as the statute "takes no account of circumstances," it unduly restrains this liberty and is therefore unconstitutional.

The precise question presented, and the only question which we can consider under this writ of error, then is whether the statute, as construed and applied in this case by the state courts, deprived the defendant of his liberty of expression in violation of the due process clause of the Fourteenth Amendment. For present purposes, we may and do assume that freedom of speech and of the press which are protected by the First Amendment from abridgment by Congress are among the fundamental personal rights and "liberties" protected by the due process clause of the Fourteenth Amendment from impairment by the States. We do not regard the incidental statement in Prudential Ins. Co. v. Cheek, 259 U. S. 530, 259 U. S. 543, that the Fourteenth Amendment imposes no restrictions on the States concerning freedom of speech, as determinative of this question.

It is a fundamental principle, long established, that the freedom of speech and of the press which is secured by the Constitution does not confer an absolute right to speak or publish, without responsibility, whatever one may choose, or an unrestricted and unbridled license that gives immunity for every possible use of language and prevents the punishment of those who abuse this freedom. That a State in the exercise of its police power may punish those who abuse this freedom by utterances inimical to the public welfare, tending to corrupt public morals, incite to crime, or disturb the public peace, is not open to question.

We cannot hold that the present statute is an arbitrary or unreasonable exercise of the police power of the State unwarrantably infringing the freedom of speech or press, and we must and do sustain its constitutionality. It was not necessary, within the meaning of the statute, that the defendant should have advocated "some definite or immediate act or acts" of force, violence or unlawfulness. It was sufficient if such acts were advocated in general terms, and it was not essential that their immediate execution should have been advocated. Nor was it necessary that the language should have been "reasonably and ordinarily calculated to incite certain persons" to acts of force, violence or unlawfulness. The advocacy need not be addressed to specific persons. Thus, the publication and circulation of a newspaper article may be an encouragement or endeavor to persuade to murder, although not addressed to any person in particular. Queen v. Most, L.R., 7 Q.B.D. 244.

We need not enter upon a consideration of the English common law rule of seditious libel or the Federal Sedition Act of 1798, to which reference is made in the defendant's brief. These are so unlike the present statute that we think the decisions under them cast no helpful light upon the questions here. And finding, for the reasons stated, that the statute is not, in itself, unconstitutional, and that it has not been applied in the present case in derogation of any constitutional right, the judgment of the Court of Appeals is Affirmed.

GARRITY V. NEW JERSEY (1967)

MR. JUSTICE DOUGLAS delivered the opinion of the Court.

Appellants were police officers in certain New Jersey boroughs. The Supreme Court of New Jersey ordered that alleged irregularities in handling cases in the municipal courts of those boroughs be investigated by the Attorney General,

U.S. Supreme Court, "Garrity v. New Jersey," 1965.

invested him with broad powers of inquiry and investigation, and directed him to make a report to the court. The matters investigated concerned alleged fixing of traffic tickets.

Before being questioned, each appellant was warned (1) that anything he said might be used against him in any state criminal proceeding; (2) that he had the privilege to refuse to answer if the disclosure would tend to incriminate him; but (3) that, if he refused to answer, he would be subject to removal from office.

Appellants answered the questions. No immunity was granted, as there is no immunity statute applicable in these circumstances. Over their objections, some of the answers given were used in subsequent prosecutions for conspiracy to obstruct the administration of the traffic laws. Appellants were convicted, and their convictions were sustained over their protests that their statements were coerced by reason of the fact that, if they refused to answer, they could lose their positions with the police department.

The choice imposed on petitioners was one between self-incrimination or job forfeiture. Coercion that vitiates a confession under Chambers v. Florida, 309 U. S. 227, and related cases can be "mental, as well as physical"; "the blood of the accused is not the only hallmark of an unconstitutional inquisition." Blackburn v. Alabama, 361 U. S. 199, 361 U. S. 206. Subtle pressures (Leyra v. Denno, 347 U. S. 556; Haynes v. Washington, 373 U. S. 503) may be as telling as coarse and vulgar ones. The question is whether the accused was deprived of his "free choice to admit, to deny, or to refuse to answer." Lisenba v. California, 314 U. S. 219, 314 U. S. 241.

The choice given petitioners was either to forfeit their jobs or to incriminate themselves. The option to lose their means of livelihood or to pay the penalty of self-incrimination is the antithesis of free choice to speak out or to remain silent. That practice, like interrogation practices we reviewed in Miranda v. Arizona, 384 U. S. 436, 384 U. S. 464–465, is "likely to exert such pressure upon an individual as to disable him from making a free and rational choice." We think the statements were infected by the coercion [Footnote 5] inherent in this scheme of questioning, and cannot be sustained as voluntary under our prior decisions.

Where the choice is "between the rock and the whirlpool," duress is inherent in deciding to "waive" one or the other.

"It always is for the interest of a party under duress to choose the lesser of two evils. But the fact that a choice was made according to interest does not exclude duress. It is the characteristic of duress properly so called."

"The privilege against self-incrimination would be reduced to a hollow mockery if its exercise could be taken as equivalent either to a confession of guilt or a conclusive presumption of perjury. ... The privilege serves to protect the innocent who otherwise might be ensnared by ambiguous circumstances."

We conclude that policemen, like teachers and lawyers, are not relegated to a watered-down version of constitutional rights. We now hold the protection of the individual under the Fourteenth Amendment against coerced statements prohibits use in subsequent criminal proceedings of statements obtained under threat of removal from office, and that it extends to all, whether they are policemen or other members of our body politic.

Reversed.

POWELL V. ALABAMA (1932)

MR. JUSTICE SUTHERLAND delivered the opinion of the Court.

The petitioners, hereinafter referred to as defendants, are negroes charged with the crime of rape, committed upon the persons of two white girls. The crime is said to have been committed on March 25, 1931. The indictment was returned in a state court of first instance on March 31, and the record recites that, on the same day, the defendants were arraigned and entered pleas of not guilty. There is a further recital to the effect that, upon the arraignment, they were represented by counsel. But no counsel had been employed, and aside from a statement made by the trial judge several days later during a colloquy immediately preceding the trial, the record does not disclose when, or under what circumstances, an appointment of counsel was made, or who was appointed. During the colloquy referred to, the trial judge, in response to a question, said that he had appointed all the members of the bar for the purpose of arraigning the defendants, and then, of course, anticipated that the members of the bar would continue to help the defendants if no counsel appeared. Upon the argument here, both sides accepted that as a correct statement of the facts concerning the matter.

U.S. Supreme Court, "Powell v. Alabama," 1932.

As each of the three cases was called for trial, each defendant was arraigned, and, having the indictment read to him, entered a plea of not guilty. Whether the original arraignment and pleas were regarded as ineffective is not shown. Each of the three trials was completed within a single day. Under the Alabama statute, the punishment for rape is to be fixed by the jury, and, in its discretion, may be from ten years' imprisonment to death. The juries found defendants guilty and imposed the death penalty upon all.

In this court, the judgments are assailed upon the grounds that the defendants, and each of them, were denied due process of law and the equal protection of the laws in contravention of the Fourteenth Amendment, specifically as follows: (1) they were not given a fair, impartial and deliberate trial; (2) they were denied the right of counsel, with the accustomed incidents of consultation and opportunity of preparation for trial, and (3) they were tried before juries from which qualified members of their own race were systematically excluded.

It is hardly necessary to say that, the right to counsel being conceded, a defendant should be afforded a fair opportunity to secure counsel of his own choice. Not only was that not done here, but such designation of counsel as was attempted was either so indefinite or so close upon the trial as to amount to a denial of effective and substantial aid in that regard. It thus will be seen that, until the very morning of the trial, no lawyer had been named or definitely designated to represent the defendants.

With this dubious understanding, the trials immediately proceeded. The defendants, young, ignorant, illiterate, surrounded by hostile sentiment, haled back and forth under guard of soldiers, charged with an atrocious crime regarded with especial horror in the community where they were to be tried, were thus put in peril of their lives within a few moments after counsel for the first time charged with any degree of responsibility began to represent them.

It is true that great and inexcusable delay in the enforcement of our criminal law is one of the grave evils of our time. Continuances are frequently granted for unnecessarily long periods of time, and delays incident to the disposition of motions for new trial and hearings upon appeal have come in many cases to be a distinct reproach to the administration of justice. The prompt disposition of criminal cases is to be commended and encouraged. But, in reaching that result, a defendant, charged with a serious crime, must not be stripped of his right to have sufficient time to advise with counsel and prepare his defense. To do that is not to proceed promptly in the calm spirit of regulated justice, but to go forward with the haste of the mob.

The Constitution of Alabama provides that, in all criminal prosecutions the accused shall enjoy the right to have the assistance of counsel, and a state statute requires the court in a capital case where the defendant is unable to employ counsel to appoint counsel for him. The state supreme court held that these provisions had not been infringed, and with that holding we are powerless to interfere. The question, however, which it is our duty, and within our power, to decide is whether the denial of the assistance of counsel contravenes the due process clause of the Fourteenth Amendment to the federal Constitution.

In Delaware, the Constitution of 1776 (Art. 25), adopted the common law of England, but expressly excepted such parts as were repugnant to the rights and privileges contained in the Declaration of Rights, and the Declaration of Rights, which was adopted on September 11, 1776, provided (Art. 14) "That in all Prosecutions for criminal Offences, every Man hath a Right ... to be allowed Counsel, ..."

It thus appears that, in at least twelve of the thirteen colonies, the rule of the English common law, in the respect now under consideration, had been definitely rejected, and the right to counsel fully recognized in all criminal prosecutions, save that, in one or two instances, the right was limited to capital offenses or to the more serious crimes, and this court seems to have been of the opinion that this was true in all the colonies.

It never has been doubted by this court, or any other, so far as we know, that notice and hearing are preliminary steps essential to the passing of an enforceable judgment, and that they, together with a legally competent tribunal having jurisdiction of the case, constitute basic elements of the constitutional requirement of due process of law. The words of Webster, so often quoted, that, by "the law of the land" is intended "a law which hears before it condemns" have been repeated in varying forms of expression in a multitude of decisions. In Holden v. Hardy, 169 U. S. 366, 169 U. S. 389, the necessity of due notice and an opportunity of being heard is described as among the "immutable principles of justice which inhere in the very idea of free government which no member of the Union may disregard." And Mr. Justice Field, in an earlier case, Galpin v. Page, 18 Wall. 350, 85 U. S. 368–369, said that the rule that no one shall be personally bound until he has had his day in court was as old as the law, and it meant that he must be cited to appear and afforded an opportunity to be heard.

In the light of the facts outlined in the forepart of this opinion—the ignorance and illiteracy of the defendants, their youth, the circumstances of public hostility, the imprisonment and the close surveillance of the defendants by the military forces, the fact that their friends and families were all in other states and communication with them necessarily difficult, and, above all, that they stood in deadly peril of their lives—we think the failure of the trial court to give them reasonable time and opportunity to secure counsel was a clear denial of due process.

But passing that, and assuming their inability, even if opportunity had been given, to employ counsel, as the trial court evidently did assume, we are of opinion that, under the circumstances just stated, the necessity of counsel was so vital and imperative that the failure of the trial court to make an effective appointment of counsel was likewise a denial of due process within the meaning of the Fourteenth Amendment. Whether this would be so in other criminal prosecutions, or under other circumstances, we need not determine. All that it is necessary now to decide, as we do decide, is that, in a capital case, where the defendant is unable to employ counsel and is incapable adequately of making his own defense because of ignorance, feeble mindedness, illiteracy, or the like, it is the duty of the court, whether requested or not, to assign counsel for him as a necessary requisite of due process of law, and that duty is not discharged by an assignment at such a time or under such circumstances as to preclude the giving of effective aid in the preparation and trial of the case.

The United States, by statute, and every state in the Union, by express provision of law or by the determination of its courts, make it the duty of the trial judge, where the accused is unable to employ counsel, to appoint counsel for him. In most states, the rule applies broadly to all criminal prosecutions; in others, it is limited to the more serious crimes; and in a very limited number, to capital cases. A rule adopted with such unanimous accord reflects, if it does not establish, the inherent right to have counsel appointed, at least in cases like the present, and lends convincing support to the conclusion we have reached as to the fundamental nature of that right.

The judgments must be reversed, and the causes remanded for further proceedings not inconsistent with this opinion.

Judgments reversed.

FURMAN V. GEORGIA (1972)

MR. JUSTICE DOUGLAS, MR. JUSTICE BRENNAN, MR. JUSTICE STEWART, MR. JUSTICE WHITE, and MR. JUSTICE MARSHALL have filed separate opinions in support of the judgments.

U.S. Supreme Court, "Furman v. Georgia," 1972.

MR. JUSTICE DOUGLAS, concurring.

In these three cases the death penalty was imposed, one of them for murder, and two for rape. In each, the determination of whether the penalty should be death or a lighter punishment was left by the State to the discretion of the judge or of the jury. In each of the three cases, the trial was to a jury. They are here on petitions for certiorari which we granted limited to the question whether the imposition and execution of the death penalty constitute "cruel and unusual punishment" within the meaning of the Eighth Amendment as applied to the States by the Fourteenth. I vote to vacate each judgment, believing that the exaction of the death penalty does violate the Eighth and Fourteenth Amendments.

The generality of a law inflicting capital punishment is one thing. What may be said of the validity of a law on the books and what may be done with the law in its application do, or may, lead to quite different conclusions.

It would seem to be incontestable that the death penalty inflicted on one defendant is "unusual" if it discriminates against him by reason of his race, religion, wealth, social position, or class, or if it is imposed under a procedure that gives room for the play of such prejudices.

Those who wrote the Eighth Amendment knew what price their forebears had paid for a system based not on equal justice, but on discrimination. In those days, the target was not the blacks or the poor, but the dissenters, those who opposed absolutism in government, who struggled for a parliamentary regime, and who opposed governments' recurring efforts to foist a particular religion on the people. Id. at 155–163. But the tool of capital punishment was used with vengeance against the opposition and those unpopular with the regime. One cannot read this history without realizing that the desire for equality was reflected in the ban against "cruel and unusual punishments" contained in the Eighth Amendment.

In a Nation committed to equal protection of the laws there is no permissible "caste" aspect of law enforcement. Yet we know that the discretion of judges and juries in imposing the death penalty enables the penalty to be selectively applied, feeding prejudices against the accused if he is poor and despised, and lacking political clout, or if he is a member of a suspect or unpopular minority, and saving those who by social position may be in a more protected position. In ancient Hindu, law a Brahman was exempt from capital punishment, and, under that law, "[g]enerally, in the law books, punishment increased in severity as social status diminished." We have, I fear, taken in practice the same position, partially as a result of making the death penalty discretionary and partially as a result of the ability of the rich to purchase the services of the most respected and most resourceful legal talent in the Nation.

Thus, these discretionary statutes are unconstitutional in their operation. They are pregnant with discrimination, and discrimination is an ingredient not compatible with the idea of equal protection of the laws that is implicit in the ban on "cruel and unusual" punishments.

∗∗∗

MR. JUSTICE BRENNAN, concurring.

We have very little evidence of the Framers' intent in including the Cruel and Unusual Punishments Clause among those restraints upon the new Government enumerated in the Bill of Rights. The absence of such a restraint from the body of the Constitution was alluded to, so far as we now know, in the debates of only two of the state ratifying conventions.

Several conclusions thus emerge from the history of the adoption of the Clause. We know that the Framers' concern was directed specifically at the exercise of legislative power. They included in the Bill of Rights a prohibition upon "cruel and unusual punishments" precisely because the legislature would otherwise have had the unfettered power to prescribe punishments for crimes. Yet we cannot now know exactly what the Framers thought "cruel and unusual punishments" were. Certainly they intended to ban torturous punishments, but the available evidence does not support the further conclusion that only torturous punishments were to be outlawed. As Livermore's comments demonstrate, the Framers were well aware that the reach of the Clause was not limited to the proscription of unspeakable atrocities. Nor did they intend simply to forbid punishments considered "cruel and unusual" at the time. The "import" of the Clause is, indeed, "indefinite," and for good reason. A constitutional provision "is enacted, it is true, from an experience of evils, but its general language hould not, therefore, be necessarily confined to the form that evil had theretofore taken. Time works changes, brings into existence new conditions and purposes. Therefore a principle, to be vital, must be capable of wider application than the mischief which gave it birth."

Ours would indeed be a simple task were we required merely to measure a challenged punishment against those that history has long condemned. That narrow and unwarranted view of the Clause, however, was left behind with the 19th century. Our task today is more complex. We know "that the words of the [Clause] are not precise, and that their scope is not static." We know, therefore, that the Clause "must draw its meaning from the evolving standards of decency that mark the progress of a maturing society."

More than the presence of pain, however, is comprehended in the judgment that the extreme severity of a punishment makes it degrading to the dignity of human beings. When we consider why they have been condemned, however, we realize that the pain involved is not the only reason. The true significance of these punishments is that they treat members of the human race as nonhumans, as objects to be toyed with and discarded. They are thus inconsistent with the fundamental premise of the Clause that even the vilest criminal remains a human being possessed of common human dignity.

In determining whether a punishment comports with human dignity, we are aided also by a second principle inherent in the Clause—that the State must not arbitrarily inflict a severe punishment. This principle derives from the notion that the State does not respect human dignity when, without reason, it inflicts upon some people a severe punishment that it does not inflict upon others.

A third principle inherent in the Clause is that a severe punishment must not be unacceptable to contemporary society. Rejection by society, of course, is a strong indication that a severe punishment doe not comport with human dignity. In applying this principle, however, we must make certain that the judicial determination is as objective as possible.

The final principle inherent in the Clause is that a severe punishment must not be excessive. A punishment is excessive under this principle if it is unnecessary: the infliction of a severe punishment by the State cannot comport with human dignity when it is nothing more than the pointless infliction of suffering. If there is a significantly less severe punishment adequate to achieve the purposes for which the punishment is inflicted.

Death is truly an awesome punishment. The calculated killing of a human being by the State involves, by its very nature, a denial of the executed person's humanity. The contrast with the plight of a person punished by imprisonment is evident. An individual in prison does not lose "the right to have rights." A prisoner retains, for example, the constitutional rights to the free exercise of religion, to be free of cruel and unusual punishments, and to treatment as a "person" for purposes of due process of law and the equal protection of the laws. A prisoner remains a member of the human family. Moreover, he retains the right of access to the courts. His punishment is not irrevocable. Apart from the common charge, grounded upon the recognition of human fallibility, that the punishment of death must inevitably be inflicted upon innocent men, we know that death has been the lot of men whose convictions were unconstitutionally secured in view of later, retroactively applied, holdings of this Court. The punishment itself may have been unconstitutionally inflicted, see Witherspoon v. Illinois, 391 U. S. 510 (1968), yet the finality of death precludes relief. An executed person has indeed "lost the right to have rights." As one 19th century proponent of punishing criminals by death declared,

> "When a man is hung, there is an end of our relations with him. His execution is a way of saying, 'You are not fit for this world, take your chance elsewhere.'

In comparison to all other punishments today, then, the deliberate extinguishment of human life by the State is uniquely degrading to human dignity. I would not hesitate to hold, on that ground alone, that death is today a "cruel and unusual" punishment, were it not that death is a punishment of longstanding usage and acceptance in this country.

The progressive decline in, and the current rarity of, the infliction of death demonstrate that our society seriously questions the appropriateness of this punishment today. The States point out that many legislatures authorize death as the punishment for certain crimes, and that substantial segments of the public, as reflected in opinion polls and referendum votes, continue to support it. Yet the availability of this punishment through statutory authorization, as well as the polls and referenda, which amount simply to approval of that authorization, simply underscores the extent to which our society has, in fact, rejected this punishment. When an unusually severe punishment is authorized for wide-scale application but not, because of society's refusal, inflicted save in a few instances, the inference is compelling that there is a deep-seated reluctance to inflict it. Indeed, the likelihood is great that the punishment is tolerated only because of its disuse. The objective indicator of society's view of an unusually severe punishment is what society does with it, and today society will inflict death upon only a small sample of the eligible criminals. Rejection could hardly be more complete without becoming absolute. At the very least, I must conclude that contemporary society views this punishment with substantial doubt.

In sum, the punishment of death is inconsistent with all four principles: death is an unusually severe and degrading punishment; there is a strong probability that it is inflicted arbitrarily; its rejection by contemporary society is virtually total; and there is no reason to believe that it serves any penal purpose more effectively than the less severe punishment of imprisonment. The function of these principles is to enable a court to determine whether a punishment comports with human dignity. Death, quite simply, does not.

When this country was founded, memories of the Stuart horrors were fresh and severe corporal punishments were common. Death was not then a unique punishment. The practice of punishing criminals by death, moreover, was widespread and by and large acceptable to society. Indeed, without developed prison systems, there was frequently no workable alternative. Since that time, successive restrictions, imposed against the background of a continuing moral controversy, have drastically curtailed the use of this punishment. Today death is a uniquely and unusually severe punishment. When examined by the principles applicable under the Cruel and Unusual Punishment Clause, death stands condemned as fatally offensive to human dignity. The punishment of death is therefore "cruel and unusual," and the States may no longer inflict it as a punishment for crimes. Rather than kill an arbitrary handful of criminals each year, the States will confine them in prison.

***

MR. JUSTICE STEWART, concurring.

On that score I would say only that I cannot agree that retribution is a constitutionally impermissible ingredient in the imposition of punishment. The instinct for retribution is part of the nature of man, and channeling that instinct in the administration of criminal justice serves an important purpose in promoting the stability of a society governed by law. When people begin to believe that organized society is unwilling or unable to impose upon criminal offenders the punishment they "deserve," then there are sown the seeds of anarchy—of self-help, vigilante justice, and lynch law.

But racial discrimination has not been proved, and I put it to one side. I simply conclude that the Eighth and Fourteenth Amendments cannot tolerate the infliction of a sentence of death under legal systems that permit this unique penalty to be so wantonly and so freakishly imposed.

***

MR. JUSTICE MARSHALL, concurring.

The criminal acts with which we are confronted are ugly, vicious, reprehensible acts. Their sheer brutality cannot and should not be minimized. But we are not called upon to condone the penalized conduct; we are asked only to examine the penalty imposed on each of the petitioners and to determine whether or not it violates the Eighth Amendment. The question then is not whether we condone rape or murder, for surely we do not; it is whether capital punishment is "a punishment no longer consistent with our own self-respect" and, therefore, violative of the Eighth Amendment.

Perhaps the most important principle in analyzing "cruel and unusual" punishment questions is one that is reiterated again and again in the prior opinions of the Court: i.e., the cruel and unusual language "must draw its meaning from the evolving standard of decency that mark the progress of a maturing society." Thus, a penalty that was permissible at one time in our Nation's history is not necessarily permissible today.

There is no holding directly in point, and the very nature of the Eighth Amendment would dictate that, unless a very recent decision existed, *stare decisis* would bow to changing values, and the question of the constitutionality of capital punishment at a given moment in history would remain open.

Capital punishment has been used to penalize various forms of conduct by members of society since the beginnings of civilization. Its precise origins are difficult to perceive, but there is some evidence that its roots lie in violent retaliation by members of a tribe or group, or by the tribe or group itself, against persons committing hostile acts toward group members. Thus, infliction of death as a penalty for objectionable conduct appears to have its beginnings in private vengeance.

As individuals gradually ceded their personal prerogatives to a sovereign power, the sovereign accepted the authority to punish wrongdoing as part of its "divine right" to rule. Individual vengeance gave way to the vengeance of the state, and capital punishment became a public function. Capital punishment worked its way into the laws of various countries, and was inflicted in a variety of macabre and horrific ways.

One great success of the abolitionist movement in the period from 1830–1900 was almost complete elimination of mandatory capital punishment. Before the legislatures formally gave juries discretion to refrain from imposing the death penalty, the phenomenon of "jury nullification," in which juries refused to convict in cases in which they believed that death was an inappropriate penalty, was experienced. [Footnote 4/73] Tennessee was the first State to give juries discretion, Tenn. Laws 1837–1838, c. 29, but other States quickly followed suit. Then, Rep. Curtis of New York introduced a federal bill that ultimately became law in 1897 which reduced the number of federal capital offenses from 60 to 3 (treason, murder, and rape) and gave the jury sentencing discretion in murder and rape cases.

The foregoing history demonstrates that capital punishment was carried from Europe to America but, once here, was tempered considerably. At times in our history, strong abolitionist movements have existed. But they have never been completely successful, as no more than one-quarter of the States of the Union have, at any one time, abolished the death penalty. They have had partial success, however, especially in reducing the number of capital crimes, replacing mandatory death sentences with jury discretion, and developing more humane methods of conducting executions.

In sum, the only support for the theory that capital punishment is an effective deterrent is found in the hypotheses with which we began and the occasional stories about a specific individual being deterred from doing a contemplated criminal act. These claims of specific deterrence are often spurious, however, and may be more than counterbalanced by the tendency of capital punishment to incite certain crimes. The United Nations Committee that studied capital punishment found that,

> "[i]t is generally agreed between the retentionists and abolitionists, whatever their opinions about the validity of comparative studies of deterrence, that the data which now exist show no correlation between the existence of capital punishment and lower rates of capital crime."

Just as Americans know little about who is executed and why, they are unaware of the potential dangers of executing an innocent man. Our "beyond a reasonable doubt" burden of proof in criminal cases is intended to protect the innocent, but we know it is not foolproof. Various studies have shown that people whose innocence is later convincingly established are convicted and sentenced to death.

Proving one's innocence after a jury finding of guilt is almost impossible. While reviewing courts are willing to entertain all kinds of collateral attacks where a sentence of death is involved, they very rarely dispute the jury's interpretation of the evidence. This is, perhaps, as it should be. But if an innocent man has been found guilty, he must then depend on the good faith of the prosecutor's office to help him establish his innocence. There is evidence, however, that prosecutors do not welcome the idea of having convictions, which they labored hard to secure, overturned, and that their cooperation is highly unlikely.

No matter how careful courts are, the possibility of perjured testimony, mistaken honest testimony, and human error remain all too real. In striking down capital punishment, this Court does not malign our system of government. On the contrary, it pays homage to it. Only in a free society could right triumph in difficult times, and could civilization record its magnificent advancement. In recognizing the humanity of our fellow beings, we pay ourselves the highest tribute. We achieve "a major milestone in the long road up from barbarism" and join the approximately 70 other jurisdictions in the world which celebrate their regard for civilization and humanity by shunning capital punishment.

GATES V. ILLINOIS (1983)

JUSTICE REHNQUIST delivered the opinion of the Court.

We granted certiorari to consider the application of the Fourth Amendment to a magistrate's issuance of a search warrant on the basis of a partially corroborated anonymous informant's tip. 454 U.S. 1140 (1982). After receiving briefs and hearing oral argument on this question, however, we requested the parties to address an additional question:

> "[W]hether the rule requiring the exclusion at a criminal trial of evidence obtained in violation of the Fourth Amendment, Mapp v. Ohio, 367 U. S. 643 (1961); Weeks v. United States, 232 U. S. 383 (1914), should to any extent be modified, so as, for example, not to require the exclusion of evidence obtained in the reasonable belief that the search and seizure at issue was consistent with the Fourth Amendment."

This totality-of-the-circumstances approach is far more consistent with our prior treatment of probable cause is any rigid demand that specific "tests" be satisfied by every informant's tip. Perhaps the central teaching of our decisions bearing on the probable cause standard is that it is a "practical, nontechnical conception." Brinegar v. United States, 338 U. S. 160, 338 U. S. 176 (1949).

"In dealing with probable cause, ... as the very name implies, we deal with probabilities. These are not technical; they are the factual and practical considerations of everyday life on which reasonable and prudent men, not legal technicians, act." Id. at 338 U. S. 175.

Our observation in United States v. Cortez, 449 U. S. 411, 449 U. S. 418 (1981), regarding "particularized suspicion," is also applicable to the probable cause standard:

> "The process does not deal with hard certainties, but with probabilities. Long before the law of probabilities was articulated as such, practical people formulated certain common sense conclusions about human

U.S. Supreme Court, "Gates v. Illinois," 1983.

behavior; jurors as factfinders are permitted to do the same—and so are law enforcement officers. Finally, the evidence thus collected must be seen and weighed not in terms of library analysis by scholars, but as understood by those versed in the field of law enforcement."

As these comments illustrate, probable cause is a fluid concept—turning on the assessment of probabilities in particular factual contexts—not readily, or even usefully, reduced to a neat set of legal rules. Informants' tips doubtless come in many shapes and sizes from many different types of persons.

As we said in Adams v. Williams, 407 U. S. 143, 407 U. S. 147 (1972):

"Informants' tips, like all other clues and evidence coming to a policeman on the scene, may vary greatly in their value and reliability."

Rigid legal rules are ill-suited to an area of such diversity. "One simple rule will not cover every situation."

Moreover, the "two-pronged test" directs analysis into two largely independent channels—the informant's "veracity" or "reliability" and his "basis of knowledge."

There are persuasive arguments against according these two elements such independent status. Instead, they are better understood as relevant considerations in the totality-of-the-circumstances analysis that traditionally has guided probable cause determinations: a deficiency in one may be compensated for, in determining the overall reliability of a tip, by a strong showing as to the other, or by some other indicia of reliability.

If, for example, a particular informant is known for the unusual reliability of his predictions of certain types of criminal activities in a locality, his failure, in a particular case, to thoroughly set forth the basis of his knowledge surely should not serve as an absolute bar to a finding of probable cause based on his tip.

Likewise, if an unquestionably honest citizen comes forward with a report of criminal activity—which, if fabricated, would subject him to criminal liability—we have found rigorous scrutiny of the basis of his knowledge unnecessary. Adams v. Williams, supra. Conversely, even if we entertain some doubt as to an informant's motives, his explicit and detailed description of alleged wrongdoing, along with a statement that the event was observed first-hand, entitles his tip to greater weight than might otherwise be the case. Unlike a totality-of-the-circumstances analysis, which permits a balanced assessment of the relative weights of all the various indicia of reliability (and unreliability) attending an informant's tip, the "two-pronged test" has encouraged an excessively technical dissection of informants' tips being focused on isolated issues that cannot sensibly be divorced from the other facts presented to the magistrate.

We also have recognized that affidavits

> "are normally drafted by nonlawyers in the midst and haste of a crim-
> inal investigation. Technical requirements of elaborate specificity once
> exacted under common law pleadings have no proper place in this area."

Likewise, search and arrest warrants long have been issued by persons who
are neither lawyers nor judges, and who certainly do not remain abreast of each
judicial refinement of the nature of "probable cause."

The rigorous inquiry into the *Spinelli* prongs and the complex superstructure
of evidentiary and analytical rules that some have seen implicit in our *Spinelli*
decision, cannot be reconciled with the fact that many warrants are—quite properly issued on the basis of nontechnical, common sense judgments of laymen
applying a standard less demanding than those used in more formal legal proceedings.

The task of the issuing magistrate is simply to make a practical, common sense
decision whether, given all the circumstances set forth in the affidavit before him,
including the "veracity" and "basis of knowledge" of persons supplying hearsay
information, there is a fair probability that contraband or evidence of a crime
will be found in a particular place. And the duty of a reviewing court is simply
to ensure that the magistrate had a "substantial basis for ... conclud[ing]" that
probable cause existed."

We are convinced that this flexible, easily applied standard will better achieve
the accommodation of public and private interests that the Fourth Amendment
requires than does the approach that has developed from *Aguilar* and *Spinelli*.

Intersectional Injustice and Rights

ROE V. WADE (1973)

MR. JUSTICE BLACKMUN delivered the opinion of the Court.

The Texas statutes that concern us here are Arts. 1191–1194 and 1196 of the
State's Penal Code. These make it a crime to "procure an abortion," as
therein defined, or to attempt one, except with respect to "an abortion procured

U.S. Supreme Court, "Roe v. Wade," 1973.

or attempted by medical advice for the purpose of saving the life of the mother." Similar statutes are in existence in a majority of the States.

On the merits, the District Court held that the "fundamental right of single women and married persons to choose whether to have children is protected by the Ninth Amendment, through the Fourteenth Amendment," and that the Texas criminal abortion statutes were void on their face because they were both unconstitutionally vague and constituted an overbroad infringement of the plaintiffs' Ninth Amendment rights. The court then held that abstention was warranted with respect to the requests for an injunction. It therefore dismissed the Does' complaint, declared the abortion statutes void, and dismissed the application for injunctive relief. 314 F. Supp. 1217, 1225 (ND Tex.1970).

The plaintiffs Roe and Doe and the intervenor Hallford, pursuant to 28 U.S.C. § 1253, have appealed to this Court from that part of the District Court's judgment denying the injunction. The defendant District Attorney has purported to cross-appeal, pursuant to the same statute, from the court's grant of declaratory relief to Roe and Hallford. Both sides also have taken protective appeals to the United States Court of Appeals for the Fifth Circuit. That court ordered the appeals held in abeyance pending decision here. We postponed decision on jurisdiction to the hearing on the merits. 402 U.S. 941 (1971).

The principal thrust of appellant's attack on the Texas statutes is that they improperly invade a right, said to be possessed by the pregnant woman, to choose to terminate her pregnancy. Appellant would discover this right in the concept of personal "liberty" embodied in the Fourteenth Amendment's Due Process Clause; or in personal, marital, familial, and sexual privacy said to be protected by the Bill of Rights or its penumbras, see Griswold v. Connecticut, 381 U. S. 479 (1965); Eisenstadt v. Baird, 405 U. S. 438 (1972); id. at 460 (WHITE, J., concurring in result); or among those rights reserved to the people by the Ninth Amendment, Griswold v. Connecticut, 381 U.S. at 486 (Goldberg, J., concurring). Before addressing this claim, we feel it desirable briefly to survey, in several aspects, the history of abortion, for such insight as that history may afford us, and then to examine the state purposes and interests behind the criminal abortion laws.

It perhaps is not generally appreciated that the restrictive criminal abortion laws in effect in a majority of States today are of relatively recent vintage. Those laws, generally proscribing abortion or its attempt at any time during pregnancy except when necessary to preserve the pregnant woman's life, are not of ancient or even of common law origin. Instead, they derive from statutory changes effected, for the most part, in the latter half of the 19th century.

Christian theology and the canon law came to fix the point of animation at 40 days for a male and 80 days for a female, a view that persisted until the 19th century, there was otherwise little agreement about the precise time of formation or animation. There was agreement, however, that, prior to this point, the fetus was to be regarded as part of the mother, and its destruction, therefore, was not homicide. Due to continued uncertainty about the precise time when animation occurred, to the lack of any empirical basis for the 40-80-day view, and perhaps to Aquinas' definition of movement as one of the two first principles of life, Bracton focused upon quickening as the critical point. The significance of quickening was echoed by later common law scholars, and found its way into the received common law in this country.

The American law. In this country, the law in effect in all but a few States until mid-19th century was the preexisting English common law. Connecticut, the first State to enact abortion legislation, adopted in 1821 that part of Lord Ellenborough's Act that related to a woman "quick with child." The death penalty was not imposed. Abortion before quickening was made a crime in that State only in 1860. In 1828, New York enacted legislation that, in two respects, was to serve as a model for early anti-abortion statutes. First, while barring destruction of an unquickened fetus as well as a quick fetus, it made the former only a misdemeanor, but the latter second-degree manslaughter. Second, it incorporated a concept of therapeutic abortion by providing that an abortion was excused if it "shall have been necessary to preserve the life of such mother, or shall have been advised by two physicians to be necessary for such purpose."

By 1840, when Texas had received the common law, only eight American States had statutes dealing with abortion. It was not until after the War Between the States that legislation began generally to replace the common law. Most of these initial statutes dealt severely with abortion after quickening, but were lenient with it before quickening. Most punished attempts equally with completed abortions. While many statutes included the exception for an abortion thought by one or more physicians to be necessary to save the mother's life, that provision soon disappeared, and the typical law required that the procedure actually be necessary for that purpose. Gradually, in the middle and late 19th century, the quickening distinction disappeared from the statutory law of most States and the degree of the offense and the penalties were increased. By the end of the 1950's, a large majority of the jurisdictions banned abortion, however and whenever performed, unless done to save or preserve the life of the mother.

It is thus apparent that, at common law, at the time of the adoption of our Constitution, and throughout the major portion of the 19th century, abortion was viewed with less disfavor than under most American statutes currently in effect. Phrasing it another way, a woman enjoyed a substantially broader right to terminate a pregnancy than she does in most States today.

The Constitution does not explicitly mention any right of privacy. In a line of decisions, however, going back perhaps as far as Union Pacific R. Co. v. Botsford, 141 U. S. 250, 251 (1891), the Court has recognized that a right of personal privacy, or a guarantee of certain areas or zones of privacy, does exist under the Constitution. In varying contexts, the Court or individual Justices have, indeed, found at least the roots of that right in the First Amendment, Stanley v. Georgia, 394 U. S. 557, 564 (1969); in the Fourth and Fifth Amendments, Terry v. Ohio, 392 U. S. 1, 8–9 (1968), Katz v. United States, 389 U. S. 347, 350 (1967), Boyd v. United States, 116 U. S. 616 (1886), see Olmstead v. United States, 277 U. S. 438, 478 (1928) (Brandeis, J., dissenting); in the penumbras of the Bill of Rights, Griswold v. Connecticut, 381 U.S. at 484–485; in the Ninth Amendment, id. at 486 (Goldberg, J., concurring); or in the concept of liberty guaranteed by the first section of the Fourteenth Amendment, see Meyer v. Nebraska, 262 U. S. 390, 399 (1923). These decisions make it clear that only personal rights that can be deemed "fundamental" or "implicit in the concept of ordered liberty," Palko v. Connecticut, 302 U. S. 319, 325 (1937), are included in this guarantee of personal privacy. They also make it clear that the right has some extension to activities relating to marriage, Loving v. Virginia, 388 U. S. 1, 12 (1967); procreation, Skinner v. Oklahoma, 316 U. S. 535, 541–542 (1942); contraception, Eisenstadt v. Baird, 405 U.S. at 453–454; id. at 460, 463–465.

We, therefore, conclude that the right of personal privacy includes the abortion decision, but that this right is not unqualified, and must be considered against important state interests in regulation.

Although the results are divided, most of these courts have agreed that the right of privacy, however based, is broad enough to cover the abortion decision; that the right, nonetheless, is not absolute, and is subject to some limitations; and that, at some point, the state interests as to protection of health, medical standards, and prenatal life, become dominant. We agree with this approach.

Where certain "fundamental rights" are involved, the Court has held that regulation limiting these rights may be justified only by a "compelling state interest," Kramer v. Union Free School District, 395 U. S. 621, 627 (1969); Shapiro v. Thompson, 394 U. S. 618, 634 (1969), Sherbert v. Verner, 374 U. S. 398, 406 (1963), and that legislative enactments must be narrowly drawn to express only the legitimate state interests at stake. Griswold v. Connecticut, 381 U.S. at 485; Aptheker

v. Secretary of State, 378 U. S. 500, 508 (1964); Cantwell v. Connecticut, 310 U. S. 296, 307–308 (1940).

In view of all this, we do not agree that, by adopting one theory of life, Texas may override the rights of the pregnant woman that are at stake. We repeat, however, that the State does have an important and legitimate interest in preserving and protecting the health of the pregnant woman, whether she be a resident of the State or a nonresident who seeks medical consultation and treatment there, and that it has still *another* important and legitimate interest in protecting the potentiality of human life. These interests are separate and distinct. Each grows in substantiality as the woman approaches term and, at a point during pregnancy, each becomes "compelling."

With respect to the State's important and legitimate interest in the health of the mother, the "compelling" point, in the light of present medical knowledge, is at approximately the end of the first trimester. It follows that, from and after this point, a State may regulate the abortion procedure to the extent that the regulation reasonably relates to the preservation and protection of maternal health. Examples of permissible state regulation in this area are requirements as to the qualifications of the person who is to perform the abortion; as to the licensure of that person; as to the facility in which the procedure is to be performed, that is, whether it must be a hospital or may be a clinic or some other place of less-than-hospital status; as to the licensing of the facility; and the like.

With respect to the State's important and legitimate interest in potential life, the "compelling" point is at viability. This is so because the fetus then presumably has the capability of meaningful life outside the mother's womb. State regulation protective of fetal life after viability thus has both logical and biological justification. If the State is interested in protecting fetal life after viability, it may go so far as to proscribe abortion during that period, except when it is necessary to preserve the life or health of the mother.

From

PLANNED PARENTHOOD OF SOUTHEASTERN PA. V. CASEY

505 U.S. 833. June 29, 1992.

Opinion by Justice O'Connor, Selections from Planned Parenthood of Southeastern Pa. v. Casey 505 U.S. 833 (1992), pp. 844-847, 850, 874.

L iberty finds no refuge in a jurisprudence of doubt.

Yet 19 years after our holding that the Constitution protects a woman's right to terminate her pregnancy in its early stages, *Roe v. Wade*, 410 U.S. 113 (1973), that definition of liberty is still questioned. Joining the respondents as *amicus curiae*, the United States, as it has done in five other cases in the last decade, again asks us to overrule *Roe*. At issue in these cases are five provisions of the Pennsylvania Abortion Control Act of 1982 as amended in 1988 and 1989. 18 Pa. Cons. Stat. §§ 3203–3220 (1990). [...] The Act requires that a woman seeking an abortion give her informed consent prior to the abortion procedure, and specifies that she be provided with certain information at least 24 hours before the abortion is performed. § 3205. For a minor to obtain an abortion, the Act requires the informed consent of one of her parents, but provides for a judicial bypass option if the minor does not wish to or cannot obtain a parent's consent. § 3206. Another provision of the Act requires that, unless certain exceptions apply, a married woman seeking an abortion must sign a statement indicating that she has notified her husband of her intended abortion. § 3209. The Act exempts compliance with these three requirements in the event of a "medical emergency," which is defined in § 3203 of the Act. See §§ 3203, 3205(a), 3206(a), 3209(c). In addition to the above provisions regulating the performance of abortions, the Act imposes certain reporting requirements on facilities that provide abortion services. §§ 3207(b), 3214(a), 3214(f).

After considering the fundamental constitutional questions resolved by *Roe*, principles of institutional integrity, and the rule of stare decisis, we are led to conclude this: the essential holding of *Roe v. Wade* should be retained and once again reaffirmed.

It must be stated at the outset and with clarity that *Roe*'s essential holding, the holding we reaffirm, has three parts. First is a recognition of the right of the woman to choose to have an abortion before viability and to obtain it without undue interference from the State. Before viability, the State's interests are not strong enough to support aprohibition of abortion or the imposition of a substantial obstacle to the woman's effective right to elect the procedure. Second is a confirmation of the State's power to restrict abortions after fetal viability, if the law contains exceptions for pregnancies which endanger a woman's life or health. And third is the principle that the State has legitimate interests from the outset of the pregnancy in protecting the health of the woman and the life of the fetus that may become a child. These principles do not contradict one another; and we adhere to each.

Constitutional protection of the woman's decision to terminate her pregnancy derives from the Due Process Clause of the Fourteenth Amendment. It declares that no State shall "deprive any person of life, liberty, or property, without due process of law." The controlling word in the case before us is "liberty." Although a literal reading of the Clause might suggest that it governs only the procedures by which a State may deprive persons of liberty, for at least 105 years, at least since *Mugler v. Kansas*, 123 U.S. 623, 660–661 (1887), the Clause has been understood to contain a substantive component as well, one "barring certain government actions regardless of the fairness of the procedures used to implement them." *Daniels v. Williams*, 474 U.S. 327, 331 (1986). As Justice Brandeis (joined by Justice Holmes) observed, "[d]espite arguments to the contrary which had seemed to me persuasive, it is settled that the due process clause of the Fourteenth Amendment applies to matters of substantive law as well as to matters of procedure. Thus all fundamental rights comprised within the term liberty are protected by the Federal Constitution from invasion by the States." *Whitney v. California*, 274 U.S. 357, 373 (1927) (Brandeis, J., concurring). "[T]he guaranties of due process, though having their roots in Magna Carta's '*per legem terrae*' and considered as procedural safeguards 'against executive usurpation and tyranny,' have in this country 'become bulwarks also against arbitrary legislation.'" *Poe v. Ullman*, 367 U.S. 497, 541 (1961) (Harlan, J., dissenting from dismissal on jurisdictional grounds) (quoting *Hurtado v. California*, 110 U.S. 516, 532 (1884)).

Men and women of good conscience can disagree, and we suppose some always shall disagree, about the profound moral and spiritual implications of terminating a pregnancy, even in its earliest stage. Some of us as individuals find abortion offensive to our most basic principles of morality, but that cannot control our decision. Our obligation is to define the liberty of all, not to mandate our own moral code. The underlying constitutional issue is whether the State can resolve these philosophic questions in such a definitive way that a woman lacks all choice in the matter, except perhaps in those rare circumstances in which the pregnancy is itself a danger to her own life or health, or is the result of rape or incest.

Numerous forms of state regulation might have the incidental effect of increasing the cost or decreasing the availability of medical care, whether for abortion or any other medical procedure. The fact that a law which serves a valid purpose, one not designed to strike at the right itself, has the incidental effect of making it more difficult or more expensive to procure an abortion cannot be enough to invalidate it. Only where state regulation imposes an undue burden on a woman's ability to make this decision does the power of the State reach into the heart of the liberty protected by the Due Process Clause. See *Hodgson v. Minnesota*, 497 U.S. 417, 458–459 (1990) (O'Connor, J., concurring in part and concurring in judgment in part); *Ohio v. Akron Center for Reproductive Health*, 497 U.S. 502.

CARHART V. GONZALEZ (2007)

JUSTICE KENNEDY delivered the opinion of the Court.

*T*he District Court in Planned Parenthood concluded the Act was unconstitutional "because it (1) pose[d] an undue burden on a woman's ability to choose a second trimester abortion; (2) [was] unconstitutionally vague; and (3) require[d] a health exception as set forth by … *Stenberg*." 320 F. Supp. 2d, at 1034–1035.

The Court of Appeals for the Ninth Circuit agreed. Like the Court of Appeals for the Eighth Circuit, it concluded the absence of a health exception rendered the Act unconstitutional. The court interpreted *Stenberg* to require a health exception unless "there is *consensus in the medical community* that the banned procedure is never medically necessary to preserve the health of women." 435 F. 3d, at 1173. Even after applying a deferential standard of review to Congress' factual findings, the Court of Appeals determined "substantial disagreement exists in the medical community regarding whether" the procedures prohibited by the Act are ever necessary to preserve a woman's health. *Id.*, at 1175–1176.

The Court of Appeals concluded further that the Act placed an undue burden on a woman's ability to obtain a second-trimester abortion. The court found the textual differences between the Act and the Nebraska statute struck down in *Stenberg* insufficient to distinguish D&E and intact D&E. 435 F. 3d, at 1178–1180. As a result, according to the Court of Appeals, the Act imposed an undue burden because it prohibited D&E. *Id.*, at 1180–1181.

Finally, the Court of Appeals found the Act void for vagueness. *Id.*, at 1181. Abortion doctors testified they were uncertain which procedures the Act made criminal. The court thus concluded the Act did not offer physicians clear warning of its regulatory reach. *Id.*, at 1181–1184. Resting on its understanding of the remedial framework established by this Court in *Ayotte v. Planned Parenthood of Northern New*

U.S. Supreme Court, "Carhart v. Gonzalez," 2007.

Eng., 546 U. S. 320, 328–330 (2006), the Court of Appeals held the Act was unconstitutional on its face and should be permanently enjoined. 435 F. 3d, at 1184–1191

***

It must be stated at the outset and with clarity that *Roe's* essential holding, the holding we reaffirm, has three parts. First is a recognition of the right of the woman to choose to have an abortion before viability and to obtain it without undue interference from the State. Before viability, the State's interests are not strong enough to support a prohibition of abortion or the imposition of a substantial obstacle to the woman's effective right to elect the procedure. Second is a confirmation of the State's power to restrict abortions after fetal viability, if the law contains exceptions for pregnancies which endanger the woman's life or health. And third is the principle that the State has legitimate interests from the outset of the pregnancy in protecting the health of the woman and the life of the fetus that may become a child. These principles do not contradict one another; and we adhere to each." 505 U. S., at 846 (opinion of the Court).

***

We assume the following principles for the purposes of this opinion. Before viability, a State "may not prohibit any woman from making the ultimate decision to terminate her pregnancy." 505 U. S., at 879 (plurality opinion). It also may not impose upon this right an undue burden, which exists if a regulation's "purpose or effect is to place a substantial obstacle in the path of a woman seeking an abortion before the fetus attains viability." *Id.*, at 878. On the other hand, "[r]egulations which do no more than create a structural mechanism by which the State, or the parent or guardian of a minor, may express profound respect for the life of the unborn are permitted, if they are not a substantial obstacle to the woman's exercise of the right to choose." *Id.*, at 877. *Casey*, in short, struck a balance. The balance was central to its holding.

***

The conclusion that the Act does not impose an undue burden is supported by other considerations. Alternatives are available to the prohibited procedure. As we have noted, the Act does not proscribe D&E. One District Court found D&E to have extremely low rates of medical complications. Planned Parenthood, supra, at 1000. Another indicated D&E was "generally the safest method of abortion during the second trimester." Carhart, 331 F. Supp. 2d, at 1031; see also Nat. Abortion Federation, supra, at 467–468 (explaining that "[e]xperts testifying for both sides" agreed D&E was safe). In addition the Act's prohibition only applies to the delivery of "a living fetus." 18 U. S. C. §1531(b)(1)(A) (2000 ed., Supp. IV). If the intact D&E procedure is truly necessary in some circumstances, it appears likely an injection that kills the fetus is an alternative under the Act that allows the doctor to perform the procedure.

* * *

Respondents have not demonstrated that the Act, as a facial matter, is void for vagueness, or that it imposes an undue burden on a woman's right to abortion based on its overbreadth or lack of a health exception. For these reasons the judgments of the Courts of Appeals for the Eighth and Ninth Circuits are reversed.

It is so ordered.

GRISWOLD V. CONNECTICUT (1965)

MR. JUSTICE DOUGLAS delivered the opinion of the Court.

Appellant Griswold is Executive Director of the Planned Parenthood League of Connecticut. Appellant Buxton is a licensed physician and a professor at the Yale Medical School who served as Medical Director for the League at its Center in New Haven—a center open and operating from November 1 to November 10, 1961, when appellants were arrested.

They gave information, instruction, and medical advice to married persons as to the means of preventing conception. They examined the wife and prescribed the best contraceptive device or material for her use. Fees were usually charged, although some couples were serviced free.

The statutes whose constitutionality is involved in this appeal are §§ 53–32 and 54–196 of the General Statutes of Connecticut (1958 rev.). The former provides:

> "Any person who uses any drug, medicinal article or instrument for the purpose of preventing conception shall be fined not less than fifty dollars or imprisoned not less than sixty days nor more than one year or be both fined and imprisoned."

Section 54–196 provides:

> "Any person who assists, abets, counsels, causes, hires or commands another to commit any offense may be prosecuted and punished as if he were the principal offender."

U.S. Supreme Court, "Griswold v. Connecticut," 1965.

The appellants were found guilty as accessories and fined $100 each, against the claim that the accessory statute, as so applied, violated the Fourteenth Amendment.

We do not sit as a super-legislature to determine the wisdom, need, and propriety of laws that touch economic problems, business affairs, or social conditions. This law, however, operates directly on an intimate relation of husband and wife and their physician's role in one aspect of that relation.

The association of people is not mentioned in the Constitution nor in the Bill of Rights. The right to educate a child in a school of the parents' choice—whether public or private or parochial—is also not mentioned. Nor is the right to study any particular subject or any foreign language. Yet the First Amendment has been construed to include certain of those rights.

By Pierce v. Society of Sisters, supra, the right to educate one's children as one chooses is made applicable to the States by the force of the First and Fourteenth Amendments. By Meyer v. Nebraska, supra, the same dignity is given the right to study the German language in a private school. In other words, the State may not, consistently with the spirit of the First Amendment, contract the spectrum of available knowledge. The right of freedom of speech and press includes not only the right to utter or to print, but the right to distribute, the right to receive, the right to read (Martin v. Struthers, 319 U. S. 141, 319 U. S. 143) and freedom of inquiry, freedom of thought, and freedom to teach (see Wiemann v. Updegraff, 344 U. S. 183, 344 U. S. 195)—indeed, the freedom of the entire university community. Sweezy v. New Hampshire, 354 U. S. 234, 354 U. S. 249–250, 354 U. S. 261–263; Barenblatt v. United States, 360 U. S. 109, 360 U. S. 112; Baggett v. Bullitt, 377 U. S. 360, 377 U. S. 369. Without those peripheral rights, the specific rights would be less secure. And so we reaffirm the principle of the Pierce and the Meyer cases.

In other words, the First Amendment has a penumbra where privacy is protected from governmental intrusion. In like context, we have protected forms of "association" that are not political in the customary sense, but pertain to the social, legal, and economic benefit of the members.

The foregoing cases suggest that specific guarantees in the Bill of Rights have penumbras, formed by emanations from those guarantees that help give them life and substance. See Poe v. Ullman, 367 U. S. 497, 367 U. S. 516–522 (dissenting opinion). Various guarantees create zones of privacy. The right of association contained in the penumbra of the First Amendment is one, as we have seen. The Third Amendment, in its prohibition against the quartering of soldiers "in any house" in time of peace without the consent of the owner, is another facet of that privacy. The Fourth Amendment explicitly affirms the "right of the people to be secure in their persons, houses, papers, and effects, against unreasonable searches and seizures." The Fifth Amendment, in its Self-Incrimination Clause, enables the citizen to create a zone of privacy which government may not force him to surrender to his detriment. The Ninth Amendment provides: "The enumeration in the Constitution, of certain rights, shall not be construed to deny or disparage others retained by the people."

Would we allow the police to search the sacred precincts of marital bedrooms for telltale signs of the use of contraceptives? The very idea is repulsive to the notions of privacy surrounding the marriage relationship. We deal with a right of privacy older than the Bill of Rights—older than our political parties, older than our school system. Marriage is a coming together for better or for worse, hopefully enduring, and intimate to the degree of being sacred. It is an association that promotes a way of life, not causes; a harmony in living, not political faiths; a bilateral loyalty, not commercial or social projects. Yet it is an association for as noble a purpose as any involved in our prior decisions.

Reversed.

MILLER V. CALIFORNIA (1973)

Miller v. California, 413 U.S. 15. June 21, 1973.

Chief Justice Burger

This much has been categorically settled by the Court, that obscene material is unprotected by the First Amendment. *Kois v. Wisconsin*, 408 U.S. 229 (1972); *United States v. Reidel*, 402 U.S. at 354; *Roth v. United States*, supra, at 485. "The First and Fourteenth Amendments have never been treated as absolutes [footnote omitted]." *Breard v. Alexandria*, 341 U.S. at 642, and cases cited. See *Times Film Corp. v. Chicago*, 365 U.S. 43, 47–50 (1961); *Joseph Burstyn, Inc. v. Wilson*, 343 U.S. at 502. We acknowledge, however, the inherent dangers of undertaking to regulate any form of expression. State statutes designed to regulate obscene materials must be carefully limited. See *Interstate Circuit, Inc. v. Dallas*, supra, at 682–685. As a result, we now confine the permissible scope of such

Chief Justice Burger, Selection from "Opinion of Chief Justice Burger," Miller v. California, Legal Information Institute, pp. 22-26.

regulation to works which depict or describe sexual conduct. That conduct must be specifically defined by the applicable state law, as written or authoritatively construed. A state offense must also be limited to works which, taken as a whole, appeal to the prurient interest in sex, which portray sexual conduct in a patently offensive way, and which, taken as a whole, do not have serious literary, artistic, political, or scientific value.

The basic guidelines for the trier of fact must be: (a) whether "the average person, applying contemporary community standards" would find that the work, taken as a whole, appeals to the prurient interest, *Kois v. Wisconsin, supra,* at 230, quoting *Roth v. United States, supra,* at 489; (b) whether the work depicts or describes, in a patently offensive way, sexual conduct specifically defined by the applicable state law; and (c) whether the work, taken as a whole, lacks serious literary, artistic, political, or scientific value. We do not adopt as a constitutional standard the "utterly without redeeming social value" test of *Memoirs v. Massachusetts,* 383 U.S. at 419; that concept has never commanded the adherence of more than three Justices at one time. *See supra* at 21. If a state law that regulates obscene material is thus limited, as written or construed, the First Amendment values applicable to the States through the Fourteenth Amendment are adequately protected by the ultimate power of appellate courts to conduct an independent review of constitutional claims when necessary. See *Kois v. Wisconsin, supra,* at 232; *Memoirs v. Massachusetts, supra,* at 459–460 (Harlan, J., dissenting); *Jacobellis v. Ohio,* 378 U.S. at 204 (Harlan, J., dissenting); *New York Times Co. v. Sullivan,* 376 U.S. 254, 284–285 (1964); *Roth v. United States, supra,* at 497–498 (Harlan, J., concurring and dissenting).

We emphasize that it is not our function to propose regulatory schemes for the States. That must await their concrete legislative efforts. It is possible, however, to give a few plain examples of what a state statute could define for regulation under part (b) of the standard announced in this opinion, *supra:*

(a) Patently offensive representations or descriptions of ultimate sexual acts, normal or perverted, actual or simulated.

(b) Patently offensive representations or descriptions of masturbation, excretory functions, and lewd exhibition of the genitals.

Sex and nudity may not be exploited without limit by films or pictures exhibited or sold in places of public accommodation any more than live sex and nudity can be exhibited or sold without limit in such public places. At a minimum, prurient, patently offensive depiction or description of sexual conduct must have serious literary, artistic, political, or scientific value to merit First Amendment protection. See *Kois v. Wisconsin, supra,* at 230–232; *Roth v.*

United States, supra, at 487; *Thornhill v. Alabama,* 310 U.S. 88, 101–102 (1940). For example, medical books for the education of physicians and related personnel necessarily use graphic illustrations and descriptions of human anatomy. In resolving the inevitably sensitive questions of fact and law, we must continue to rely on the jury system, accompanied by the safeguards that judges, rules of evidence, presumption of innocence, and other protective features provide, as we do with rape, murder, and a host of other offenses against society and its individual members.

TEXAS V. LAWRENCE (2003)

MR. JUSTICE KENNEDY delivered the opinion of the Court.

Liberty protects the person from unwarranted government intrusions into a dwelling or other private places. In our tradition the State is not omnipresent in the home. And there are other spheres of our lives and existence, outside the home, where the State should not be a dominant presence. Freedom extends beyond spatial bounds. Liberty presumes an autonomy of self that includes freedom of thought, belief, expression, and certain intimate conduct. The instant case involves liberty of the person both in its spatial and more transcendent dimensions.

The question before the Court is the validity of a Texas statute making it a crime for two persons of the same sex to engage in certain intimate sexual conduct. The complaints described their crime as "deviate sexual intercourse, namely anal sex, with a member of the same sex (man)." App. to Pet. for Cert. 127a, 139a. The applicable state law is Tex. Penal Code Ann. § 21.06(a) (2003). It provides: "A person commits an offense if he engages in deviate sexual intercourse with another individual of the same sex." The statute defines "[d]eviate sexual intercourse" as follows:

"(A) any contact between any part of the genitals of one person and the mouth or anus of another person; or

"(B) the penetration of the genitals or the anus of another person with an object." § 21.01(1).

We conclude the case should be resolved by determining whether the petitioners were free as adults to engage in the private conduct in the exercise of their liberty under the Due Process Clause of the Fourteenth Amendment to the Constitution. For this inquiry we deem it necessary to reconsider the Court's holding in Bowers.

There are broad statements of the substantive reach of liberty under the Due Process Clause in earlier cases, including Pierce v. Society of Sisters, 268 U.S. 510 (1925), and Meyer v. Nebraska, 262 U.S. 390 (1923); but the most pertinent beginning point is our decision in Griswold v. Connecticut, 381 U.S. 479 (1965).

In Griswold the Court invalidated a state law prohibiting the use of drugs or devices of contraception and counseling or aiding and abetting the use of contraceptives. The Court described the protected interest as a right to privacy and placed emphasis on the marriage relation and the protected space of the marital bedroom. Id., at 485.

American laws targeting same-sex couples did not develop until the last third of the 20th century. The reported decisions concerning the prosecution of consensual, homosexual sodomy between adults for the years 1880–1995 are not always clear in the details, but a significant number involved conduct in a public place. It was not until the 1970's that any State singled out same-sex relations for criminal prosecution, and only nine States have done so.

Of even more importance, almost five years before Bowers was decided the European Court of Human Rights considered a case with parallels to Bowers and to today's case. An adult male resident in Northern Ireland alleged he was a practicing homosexual who desired to engage in consensual homosexual conduct. The laws of Northern Ireland forbade him that right. He alleged that he had been questioned, his home had been searched, and he feared criminal prosecution. The court held that the laws proscribing the conduct were invalid under the European Convention on Human Rights. Dudgeon v. United Kingdom, 45 Eur. Ct. H.R. (1981) ¶ 52. Authoritative in all countries that are members of the Council of Europe (21 nations then, 45 nations now), the decision is at odds with the premise in Bowers that the claim put forward was insubstantial in our Western civilization.

Two principal cases decided after Bowers cast its holding into even more doubt. In Planned Parenthood of Southeastern Pa. v. Casey, 505 U.S. 833 (1992), the Court reaffirmed the substantive force of the liberty protected by the Due Process Clause. The Casey decision again confirmed that our laws and tradition afford constitutional protection to personal decisions relating to marriage, procreation, contraception, family relationships, child rearing, and education. Id., at 851. In explaining the respect the Constitution demands for the autonomy of the person in making these choices, we stated as follows:

> "These matters, involving the most intimate and personal choices a person may make in a lifetime, choices central to personal dignity and autonomy, are central to the liberty protected by the Fourteenth Amendment. At the heart of liberty is the right to define one's own concept of existence, of meaning, of the universe, and of the mystery of human life. Beliefs about these matters could not define the attributes of personhood were they formed under compulsion of the State." Ibid.

Persons in a homosexual relationship may seek autonomy for these purposes, just as heterosexual persons do. The decision in Bowers would deny them this right. The second post-Bowers case of principal relevance is Romer v. Evans, 517 U.S. 620 (1996). There the Court struck down class-based legislation directed at homosexuals as a violation of the Equal Protection Clause. Romer invalidated an amendment to Colorado's constitution which named as a solitary class persons who were homosexuals, lesbians, or bisexual either by "orientation, conduct, practices or relationships," id., at 624 (internal quotation marks omitted), and deprived them of protection under state antidiscrimination laws. We concluded that the provision was "born of animosity toward the class of persons affected" and further that it had no rational relation to a legitimate governmental purpose. Id., at 634.

The quality of treatment and the due process right to demand respect for conduct protected by the substantive guarantee of liberty are linked in important respects, and a decision on the latter point advances both interests. If protected conduct is made criminal and the law which does so remains unexamined for its substantive validity, its stigma might remain even if it were not enforceable as drawn for equal protection reasons. When homosexual conduct is made criminal by the law of the State, that declaration in and of itself is an invitation to subject homosexual persons to discrimination both in the public and in the private spheres. The central holding of Bowers has been brought in question by this case, and it should be addressed. Its continuance as precedent demeans the lives of homosexual persons.

The doctrine of stare decisis is essential to the respect accorded to the judgments of the Court and to the stability of the law. It is not, however, an inexorable command. Payne v. Tennessee, 501 U.S. 808, 828 (1991) ("Stare decisis is not an inexorable command; rather, it 'is a principle of policy and not a mechanical formula of adherence to the latest decision'") (quoting Helvering v. Hallock, 309 U.S. 106, 119 (1940))). In Casey we noted that when a Court is asked to overrule a precedent recognizing a constitutional liberty interest, individual or societal reliance on the existence of that liberty cautions with particular strength against reversing course. 505 U.S., at 855–856; see also id., at 844 ("Liberty finds no refuge in a jurisprudence of doubt"). The holding in Bowers, however, has not induced detrimental reliance comparable to some instances where recognized individual rights are involved. Indeed, there has been no individual or societal reliance on Bowers of the sort that could counsel against overturning its holding once there are compelling reasons to do so. Bowers itself causes uncertainty, for the precedents before and after its issuance contradict its central holding.

The case does involve two adults who, with full and mutual consent from each other, engaged in sexual practices common to a homosexual lifestyle. The petitioners are entitled to respect for their private lives. The State cannot demean their existence or control their destiny by making their private sexual conduct a crime. Their right to liberty under the Due Process Clause gives them the full right to engage in their conduct without intervention of the government. "It is a promise of the Constitution that there is a realm of personal liberty which the government may not enter." Casey, supra, at 847. The Texas statute furthers no legitimate state interest which can justify its intrusion into the personal and private life of the individual.

Had those who drew and ratified the Due Process Clauses of the Fifth Amendment or the Fourteenth Amendment known the components of liberty in its manifold possibilities, they might have been more specific. They did not presume to have this insight. They knew times can blind us to certain truths and later generations can see that laws once thought necessary and proper in fact serve only to oppress. As the Constitution endures, persons in every generation can invoke its principles in their own search for greater freedom. The judgment of the Court of Appeals for the Texas Fourteenth District is reversed, and the case is remanded for further proceedings not inconsistent with this opinion.

It is so ordered.

LOVING V. VIRGINIA (1967)

MR. CHIEF JUSTICE WARREN delivered the opinion of the Court.

This case presents a constitutional question never addressed by this Court: whether a statutory scheme adopted by the State of Virginia to prevent marriages between persons solely on the basis of racial classifications violates the Equal Protection and Due Process Clauses of the Fourteenth Amendment. For reasons which seem to us to reflect the central meaning of those constitutional commands, we conclude that these statutes cannot stand consistently with the Fourteenth Amendment.

In June, 1958, two residents of Virginia, Mildred Jeter, a Negro woman, and Richard Loving, a white man, were married in the District of Columbia pursuant to its laws. Shortly after their marriage, the Lovings returned to Virginia and established their marital abode in Caroline County. At the October Term, 1958, of the Circuit Court of Caroline County, a grand jury issued an indictment charging the Lovings with violating Virginia's ban on interracial marriages. On January 6, 1959, the Lovings pleaded guilty to the charge, and were sentenced to one year in jail; however, the trial judge suspended the sentence for a period of 25 years on the condition that the Lovings leave the State and not return to Virginia together for 25 years. He stated in an opinion that:

> "Almighty God created the races white, black, yellow, malay and red, and he placed them on separate continents. And, but for the interference with his arrangement, there would be no cause for such marriage. The fact that he separated the races shows that he did not intend for the races to mix."

The Supreme Court of Appeals upheld the constitutionality of the anti-miscegenation statutes and, after modifying the sentence, affirmed the convictions. The Lovings appealed this decision, and we noted probable jurisdiction on December 12, 1966, 385 U.S. 986.

Virginia is now one of 16 States which prohibit and punish marriages on the basis of racial classifications. Penalties for miscegenation arose as an incident to slavery, and have been common in Virginia since the colonial period. The present statutory scheme dates from the adoption of the Racial Integrity Act of 1924, passed during the period of extreme nativism which followed the end of the First World War. The central features of this Act, and current Virginia law, are

U.S. Supreme Court, "Loving v. Virginia," 1967.

the absolute prohibition of a "white person" marrying other than another "white person," a prohibition against issuing marriage licenses until the issuing official is satisfied that the applicants' statements as to their race are correct, certificates of "racial composition" to be kept by both local and state registrars, and the carrying forward of earlier prohibitions against racial intermarriage.

These statutes also deprive the Lovings of liberty without due process of law in violation of the Due Process Clause of the Fourteenth Amendment. The freedom to marry has long been recognized as one of the vital personal rights essential to the orderly pursuit of happiness by free men.

Marriage is one of the "basic civil rights of man," fundamental to our very existence and survival. Skinner v. Oklahoma, 316 U. S. 535, 316 U. S. 541 (1942). See also Maynard v. Hill, 125 U. S. 190 (1888). To deny this fundamental freedom on so unsupportable a basis as the racial classifications embodied in these statutes, classifications so directly subversive of the principle of equality at the heart of the Fourteenth Amendment, is surely to deprive all the State's citizens of liberty without due process of law. The Fourteenth Amendment requires that the freedom of choice to marry not be restricted by invidious racial discriminations. Under our Constitution, the freedom to marry, or not marry, a person of another race resides with the individual, and cannot be infringed by the State. These convictions must be reversed.

It is so ordered.

Economic and Global Challenges

WICKARD V. FILBURN (1942)

MR. JUSTICE JACKSON delivered the opinion of the Court.

The appellee for many years past has owned and operated a small farm in Montgomery County, Ohio, maintaining a herd of dairy cattle, selling milk, raising poultry, and selling poultry and eggs. It has been his practice to raise a small acreage of winter wheat, sown in the Fall and harvested in the following

U.S. Supreme Court, "Wickard v. Filburn," 1942.

July; to sell a portion of the crop; to feed part to poultry and livestock on the farm, some of which is sold; to use some in making flour for home consumption, and to keep the rest for the following seeding. The intended disposition of the crop here involved has not been expressly stated.

In July of 1940, pursuant to the Agricultural Adjustment Act of 1938, as then amended, there were established for the appellee's 1941 crop a wheat acreage allotment of 11.1 acres and a normal yield of 20.1 bushels of wheat an acre. He was given notice of such allotment in July of 1940, before the Fall planting of his 1941 crop of wheat, and again in July of 1941, before it was harvested. He sowed, however, 23 acres, and harvested from his 11.9 acres of excess acreage 239 bushels, which, under the terms of the Act as amended on May 26, 1941, constituted farm marketing excess, subject to a penalty of 49 cents a bushel, or $117.11 in all. The appellee has not paid the penalty, and he has not postponed or avoided it by storing the excess under regulations of the Secretary of Agriculture, or by delivering it up to the Secretary. The Committee, therefore, refused him a marketing card, which was, under the terms of Regulations promulgated by the Secretary, necessary to protect a buyer from liability to the penalty and upon its protecting lien.

The court below held, with one judge dissenting, that the speech of the Secretary invalidated the referendum, and that the amendment of May 26, 1941,

> "insofar as it increased the penalty for the farm marketing excess over the fifteen cents per bushel prevailing at the time of planting and subjected the entire crop to a lien for the payment thereof,"

should not be applied to the appellee because, as so applied, it was retroactive, and in violation of the Fifth Amendment, and, alternatively, because the equities of the case so required. 43 F. Supp. 1017. Its Judgment permanently enjoined appellants from collecting a marketing penalty of more than 15 cents a bushel on the farm marketing excess of appellee's 1941 wheat crop, from subjecting appellee's entire 1941 crop to a lien for the payment of the penalty, and from collecting a 15-cent penalty except in accordance with the provisions of § 339 of the Act as that section stood prior to the amendment of May 26, 1941. The Secretary and his codefendants have appealed.

At the beginning, Chief Justice Marshall described the federal commerce power with a breadth never yet exceeded. Gibbons v. Ogden, 9 Wheat. 1, 22 U. S. 194–195. He made emphatic the embracing and penetrating nature of this power by warning that effective restraints on its exercise must proceed from political, rather than from judicial, processes. Id. at 22 U. S. 197.

For nearly a century, however, decisions of this Court under the Commerce Clause dealt rarely with questions of what Congress might do in the exercise of its granted power under the Clause, and almost entirely with the permissibility of state activity which it was claimed discriminated against or burdened interstate commerce. During this period, there was perhaps little occasion for the affirmative exercise of the commerce power, and the influence of the Clause on American life and law was a negative one, resulting almost wholly from its operation as a restraint upon the powers of the states. In discussion and decision, the point of reference, instead of being what was "necessary and proper" to the exercise by Congress of its granted power, was often some concept of sovereignty thought to be implicit in the status of statehood. Certain activities such as "production," "manufacturing," and "mining" were occasionally said to be within the province of state governments and beyond the power of Congress under the Commerce Clause.

It was not until 1887, with the enactment of the Interstate Commerce Act, that the interstate commerce power began to exert positive influence in American law and life. This first important federal resort to the commerce power was followed in 1890 by the Sherman Anti-Trust Act and, thereafter, mainly after 1903, by many others. These statutes ushered in new phases of adjudication, which required the Court to approach the interpretation of the Commerce Clause in the light of an actual exercise by Congress of its power thereunder.

Appellee's claim that the Act works a deprivation of due process even apart from its allegedly retroactive effect is not persuasive. Control of total supply, upon which the whole statutory plan is based, depends upon control of individual supply. Appellee's claim is not that his quota represented less than a fair share of the national quota, but that the Fifth Amendment requires that he be free from penalty for planting wheat and disposing of his crop as he sees fit.

We do not agree. In its effort to control total supply, the Government gave the farmer a choice which was, of course, designed to encourage cooperation and discourage noncooperation. The farmer who planted within his allotment was, in effect, guaranteed a minimum return much above what his wheat would have brought if sold on a world market basis. Exemption from the applicability of quotas was made in favor of small producers. The farmer who produced in excess of his quota might escape penalty by delivering his wheat to the Secretary, or by storing it with the privilege of sale without penalty in a later year to fill out his quota, or irrespective of quotas if they are no longer in effect, and he could obtain a loan of 60 percent of the rate for cooperators, or about 59 cents a bushel, on so much of his wheat as would be subject to penalty if marketed. Finally, he might make other disposition of his wheat, subject to the penalty. It is agreed that, as the result of the wheat programs, he is able to market his wheat at a price "far above any world price based on the natural reaction of supply and demand." We can hardly find a denial of due process in these circumstances, particularly since it is even doubtful that appellee's burdens under the program outweigh his benefits. It is hardly lack of due process for the Government to regulate that which it subsidizes.

Only when he threshed, and thereby made it a part of the bulk of wheat overhanging the market, did he become subject to penalty. He has made no effort to show that the value of his excess wheat consumed without threshing was less than it would have been had it been threshed while subject to the statutory provisions in force at the time of planting. Concurrently with the increase in the amount of the penalty, Congress authorized a substantial increase in the amount of the loan which might be made to cooperators upon stored farm marketing excess wheat. That appellee is the worse off for the aggregate of this legislation does not appear; it only appears that, if he could get all that the Government gives and do nothing that the Government asks, he would be better off than this law allows. To deny him this is not to deny him due process of law. Cf. Mulford v. Smith, 307 U. S. 38.

Reversed.

CITIZENS UNITED V. FEDERAL ELECTION COMM'N (2010)

Justice Kennedy delivered the opinion of the Court.

Federal law prohibits corporations and unions from using their general treasury funds to make independent expenditures for speech defined as an "electioneering communication" or for speech expressly advocating the election or defeat of a candidate. 2 U. S. C. §441b. Limits on electioneering communications were upheld in McConnell v. Federal Election Comm'n, 540 U. S. 93, 203–209 (2003). The holding of McConnell rested to a large extent on an earlier case, Austin v. Michigan Chamber of Commerce, 494 U. S. 652 (1990). Austin had held that political speech may be banned based on the speaker's corporate identity.

U.S. Supreme Court, "Citizens United v. Federal Election Commission," 2010.

In this case we are asked to reconsider Austin and, in effect, McConnell. It has been noted that "Austin was a significant departure from ancient First Amendment principles," Federal Election Comm'n v. Wisconsin Right to Life, Inc., 551 U. S. 449, 490 (2007) (WRTL) (Scalia, J., concurring in part and concurring in judgment). We agree with that conclusion and hold that stare decisis does not compel the continued acceptance of Austin. The Government may regulate corporate political speech through disclaimer and disclosure requirements, but it may not suppress that speech altogether.

***

The First Amendment provides that "Congress shall make no law ... abridging the freedom of speech." Laws enacted to control or suppress speech may operate at different points in the speech process. The following are just a few examples of restrictions that have been attempted at different stages of the speech process—all laws found to be invalid: restrictions requiring a permit at the outset, Watchtower Bible & Tract Soc. of N. Y., Inc. v. Village of Stratton, 536 U. S. 150, 153 (2002); imposing a burden by impounding proceeds on receipts or royalties, Simon & Schuster, Inc. v. Members of N. Y. State Crime Victims Bd., 502 U. S. 105, 108, 123 (1991); seeking to exact a cost after the speech occurs, New York Times Co. v. Sullivan, 376 U. S., at 267; and subjecting the speaker to criminal penalties, Brandenburg v. Ohio, 395 U. S. 444, 445 (1969) (per curiam).

The law before us is an outright ban, backed by criminal sanctions. Section 441b makes it a felony for all corporations—including nonprofit advocacy corporations—either to expressly advocate the election or defeat of candidates or to broadcast electioneering communications within 30 days of a primary election and 60 days of a general election. Thus, the following acts would all be felonies under §441b: The Sierra Club runs an ad, within the crucial phase of 60 days before the general election, that exhorts the public to disapprove of a Congressman who favors logging in national forests; the National Rifle Association publishes a book urging the public to vote for the challenger because the incumbent U. S. Senator supports a handgun ban; and the American Civil Liberties Union creates a Web site telling the public to vote for a Presidential candidate in light of that candidate's defense of free speech. These prohibitions are classic examples of censorship.

Section 441b is a ban on corporate speech notwithstanding the fact that a PAC created by a corporation can still speak. See McConnell, 540 U. S., at 330–333 (opinion of Kennedy, J.). A PAC is a separate association from the corporation. So the PAC exemption from §441b's expenditure ban, §441b(b)(2), does not allow corporations to speak. Even if a PAC could somehow allow a corporation to speak—and it does not—the option to form PACs does not alleviate the First Amendment problems with §441b. PACs are burdensome alternatives; they are expensive to administer and subject to extensive regulations. For example, every PAC must appoint a treasurer, forward donations to the treasurer promptly, keep detailed records of the identities of the persons making donations, preserve receipts for three years, and file an organization statement and report changes to this information within 10 days. See id., at 330–332 (quoting MCFL, 479 U. S., at 253–254).

And that is just the beginning. PACs must file detailed monthly reports with the FEC, which are due at different times depending on the type of election that is about to occur:

> "'These reports must contain information regarding the amount of cash on hand; the total amount of receipts, detailed by 10 different categories; the identification of each political committee and candidate's authorized or affiliated committee making contributions, and any persons making loans, providing rebates, refunds, dividends, or interest or any other offset to operating expenditures in an aggregate amount over $200; the total amount of all disbursements, detailed by 12 different categories; the names of all authorized or affiliated committees to whom expenditures aggregating over $200 have been made; persons to whom loan repayments or refunds have been made; the total sum of all contributions, operating expenses, outstanding debts and obligations, and the settlement terms of the retirement of any debt or obligation.'" 540 U. S., at 331–332 (quoting MCFL, supra, at 253–254).

PACs have to comply with these regulations just to speak. This might explain why fewer than 2,000 of the millions of corporations in this country have PACs. See Brief for Seven Former Chairmen of FEC et al. as Amici Curiae 11 (citing FEC, Summary of PAC Activity 1990–2006, online at http://www.fec.gov/press/press2007/ 20071009pac/sumhistory.pdf); IRS, Statistics of Income: 2006, Corporation Income Tax Returns 2 (2009) (hereinafter Statistics of Income) (5.8 million for-profit corporations filed 2006 tax returns). PACs, furthermore, must exist before they can speak. Given the onerous restrictions, a corporation may not be able to establish a PAC in time to make its views known regarding candidates and issues in a current campaign.

Section 441b's prohibition on corporate independent expenditures is thus a ban on speech. As a "restriction on the amount of money a person or group can spend on political communication during a campaign," that statute "necessarily reduces the quantity of expression by restricting the number of issues discussed, the depth of their exploration, and the size of the audience reached." Buckley v. Valeo, 424 U. S. 1, 19 (1976) (per curiam). Were the Court to uphold these restrictions, the Government could repress speech by silencing certain voices at any of the various points in the speech process. See McConnell, supra, at 251 (opinion of Scalia, J.) (Government could repress speech by "attacking all levels of the production and dissemination of ideas," for "effective public communication requires the speaker to make use of the services of others"). If §441b applied to individuals, no one would believe that it is merely a time, place, or manner restriction on speech. Its purpose and effect are to silence entities whose voices the Government deems to be suspect.

Speech is an essential mechanism of democracy, for it is the means to hold officials accountable to the people. See Buckley, supra, at 14–15 ("In a republic where the people are sovereign, the ability of the citizenry to make informed choices among candidates for office is essential"). The right of citizens to inquire, to hear, to speak, and to use information to reach consensus is a precondition to enlightened self-government and a necessary means to protect it. The First Amendment "'has its fullest and most urgent application' to speech uttered during a campaign for political office." Eu v. San Francisco County Democratic Central Comm., 489 U. S. 214, 223 (1989) (quoting Monitor Patriot Co. v. Roy, 401 U. S. 265, 272 (1971)); see Buckley, supra, at 14 ("Discussion of public issues and debate on the qualifications of candidates are integral to the operation of the system of government established by our Constitution").

For these reasons, political speech must prevail against laws that would suppress it, whether by design or inadvertence. Laws that burden political speech are "subject to strict scrutiny," which requires the Government to prove that the restriction "furthers a compelling interest and is narrowly tailored to achieve that interest." WRTL, 551 U. S., at 464 (opinion of Roberts, C. J.). While it might be maintained that political speech simply cannot be banned or restricted as a categorical matter, see Simon & Schuster, 502 U. S., at 124 (Kennedy, J., concurring in judgment), the quoted language from WRTL provides a sufficient framework for protecting the relevant First Amendment interests in this case. We shall employ it here.

Premised on mistrust of governmental power, the First Amendment stands against attempts to disfavor certain subjects or viewpoints. See, e.g., United States v. Playboy Entertainment Group, Inc., 529 U. S. 803, 813 (2000) (striking down content-based restriction). Prohibited, too, are restrictions distinguishing among different speakers, allowing speech by some but not others. See First Nat. Bank of Boston v. Bellotti, 435 U. S. 765, 784 (1978). As instruments to censor, these categories are interrelated: Speech restrictions based on the identity of the speaker are all too often simply a means to control content.

Quite apart from the purpose or effect of regulating content, moreover, the Government may commit a constitutional wrong when by law it identifies certain preferred speakers. By taking the right to speak from some and giving it to others, the Government deprives the disadvantaged person or class of the right to use speech to strive to establish worth, standing, and respect for the speaker's voice. The Government may not by these means deprive the public of the right and privilege to determine for itself what speech and speakers are worthy of consideration. The First Amendment protects speech and speaker, and the ideas that flow from each.

The Court has upheld a narrow class of speech restrictions that operate to the disadvantage of certain persons, but these rulings were based on an interest in allowing governmental entities to perform their functions. See, e.g., Bethel School Dist. No. 403 v. Fraser, 478 U. S. 675, 683 (1986) (protecting the "function of public school education"); Jones v. North Carolina Prisoners' Labor Union, Inc., 433 U. S. 119, 129 (1977) (furthering "the legitimate penological objectives of the corrections system" (internal quotation marks omitted)); Parker v. Levy, 417 U. S. 733, 759 (1974) (ensuring "the capacity of the Government to discharge its [military] responsibilities" (internal quotation marks omitted)); Civil Service Comm'n v. Letter Carriers, 413 U. S. 548, 557 (1973) ("[F]ederal service should depend upon meritorious performance rather than political service"). The corporate independent expenditures at issue in this case, however, would not interfere with governmental functions, so these cases are inapposite. These precedents stand only for the proposition that there are certain governmental functions that cannot operate without some restrictions on particular kinds of speech. By contrast, it is inherent in the nature of the political process that voters must be free to obtain information from diverse sources in order to determine how to cast their votes. At least before Austin, the Court had not allowed the exclusion of a class of speakers from the general public dialogue.

We find no basis for the proposition that, in the context of political speech, the Government may impose restrictions on certain disfavored speakers. Both history and logic lead us to this conclusion.

PLYLER V. DOE (1982)

JUSTICE BRENNAN delivered the opinion of the Court.

The question presented by these cases is whether, consistent with the Equal Protection Clause of the Fourteenth Amendment, Texas may deny to undocumented school-age children the free public education that it provides to children who are citizens of the United States or legally admitted aliens.

Since the late 19th century, the United States has restricted immigration into this country. Unsanctioned entry into the United States is a crime, 8 U.S.C. § 1325, and those who have entered unlawfully are subject to deportation, 8 U.S.C. §§ 1251, 1252 (1976 ed. and Supp. IV). But despite the existence of these legal restrictions, a substantial number of persons have succeeded in unlawfully entering the United States, and now live within various States, including the State of Texas.

In May, 1975, the Texas Legislature revised its education laws to withhold from local school districts any state funds for the education of children who were not "legally admitted" into the United States. The 1975 revision also authorized local school districts to deny enrollment in their public schools to children not "legally admitted" to the country. Tex. Educ. Code Ann. § 21.031 (Vernon Supp. 1981). These cases involve constitutional challenges to those provisions.

The Fourteenth Amendment provides that

> "[n]o State shall ... deprive any person of life, liberty, or property, without due process of law; nor deny to any person within its jurisdiction the equal protection of the laws."

Appellants argue at the outset that undocumented aliens, because of their immigration status, are not "persons within the jurisdiction" of the State of Texas, and that they therefore have no right to the equal protection of Texas law. We reject this argument. Whatever his status under the immigration laws, an alien is surely a "person" in any ordinary sense of that term. Aliens, even aliens whose presence in this country is unlawful, have long been recognized as "persons" guaranteed due process of law by the Fifth and Fourteenth Amendments. Shaughnessv v. Mezei, 345 U. S. 206, 345 U. S. 212 (1953); Wong Wing v. United States, 163 U. S. 228, 163 U. S. 238 (1896); Yick Wo v. Hopkins, 118 U. S. 356, 118 U. S. 369 (1886). Indeed, we have clearly held that the Fifth

U.S. Supreme Court, "Plyler v. Doe," 1982.

Amendment protects aliens whose presence in this country is unlawful from invidious discrimination by the Federal Government. Mathews v. Diaz, 426 U. S. 67, 426 U. S. 77 (1976).

"The Fourteenth Amendment to the Constitution is not confined to the protection of citizens. It says:"

> "Nor shall any state deprive any person of life, liberty, or property without due process of law; nor deny to any person within its jurisdiction the equal protection of the laws."

> "These provisions are universal in their application, to all persons within the territorial jurisdiction, without regard to any differences of race, of color, or of nationality, and the protection of the laws is a pledge of the protection of equal laws." Yick Wo, supra, at 118 U. S. 369.

In concluding that "all persons within the territory of the United States," including aliens unlawfully present, may invoke the Fifth and Sixth Amendments to challenge actions of the Federal Government, we reasoned from the understanding that the Fourteenth Amendment was designed to afford its protection to all within the boundaries of a State. Wong Wing, supra, at 163 U. S. 238. Our cases applying the Equal Protection Clause reflect the same territorial theme:

> "Manifestly, the obligation of the State to give the protection of equal laws can be performed only where its laws operate, that is, within its own jurisdiction. It is there that the equality of legal right must be maintained. That obligation is imposed by the Constitution upon the States severally as governmental entities, each responsible for its own laws establishing the rights and duties of persons within its borders." Missouri ex rel. Gaines v. Canada, 305 U. S. 337, 305 U. S. 350 (1938).

Although the congressional debate concerning § 1 of the Fourteenth Amendment was limited, that debate clearly confirms the understanding that the phrase "within its jurisdiction" was intended in a broad sense to offer the guarantee of equal protection to all within a State's boundaries, and to all upon whom the State would impose the obligations of its laws. Indeed, it appears from those debates that Congress, by using the phrase "person within its jurisdiction," sought expressly to ensure that the equal protection of the laws was provided to the alien population. Representative Bingham reported to the House the draft resolution of the Joint Committee of Fifteen on Reconstruction (H.R. 63) that was to become the Fourteenth Amendment. Cong. Globe, 39th Cong., 1st Sess., 1033

(1866). Two days later, Bingham posed the following question in support of the resolution:

> "Is it not essential to the unity of the people that the citizens of each
> State shall be entitled to all the privileges and immunities of citizens in
> the several States? Is it not essential to the unity of the Government and
> the unity of the people that all persons, whether citizens or strangers,
> within this land, shall have equal protection in every State in this Union
> in the rights of life and liberty and property?" Id. at 1090.

Sheer incapability or lax enforcement of the laws barring entry into this country, coupled with the failure to establish an effective bar to the employment of undocumented aliens, has resulted in the creation of a substantial "shadow population" of illegal migrants—numbering in the millions—within our borders. This situation raises the specter of a permanent caste of undocumented resident aliens, encouraged by some to remain here as a source of cheap labor, but nevertheless denied the benefits that our society makes available to citizens and lawful residents. The existence of such an underclass presents most difficult problems for a Nation that prides itself on adherence to principles of equality under law.

Public education is not a "right" granted to individuals by the Constitution. San Antonio Independent School Dist. v. Rodriguez, 411 U. S. 1, 411 U. S. 35 (1973). But neither is it merely some governmental "benefit" indistinguishable from other forms of social welfare legislation. Both the importance of education in maintaining our basic institutions and the lasting impact of its deprivation on the life of the child mark the distinction. The "American people have always regarded education and [the] acquisition of knowledge as matters of supreme importance." Meyer v. Nebraska, 262 U. S. 390, 262 U. S. 400 (1923). We have recognized "the public schools as a most vital civic institution for the preservation of a democratic system of government," Abington School District v. Schempp, 374 U. S. 203, 374 U. S. 230 (1963) (BRENNAN, J., concurring), and as the primary vehicle for transmitting "the values on which our society rests." Ambach v. Norwick, 441 U. S. 68, 441 U. S. 76 (1979).

These well-settled principles allow us to determine the proper level of deference to be afforded § 21.031. Undocumented aliens cannot be treated as a suspect class, because their presence in this country in violation of federal law is not a "constitutional irrelevancy." Nor is education a fundamental right; a State need not justify by compelling necessity every variation in the manner in which education is provided to its population. See San Antonio Independent School Dist. v. Rodriguez, supra, at 411 U. S. 28–39. But more is involved in these cases than the abstract question whether § 21.031 discriminates against a suspect class, or whether education is a fundamental right. Section 21.031 imposes a lifetime hardship on a discrete class of children not accountable for their disabling status. The stigma of illiteracy will mark them for the rest of their lives. By denying these children a basic education, we deny them the ability to live within the structure of our civic institutions, and foreclose any realistic possibility that they will contribute in even the smallest way to the progress of our Nation. In determining the rationality of § 21. 031, we may appropriately take into account its costs to the Nation and to the innocent children who are its victims. In light of these countervailing costs, the discrimination contained in § 21.031 can hardly be considered rational unless it furthers some substantial goal of the State.

To be sure, like all persons who have entered the United States unlawfully, these children are subject to deportation. 8 U.S.C. §§ 1251, 1252 (1976 ed. and Supp. IV). But there is no assurance that a child subject to deportation will ever be deported. An illegal entrant might be granted federal permission to continue to reside in this country, or even to become a citizen. See, e.g., 8 U.S.C. §§ 1252, 1253(h), 1254 (1976 ed. and Supp. IV). In light of the discretionary federal power to grant relief from deportation, a State cannot realistically determine that any particular undocumented child will in fact be deported until after deportation proceedings have been completed. It would, of course, be most difficult for the State to justify a denial of education to a child enjoying an inchoate federal permission to remain.

First, appellants appear to suggest that the State may seek to protect itself from an influx of illegal immigrants. While a State might have an interest in mitigating the potentially harsh economic effects of sudden shifts in population, [Footnote 23] § 21.031 hardly offers an effective method of dealing with an urgent demographic or economic problem. There is no evidence in the record suggesting that illegal entrants impose any significant burden on the State's economy. To the contrary, the available evidence suggests that illegal aliens underutilize public services, while contributing their labor to the local economy and tax money to the state fisc. 458 F. Supp. at 578; 501 F. Supp. at 570–571. The dominant incentive for illegal entry into the State of Texas is the availability of employment; few if any illegal immigrants come to this country, or presumably to the State of Texas, in order to avail themselves of a free education. [Footnote 24] Thus, even making the doubtful assumption that the net impact of illegal aliens on the economy of the State is negative, we think it clear that "[c]harging tuition to undocumented children constitutes a ludicrously ineffectual attempt to stem the tide of illegal immigration," at least when compared with the alternative of prohibiting the employment of illegal aliens. 458 F. Supp. at 585. See 628 F.2d at 461; 501 F. Supp. at 579, and n. 88.

Second, while it is apparent that a State may "not ... reduce expenditures for education by barring [some arbitrarily chosen class of] children from its schools," Shapiro v. Thompson, 394 U. S. 618, 394 U. S. 633 (1969), appellants suggest that undocumented children are appropriately singled out for exclusion because of the special burdens they impose on the State's ability to provide high-quality public education. But the record in no way supports the claim that exclusion of undocumented children is likely to improve the overall quality of education in the State.

As the District Court in No. 801934 noted, the State failed to offer any "credible supporting evidence that a proportionately small diminution of the funds spent on each child [which might result from devoting some state funds to the education of the excluded group] will have a grave impact on the quality of education." 501 F. Supp. at 583. And, after reviewing the State's school financing mechanism, the District Court in No. 80–1538 concluded that barring undocumented children from local schools would not necessarily improve the quality of education provided in those schools. 458 F. Supp. at 577.

Of course, even if improvement in the quality of education were a likely result of barring some number of children from the schools of the State, the State must support its selection of this group as the appropriate target for exclusion. In terms of educational cost and need, however, undocumented children are "basically indistinguishable" from legally resident alien children. Id. at 589; 501 F. Supp. at 583, and n. 104.

Finally, appellants suggest that undocumented children are appropriately singled out because their unlawful presence within the United States renders them less likely than other children to remain within the boundaries of the State, and to put their education to productive social or political use within the State. Even assuming that such an interest is legitimate, it is an interest that is most difficult to quantify. The State has no assurance that any child, citizen or not, will employ the education provided by the State within the confines of the State's borders. In any event, the record is clear that many of the undocumented children disabled by this classification will remain in this country indefinitely, and that some will become lawful residents or citizens of the United States. It is difficult to understand precisely what the State hopes to achieve by promoting the creation and perpetuation of a subclass of illiterates within our boundaries, surely adding to the problems and costs of unemployment, welfare, and crime. It is thus clear that whatever savings might be achieved by denying these children an education, they are wholly insubstantial in light of the costs involved to these children, the State, and the Nation.

If the State is to deny a discrete group of innocent children the free public education that it offers to other children residing within its borders, that denial must be justified by a showing that it furthers some substantial state interest. No such showing was made here. Accordingly, the judgment of the Court of Appeals in each of these cases is.

Affirmed.

E.P.A. V. EME HOMER CITY GENERATION (2014)

Justice Ginsburg delivered the opinion of the Court.

These cases concern the efforts of Congress and the Environmental Protection Agency (EPA or Agency) to cope with a complex problem: air pollution emitted in one State, but causing harm in other States. Left unregulated, the emitting or upwind State reaps the benefits of the economic activity causing the pollution without bearing all the costs. See Revesz, Federalism and Interstate Environmental Externalities, 144 U. Pa. L. Rev. 2341, 2343 (1996). Conversely, downwind States to which the pollution travels are unable to achieve clean air because of the influx of out-of-state pollution they lack authority to control. See S. Rep. No. 101–228, p. 49 (1989). To tackle the problem, Congress included a Good Neighbor Provision in the Clean Air Act (Act or CAA). That provision, in its current phrasing, instructs States to prohibit in-state sources "from emitting any air pollutant in amounts which will ... contribute significantly" to downwind States' "nonattainment ... , or interfere with maintenance," of any EPA-promulgated national air quality standard. 42 U. S. C. §7410(a)(2)(D)(i).

Interpreting the Good Neighbor Provision, EPA adopted the Cross-State Air Pollution Rule (commonly and hereinafter called the Transport Rule). The rule calls for consideration of costs, among other factors, when determining the emission reductions an upwind State must make to improve air quality in polluted downwind areas. The Court of Appeals for the D. C. Circuit vacated the rule in its entirety. It held, 2 to 1, that the Good Neighbor Provision requires EPA to consider only each upwind State's physically proportionate responsibility for

U.S. Supreme Court, "EPA v. Homer City Generation," 2014.

each downwind State's air quality problem. That reading is demanded, according to the D. C. Circuit, so that no State will be required to decrease its emissions by more than its ratable share of downwind-state pollution.

In Chevron U. S. A. Inc. v. Natural Resources Defense Council, Inc., 467 U. S. 837 (1984), we reversed a D. C. Circuit decision that failed to accord deference to EPA's reasonable interpretation of an ambiguous Clean Air Act provision. Satisfied that the Good Neighbor Provision does not command the Court of Appeals' cost-blind construction, and that EPA reasonably interpreted the provision, we reverse the D. C. Circuit's judgment.

***

Under the Transport Rule, EPA employed a "two-step approach" to determine when upwind States "contribute[d] significantly to nonattainment," id., at 48254, and therefore in "amounts" that had to be eliminated. At step one, called the "screening" analysis, the Agency excluded as de minimis any upwind State that contributed less than one percent of the three NAAQS[3] to any downwind State "receptor," a location at which EPA measures air quality. See id., at 48236–48237. [4] If all of an upwind State's contributions fell below the one-percent threshold, that State would be considered not to have "contribute[d] significantly" to the nonattainment of any downwind State. Id., at 48236. States in that category were screened out and exempted from regulation under the rule.

***

Once EPA has calculated emission budgets, the D. C. Circuit held, the Agency must give upwind States the opportunity to propose SIPs allocating those budgets among in-state sources before issuing a FIP. 696 F. 3d, at 37. As the State respondents put it, a FIP allocating a State's emission budget "must issue after EPA has quantified the States' good-neighbor obligations [in an emission budget] and given the States a reasonable opportunity to meet those obligations in SIPs." Brief for State Respondents 20.

***

... Most upwind States contribute pollution to multiple downwind States in varying amounts. See 76 Fed. Reg. 48239–48246. See also Brief for Respondent Calpine Corp. et al. in Support of Petitioners 48–49 (offering examples). Suppose then that States X and Y also contribute pollutants to a second downwind State (State B), this time in a ratio of seven to one. Though State Y contributed a relatively larger share of pollution to State A, with respect to State B, State X is the greater offender. Following the proportionality approach with respect to State B would demand that State X reduce its emissions by seven times as much as State Y. Recall, however, that State Y, as just hypothesized, had to effect five times as large a reduction with respect to State A. The Court of Appeals' proportionality edict with respect to both State A and State B appears to work neither mathematically nor in practical application. Proportionality as to one down-wind State will not achieve proportionality as to others. Quite the opposite. And where, as is generally true, upwind States contribute pollution to more than two downwind receptors, proportionality becomes all the more elusive.

***

We agree with the Court of Appeals to this extent: EPA cannot require a State to reduce its output of pollution by more than is necessary to achieve attainment in every downwind State or at odds with the one-percent threshold the Agency has set. If EPA requires an upwind State to reduce emissions by more than the amount necessary to achieve attainment in every downwind State to which it is linked, the Agency will have overstepped its authority, under the Good Neighbor Provision, to eliminate those "amounts [that] contribute ... to nonattainment." Nor can EPA demand reductions that would drive an upwind State's contribution to every downwind State to which it is linked below one percent of the relevant NAAQS. Doing so would be counter to step one of the Agency's interpretation of the Good Neighbor Provision. See 76 Fed. Reg. 48236 ("[S]tates whose contributions are below th[e] thresholds do not significantly contribute to nonattainment ... of the relevant NAAQS.").

Neither possibility, however, justifies wholesale invalidation of the Transport Rule. First, instances of "over-control" in particular downwind locations, the D. C. Circuit acknowledged, see 696 F. 3d, at 22, may be incidental to reductions necessary to ensure attainment elsewhere. Because individual upwind States often "contribute significantly" to nonattainment in multiple downwind locations, the emissions reduction required to bring one linked downwind State into attainment may well be large enough to push other linked downwind States over the attainment line.[22] As the Good Neighbor Provision seeks attainment in every downwind State, however, exceeding attainment in one State cannot rank as "over-control" unless unnecessary to achieving attainment in any downwind State. Only reductions unnecessary to downwind attainment anywhere fall outside the Agency's statutory authority.[23]

Second, while EPA has a statutory duty to avoid over-control, the Agency also has a statutory obligation to avoid "under-control," i.e., to maximize achievement of attainment downwind. For reasons earlier explained, see supra, at 3–4, a degree of imprecision is inevitable in tackling the problem of interstate air pollution. Slight changes in wind patterns or energy consumption, for example, may vary downwind air quality in ways EPA might not have anticipated. The Good Neighbor Provision requires EPA to seek downwind attainment of NAAQS notwithstanding the uncertainties. Hence, some amount of over-control, i.e., emission budgets that turn out to be more demanding than necessary, would not be surprising. Required to balance the possibilities of under-control and over-control, EPA must have leeway in fulfilling its statutory mandate.

Finally, in a voluminous record, involving thousands of upwind-to-downwind linkages, respondents point to only a few instances of "unnecessary" emission reductions, and even those are contested by EPA. Compare Brief for Industry Respondents 19 with Reply Brief for Federal Petitioners 21–22. EPA, for its part, offers data, contested by respondents, purporting to show that few (if any) upwind States have been required to limit emissions below the one-percent threshold of significance. Compare Brief for Federal Petitioners 37, 54–55, with Brief for Industry Respondents 40.

If any upwind State concludes it has been forced to regulate emissions below the one-percent threshold or beyond the point necessary to bring all downwind States into attainment, that State may bring a particularized, as-applied challenge to the Transport Rule, along with any other as-applied challenges it may have. Cf. Babbitt v. Sweet Home Chapter, Communities for Great Ore., 515 U. S. 687–700 (1995) (approving agency's reasonable interpretation of statute despite possibility of improper applications); American Hospital Assn. v. NLRB, 499 U. S. 606, 619 (1991) (rejecting facial challenge to National Labor Relations Board rule despite possible arbitrary applications). Satisfied that EPA's cost-based methodology, on its face, is not "arbitrary, capricious, or manifestly contrary to the statute," Chevron, 467 U. S., at 844, we uphold the Transport Rule. The possibility that the rule, in uncommon particular applications, might exceed EPA's statutory authority does not warrant judicial condemnation of the rule in its entirety.

In sum, we hold that the CAA does not command that States be given a second opportunity to file a SIP after EPA has quantified the State's interstate pollution obligations. We further conclude that the Good Neighbor Provision does not require EPA to disregard costs and consider exclusively each upwind State's physically proportionate responsibility for each downwind air quality problem. EPA's cost-effective allocation of emission reductions among upwind States, we hold, is a permissible, work-able, and equitable interpretation of the Good Neighbor Provision.

***

For the reasons stated, the judgment of the United States Court of Appeals for the D. C. Circuit is reversed, and the cases are remanded for further proceedings consistent with this opinion.

It is so ordered.

SUMMARY

You have reviewed many cases that introduced you to the dilemma of constitutional interpretation in the attempt to resolve social problems. As the justices of the supreme court engaged in the critical application of both constitutional text and the broader principles, or the spirit of the constitutional order, you should see that certain contradictions develop through these social controversies. The first involved the contradiction between fundamental rights of the individual and the exclusion of Africans from these rights. The next set of cases examined central issues that arise through the criminal justice system. These cases bring light to the gap between the ideals of the Bill of Rights and the injustices that occur through the practice of actual policing and corrections. These controversies raise philosophical questions about how people should be treated as well as how a state functions in a modern economy.

These questions persist in the age of intersectional social movements arguing against racial, gender, and class-based discrimination. These claims of rights are fully captured in the battles between state interventions into the personal life of women, homosexuals, and interracial relationships. The court wrestles with the needs of the state on the one hand and the infringement on personal liberty on the other hand. In the final set of cases, you saw that this ongoing contradiction extends to agriculture and commerce, corporate campaign finance and elections, immigration challenges in education, and the future labor force, and how state and federal government agencies should respond to climate change and pollution.

These case excerpts were edited to help you examine the different approaches that were taken by different judges and at different historical moments. It also showed you the textual space that judges operate within. In other words, judges exercise a great deal of subjective decision-making influenced by the backgrounds, culture, experience, education, and training. Much of this can be discerned by the careful reader through the language the justices use and the ways in which they frame the constitutional controversies. Judges are also constrained by previous cases and the logic of legal precedent. As you read you should have noticed that the judges use previous cases to both support their reasoning but also to draw distinctions and, in some cases, to overturn previous reasoning through a new analysis or a more critical approach.

Each set of readings gave you the opportunity to use an intersectional analytical framework to better understand how our identities are constituted by the legal order and how we form new conceptions of constitutional rights through our experiences in everyday social settings. This sociolegal tool is useful in both academic spaces, where you might gain a deeper and more comprehensive understanding of the polyvocality of legality but also in our everyday lives where we practice democratic engagement. The ability to better see how we might engender agency with others is a fundamental principle of self-governance and the full enjoyment of political life.

UNIT IV

Constitutional Contradiction

LEARNING OUTCOMES _____

1. Students will be able to explain how systemic contradictions influence interpretation of the US Constitution.
2. Students will be able to describe how judges interpret constitutional text to maintain the system over both individual liberty and social good.
3. Students will be able to see how formal legal rules work against social change.
4. Students will be able to better evaluate how judicial decisions affect social relations.

I magine it is the year 2050. The global temperature and the oceans have risen beyond the predictions of scientists. Extreme weather and storms have increased and the US Government has failed to maintain order. These natural disasters have led to mass migration across the globe and individual countries have militarized boundaries leading to outbreaks in small-scale battles among border countries. Misinformation is commonly used to defend injustices committed by private corporations as they seize land and housing from everyday people. Many communities have declared sovereignty based on local jurisdictions and defend their territory against outsiders, including government agents and police.

Such a dystopian future is often raised as a reason for law. However, it is not too difficult to see how different stories of law could coexist with the chaos outline above and how social movements might construct new social relations in contrast to the stories of law. What is harder to imagine is how the US Constitution, without dramatic reforms would be able to govern the emerging challenges.

The controversies of the past are linked to the problems of the future. There are inherent contradictions rooted in the tension between private property, social good, and textual interpretation. In this conclusion, you will examine how these tensions have persisted and what role judges play in maintaining a system built upon these systemic contradictions. This becomes especially important when we examine how legal education is presented. For example, in the case of *Marbury v. Madison*, did you know that all parties to the litigation were slaveholders? They were also political adversaries. How do these identities and interests affect the case? These questions are rarely raised in elite law school courses. Thus, we must also consider the identities of diverse students, especially those whom are first in their family to attend college or who are not attending wealthy, elite institutions. As you have learned throughout this text, your experiences form your beliefs and interpretations of constitutional values.

In the next reading, bell hooks presents an urgent question for critical social science research from a humanities perspective: How can the institution of higher education better integrate those from the working class and how can educators better understand the point of view of the working class when so many educators in higher education are from privileged backgrounds, often White, and with parents who attended college?

From

CONFRONTING CLASS IN THE CLASSROOM

bell hooks

Class is rarely talked about in the United States; nowhere is there a more intense silence about the reality of class differences than in educational settings. Significantly, class differences are particularly ignored in classrooms. From grade school on, we are all encouraged to cross the threshold of the classroom believing we are entering a democratic space—a free zone where the desire to study and learn makes us all equal. And even if we enter accepting the reality of class differences, most of us still believe knowledge will be meted out in fair and equal proportions. In those rare cases where it is acknowledged that students and professors do not share the same class back grounds, the underlying assumption is still that we are all equally committed to getting ahead, to moving up the ladder of success to the top. And even though many of us will not make it to the top, the unspoken understanding is that we will land somewhere in the middle, between top and bottom.

Coming from a nonmaterially privileged background, from the working poor, I entered college acutely aware of class. When I received notice of my acceptance at Stanford University, the first question that was raised in my household was how I would pay for it. My parents understood that I had been awarded scholarships, and allowed to take out loans, but they wanted to know where the money would come from for transportation, clothes, books. Given these concerns, I went to Stanford thinking that class was mainly about materiality. It only took me a short while to understand that class was more than just a question of money, that it shaped values, attitudes, social relations, and the biases that informed the way knowledge would be given and received. These same realizations about class in the academy are expressed again and again by academics from working-class backgrounds in the collection of essays *Strangers in Paradise* edited by Jake Ryan and Charles Sackrey.

During my college years it was tacitly assumed that we all agreed that class should not be talked about, that there would be no critique of the bourgeois class biases shaping and informing pedagogical process (as well as social etiquette) in the classroom. Although no one ever directly stated the rules that would govern our conduct, it was taught by example and reinforced by a system of rewards. As silence and obedience to authority were most rewarded, students learned that this was the appropriate demeanor in the classroom. Loudness, anger, emotional outbursts, and even something as seemingly innocent as unrestrained laughter were deemed unacceptable, vulgar disruptions of classroom social order. These traits were also associated with being a member of the lower classes. If one was not from a privileged class group, adopting a demeanor similar to that of the group could help one to advance. It is still necessary for students to assimilate bourgeois values in order to be deemed acceptable.

Bourgeois values in the classroom create a barrier, blocking the possibility of confrontation and conflict, warding off dissent. Students are often silenced by means of their acceptance of class values that teach them to maintain order at all costs. When the obsession with maintaining order is coupled with the fear of "losing face," of not being thought well of by one's professor and peers, all possibility of constructive dialogue is undermined. Even though students enter the "democratic" classroom believing they have the right to "free speech," most students are not comfortable exercising this right to "free speech." Most students are not comfortable exercising this right—especially if it means they must give voice to thoughts, ideas, feelings that go against the grain, that are unpopular. This censoring process is only one way bourgeois values overdetermine social behavior in the classroom and undermine the democratic exchange of ideas. Writing about his experience in the section of *Strangers in Paradise* entitled "Outsiders," Karl Anderson confessed:

> Power and hierarchy, and not teaching and learning, dominated the graduate school I found myself in. "Knowledge" was one-upmanship, and no one disguised the fact. ... The one thing I learned absolutely was the inseparability of free speech and free thought. I, as well as some of my peers, were refused the opportunity to speak and sometimes to ask questions deemed "irrelevant" when the instructors didn't wish to discuss or respond to them.

Students who enter the academy unwilling to accept without question the assumptions and values held by privileged classes tend to be silenced, deemed troublemakers.

Conservative discussions of censorship in contemporary university settings often suggest that the absence of constructive dialogue, enforced silencing, takes place as a by-product of progressive efforts to question canonical knowledge, critique relations of domination, or subvert bourgeois class biases. There is little or no discussion of the way in which the attitudes and values of those from materially privileged classes are imposed upon everyone via biased pedagogical strategies. Reflected in choice of subject matter and the manner in which ideas are shared, these biases need never be overtly stated. In his essay Karl Anderson states that silencing is "the most oppressive aspect of middle-class life." He maintains:

> It thrives upon people keeping their mouths shut, unless they are actually endorsing whatever powers exist. The free marketplace of "ideas" that is so beloved of liberals is as much a fantasy as a free market place in oil or automobiles; a more harmful fantasy, because it breeds even more hypocrisy and cynicism. Just as teachers can control what is said in their class rooms, most also have ultra-sensitive antennae as to what will be rewarded or punished that is said outside them. And these antennae control them.

Silencing enforced by bourgeois values is sanctioned in the classroom by everyone.

Even those professors who embrace the tenets of critical pedagogy (many of whom are white and male) still conduct their classrooms in a manner that only reinforces bourgeois models of decorum. At the same time, the subject matter taught in such classes might reflect professorial awareness of intellectual perspectives that critique domination, that emphasize an understanding of the politics of difference, of race, class, gender, even though classroom dynamics remain conventional, business as usual. When contemporary feminist movement made its initial presence felt in the academy there was both an ongoing critique of conventional classroom dynamics and an attempt to create alternative pedagogical strategies. However, as feminist scholars endeavored to make Women's Studies a discipline administrators and peers would respect, there was a shift in perspective.

Significantly, feminist classrooms were the first spaces in the university where I encountered any attempt to acknowledge class difference. The focus was usually on the way class differences are structured in the larger society, not on our class position. Yet the focus on gender privilege in patriarchal society often meant that there was a recognition of the ways women were economically disenfranchised and therefore more likely to be poor or working class. Often, the feminist classroom was the only place where students (mostly female) from materially disadvantaged circumstances would speak from that class positionality, acknowledging both the impact of class on our social status as well as critiquing the class biases of feminist thought.

When I first entered university settings I felt estranged from this new environment. Like most of my peers and professors, I initially believed those feelings were there because of differences in racial and cultural background. However, as time passed it was more evident that this estrangement was in part a reflection of class difference. At Stanford, I was often asked by peers and professors if I was there on a scholarship. Underlying this question was the implication that receiving financial aid "diminished" one in some way. It was not just this experience that intensified my awareness of class difference, it was the constant evocation of materially privileged class experience (usually that of the middle class) as a universal norm that not only set those of us from working-class backgrounds apart but effectively excluded those who were not privileged from discussions, from social activities. To avoid feelings of estrangement, students from working-class backgrounds could assimilate into the mainstream, change speech patterns, points of reference, drop any habit that might reveal them to be from a nonmaterially privileged background.

Of course I entered college hoping that a university degree would enhance my class mobility. Yet I thought of this solely in economic terms. Early on I did not realize that class was much more than one's economic standing, that it determined values, standpoint, and interests. It was assumed that any student coming from a poor or working-class background would willingly surrender all values and habits of being associated with this background. Those of us from diverse ethnic/racial backgrounds learned that no aspect of our vernacular culture could be voiced in elite settings. This was especially the case with vernacular language or a first language that was not English. To insist on speaking in any manner that did not conform to privileged class ideals and mannerisms placed one always in the position of interloper.

Demands that individuals from class backgrounds deemed undesirable surrender all vestiges of their past create psychic turmoil. We were encouraged, as many students are today, to betray our class origins. Rewarded if we chose to assimilate, estranged if we chose to maintain those aspects of who we were, some were all too often seen as outsiders. Some of us rebelled by clinging to exaggerated manners and behavior clearly marked as outside the accepted bourgeois norm. During my student years, and now as a professor, I see many students from "undesirable" class backgrounds become unable to complete their studies because the contradictions between the behavior necessary to "make it" in the academy and those that allowed them to be comfortable at home, with their families and friends, are just too great.

Often, African Americans are among those students I teach from poor and working-class backgrounds who are most vocal about issues of class. They express frustration, anger, and sadness about the tensions and stress they experience trying to conform to acceptable white, middle-class behaviors in university settings while retaining the ability to "deal" at home. Sharing strategies for coping from my own experience, I encourage students to reject the notion that they must choose between experiences. They must believe they can inhabit comfortably two different worlds, but they must make each space one of comfort. They must creatively invent ways to cross borders. They must believe in their capacity to alter the bourgeois settings they enter. All too often, students from nonmaterially privileged backgrounds assume a position of passivity—they behave as victims, as though they can only be acted upon against their will. Ultimately, they end up feeling they can only reject or accept the norms imposed upon them. This either/ or often sets them up for disappointment and failure.

Those of us in the academy from working-class backgrounds are empowered when we recognize our own agency, our capacity to be active participants in the pedagogical process. This process is not simple or easy: it takes courage to embrace a vision of wholeness of being that does not reinforce the capitalist version that suggests that one must always give something up to gain another. In the introduction to the section of their book titled "Class Mobility and Internalized Conflict," Ryan and Sackrey remind readers that "the academic work process is essentially antagonistic to the working class, and academics for the most part live in a different world of culture, different ways that make it, too, antagonistic to working class life." Yet those of us from working-class backgrounds cannot allow class antagonism to prevent us from gaining knowledge, degrees and enjoying the aspects of higher education that are fulfilling. Class antagonism can be constructively used, not made to reinforce the notion that students and professors from working-class backgrounds are "outsiders" and "interlopers," but to subvert and challenge the existing structure.

When I entered my first Women's Studies classes at Stanford, white professors talked about "women" when they were making the experience of materially privileged white women a norm. It was both a matter of personal and intellectual integrity for me to challenge this biased assumption. By challenging, I refused to be complicit in the erasure of black and/or working-class women of all ethnicities. Personally, that meant I was not able just to sit in class, grooving on the good feminist vibes—that was a loss. The gain was that I was honoring the experience of poor and working-class women in my own family, in that very community that had encouraged and supported me in my efforts to be better educated. Even though my intervention was not wholeheartedly welcomed, it created a context for critical thinking, for dialectical exchange.

Any attempt on the part of individual students to critique the bourgeois biases that shape pedagogical process, particularly as they relate to epistemological perspectives (the points from which information is shared) will, in most cases, no doubt, be viewed as negative and disruptive. Given the presumed radical or liberal nature of early feminist classrooms, it was shocking to me to find those settings were also often closed to different ways of thinking. While it was acceptable to critique patriarchy in that context, it was not acceptable to confront issues of class, especially in ways that were not simply about the evocation of guilt. In general, despite their participation in different disciplines and the diversity of class backgrounds, African American scholars and other nonwhite professors have been no more willing to confront issues of class. Even when it became more acceptable to give at least lip service to the recognition of race, gender, and class, most professors and students just did not feel they were able to address class in anything more than a simplistic way. Certainly, the primary area where there was the possibility of meaningful critique and change was in relation to biased scholarship, work that used the experiences and thoughts of materially privileged people as normative.

In recent years, growing awareness of class differences in progressive academic circles has meant that students and professors committed to critical and feminist pedagogy have the opportunity to make spaces in the academy where class can receive attention. Yet there can be no intervention that challenges the status quo if we are not willing to interrogate the way our presentation of self as well as our pedagogical process is often shaped by middle-class norms. My awareness of class has been continually reinforced by my efforts to remain close to loved ones who remain in materially underprivileged class positions. This has helped me to employ pedagogical strategies that create ruptures in the established order, that promote modes of learning which challenge bourgeois hegemony.

One such strategy has been the emphasis on creating in classrooms learning communities where everyone's voice can be heard, their presence recognized and valued. In the section of *Strangers in Paradise* entitled "Balancing Class Locations," Jane Ellen Wilson shares the way an emphasis on personal voice strengthened her.

> Only by coming to terms with my own past, my own background, and seeing that in the context of the world at large, have I begun to find my true voice and to understand that, since it is my own voice, that no pre-cut niche exists for it; that part of the work to be done is making a place, with others, where my and our voices, can stand clear of the background noise and voice our concerns as part of a larger song.

When those of us in the academy who are working class or from working-class backgrounds share our perspectives, we subvert the tendency to focus only on the thoughts, attitudes, and experiences of those who are materially privileged. Feminist and critical pedagogy are two alternative paradigms for teaching which have really emphasized the issue of coming to voice. That focus emerged as central, precisely because it was so evident that race, sex, and class privilege empower some students more than others, granting "authority" to some voices more than others.

A distinction must be made between a shallow emphasis on coming to voice, which wrongly suggests there can be some democratization of voice wherein everyone's words will be given equal time and be seen as equally valuable (often the model applied in feminist classrooms), and the more complex recognition of the uniqueness of each voice and a willingness to create spaces in the classroom where all voices can be heard because all students are free to speak, knowing their presence will be recognized and valued. This does not mean that anything can be said, no matter how irrelevant to classroom subject matter, and receive attention—or that something meaningful takes place if everyone has equal time to voice an opinion. In the classes I teach, I have students write short paragraphs that they read aloud so that we all have a chance to hear unique perspectives and we are all given an opportunity to pause and listen to one another. Just the physical experience of hearing, of listening intently, to each particular voice strengthens our capacity to learn together. Even though a student may not speak again after this moment, that student's presence has been acknowledged.

Hearing each other's voices, individual thoughts, and sometimes associating theses voices with personal experience makes us more acutely aware of each other. That moment of collective participation and dialogue means that students and professor respect—and here I invoke the root meaning of the word, "to look at"—each other, engage in acts of recognition with one another, and do not just talk to the professor. Sharing experiences and confessional narratives in the classroom helps establish communal commitment to learning. These narrative moments usually are the space where the assumption that we share a common class background and perspective is disrupted. While students may be open to the idea that they do not all come from a common class background, they may still expect that the values of materially privileged groups will be the class's norm.

Some students may feel threatened if awareness of class difference leads to changes in the classroom. Today's students all dress alike, wearing clothes from stores such as the Gap and Benetton; this acts to erase the markers of class difference that older generations of students experienced. Young students are more eager to deny the impact of class and class differences in our society. I have found that students from upper- and middle-class backgrounds are disturbed if heated exchange takes place in the classroom. Many of them equate loud talk or interruptions with rude and threatening behavior. Yet those of us from working-class backgrounds may feel that discussion is deeper and richer if it arouses intense responses. In class, students are often disturbed if anyone is interrupted while speaking, even though outside class most of them are not threatened. Few of us are taught to facilitate heated discussions that may include useful interruptions and digressions, but it is often the professor who is most invested in maintaining order in the classroom. Professors cannot empower students to embrace diversities of experience, standpoint, behavior, or style if our training has disempowered us, socialized us to cope effectively only with a single mode of interaction based on middle-class values.

Most progressive professors are more comfortable striving to challenge class biases through the material studied than they are with interrogating how class biases shape conduct in the classroom and transforming their pedagogical process. When I entered my first classroom as a college professor and a feminist, I was deeply afraid of using authority in a way that would perpetuate class elitism and other forms of domination. Fearful that I might abuse power, I falsely pretended that no power difference existed between students and myself. That was a mistake. Yet it was only as I began to interrogate my fear of "power"—the way that fear was related to my own class background where I had so often seen those with class power coerce, abuse, and dominate those without—that I began to understand that power was not itself negative. It depended what one did with it. It was up to me to create ways within my professional power constructively, precisely because I was teaching in institutional structures that affirm it is fine to use power to reinforce and maintain coercive hierarchies.

Fear of losing control in the classroom often leads individual professors to fall into a conventional teaching pattern wherein power is used destructively. It is this fear that leads to collective professorial investment in bourgeois decorum as a means of maintaining a fixed notion of order, of ensuring that the teacher will have absolute authority. Unfortunately, this fear of losing control shapes and informs the professorial pedagogical process to the extent that it acts a barrier preventing any constructive grappling with issues of class.

Sometimes students who want professors to grapple with class differences often simply desire that individuals from less materially privileged backgrounds be given center stage so that an inversion of hierarchical structures takes place, not a disruption. One semester, a number of black female students from working-class backgrounds attended a course I taught on African American women writers. They arrived hoping I would use my professorial power to decenter the voices of privileged white students in nonconstructive ways so that those students would experience what it is like to be an outsider. Some of these black students rigidly resisted attempts to involve the others in an engaged pedagogy where space is created for everyone. Many of the black students feared that learning new terminology or new perspectives would alienate them from familiar social relations. Since these fears are rarely addressed as part of progressive pedagogical process, students caught in the grip of such anxiety often sit in classes feeling hostile, estranged, refusing to participate. I often face students who think that in my classes they will "naturally" not feel estranged and that part of this feeling of comfort, or being "at home," is that they will not have to work as hard as they do in other classes. These students are not expecting to find alternative pedagogy in my classes but merely "rest" from the negative tensions they may feel in the majority of other courses. It is my job to address these tensions.

If we can trust the demographics, we must assume that the academy will be full of students from diverse classes, and that more of our students than ever before will be from poor and working-class backgrounds. This change will not be reflected in the class background of professors. In my own experience, I encounter fewer and fewer academics from working-class backgrounds. Our absence is no doubt related to the way class politics and class struggle shapes who will receive graduate degrees in our society. However, constructively confronting issues of class is not simply a task for those of us who came from working-class and poor backgrounds; it is a challenge for all professors. Critiquing the way academic settings are structured to reproduce class hierarchy, Jake Ryan and Charles Sackrey emphasize "that no matter what the politics or ideological stripe of the individual professor, of what the content of his or her teaching, Marxist, anarchist, or nihilist, he or she nonetheless participates in the reproduction of the cultural and class relations of capitalism." Despite this bleak assertion they are willing to acknowledge that "nonconformist intellectuals can, through research and publication, chip away with some success at the conventional orthodoxies, nurture students with comparable ideas and intentions, or find ways to bring some fraction of the resources of the university to the service of the ... class interests of the workers and others below." Any professor who commits to engaged pedagogy recognizes the importance of constructively confronting issues of class. That means welcoming the opportunity to alter our classroom practices creatively so that the democratic ideal of education for everyone can be realized.

Systemic Contradiction: Profit Over People

As sociolegal scholar William Chamblis (1993) noted there is a fundamental contradiction in a society committed to rapid industrialization and to social equality; these two goals cannot simultaneously be maximized. People can debate the relative value of each of these goals; however, whether the contradiction might be resolved dramatically affects the life outcomes of many people. Revolutionary movements seek to transform the social relations toward a more equitable and just distribution of power. As you have read throughout this reader, judges occupy an influential position in this complex structure of governance. It is a weight many judges have said is an uneasy one to hold.

On the one hand, judges have taken an oath to uphold justice for rich and poor alike; on the other hand, those with wealth and power have greater access to and influence over the court system. How then can we expect judges to be able to strike a balance between political struggles and limiting injustices? Justice John Marshall explained how he saw the role of the court in *Marbury v. Madison*. Pay special attention to how he perceived what approach judges should take when confronted with controversies between state action and individual liberty. You should also examine how this theory of judicial power influences the delicate balance of democratic politics and how that influences controversies today.

From

MARBURY V. MADISON

5 U.S. 137, 1803.

The Government of the United States has been emphatically termed a government of laws, and not of men. It will certainly cease to deserve this high appellation if the laws furnish no remedy for the violation of a vested legal right (163).

The question whether an act repugnant to the Constitution can become the law of the land is a question deeply interesting to the United States, but, happily, not of an intricacy proportioned to its interest. It seems only necessary to recognize certain principles, supposed to have been long and well established, to decide it.

That the people have an original right to establish for their future government such principles as, in their opinion, shall most conduce to their own happiness is the basis on which the whole American fabric has been erected. The exercise of this original right is a very great exertion; nor can it nor ought it to be frequently repeated. The principles, therefore, so established are deemed fundamental. And as the authority from which they proceed, is supreme, and can seldom act, they are designed to be permanent.

This original and supreme will organizes the government and assigns to different departments their respective powers. It may either stop here or establish certain limits not to be transcended by those departments.

The Government of the United States is of the latter description. The powers of the Legislature are defined and limited; and that those limits may not be mistaken or forgotten, the Constitution is written. To what purpose are powers limited, and to what purpose is that limitation committed to writing, if these limits may at any time be passed by those intended to be restrained? The distinction between a government with limited and unlimited powers is abolished if those limits do not confine the persons on whom they are imposed, and if acts prohibited and acts allowed are of equal obligation. It is a proposition too plain to be contested that the Constitution controls any legislative act repugnant to it, or that the Legislature may alter the Constitution by an ordinary act.

Chief Justice Marshall, Selections from Marbury v. Madison, pp. 163-180.

Between these alternatives there is no middle ground. The Constitution is either a superior, paramount law, unchangeable by ordinary means, or it is on a level with ordinary legislative acts, and, like other acts, is alterable when the legislature shall please to alter it.

If the former part of the alternative be true, then a legislative act contrary to the Constitution is not law; if the latter part be true, then written Constitutions are absurd attempts on the part of the people to limit a power in its own nature illimitable.

Certainly all those who have framed written Constitutions contemplate them as forming the fundamental and paramount law of the nation, and consequently the theory of every such government must be that an act of the Legislature repugnant to the Constitution is void.

This theory is essentially attached to a written Constitution, and is consequently to be considered by this Court as one of the fundamental principles of our society. It is not, therefore, to be lost sight of in the further consideration of this subject.

If an act of the Legislature repugnant to the Constitution is void, does it, notwithstanding its invalidity, bind the Courts and oblige them to give it effect? Or, in other words, though it be not law, does it constitute a rule as operative as if it was a law? This would be to overthrow in fact what was established in theory, and would seem, at first view, an absurdity too gross to be insisted on. It shall, however, receive a more attentive consideration.

It is emphatically the province and duty of the Judicial Department to say what the law is. Those who apply the rule to particular cases must, of necessity, expound and interpret that rule. If two laws conflict with each other, the Courts must decide on the operation of each.

So, if a law be in opposition to the Constitution, if both the law and the Constitution apply to a particular case, so that the Court must either decide that case conformably to the law, disregarding the Constitution, or conformably to the Constitution, disregarding the law, the Court must determine which of these conflicting rules governs the case. This is of the very essence of judicial duty.

If, then, the Courts are to regard the Constitution, and the Constitution is superior to any ordinary act of the Legislature, the Constitution, and not such ordinary act, must govern the case to which they both apply.

Those, then, who controvert the principle that the Constitution is to be considered in court as a paramount law are reduced to the necessity of maintaining that courts must close their eyes on the Constitution, and see only the law.

This doctrine would subvert the very foundation of all written Constitutions. It would declare that an act which, according to the principles and theory of our government, is entirely void, is yet, in practice, completely obligatory. It would declare that, if the Legislature shall do what is expressly forbidden, such act, notwithstanding the express prohibition, is in reality effectual. It would be giving to the Legislature a practical and real omnipotence with the same breath which professes to restrict their powers within narrow limits. It is prescribing limits, and declaring that those limits may be passed at pleasure.

That it thus reduces to nothing what we have deemed the greatest improvement on political institutions—a written Constitution, would of itself be sufficient, in America where written Constitutions have been viewed with so much reverence, for rejecting the construction. But the peculiar expressions of the Constitution of the United States furnish additional arguments in favor of its rejection.

The judicial power of the United States is extended to all cases arising under the Constitution.

Could it be the intention of those who gave this power to say that, in using it, the Constitution should not be looked into? That a case arising under the Constitution should be decided without examining the instrument under which it arises? This is too extravagant to be maintained.

In some cases then, the Constitution must be looked into by the judges. And if they can open it at all, what part of it are they forbidden to read or to obey?

There are many other parts of the Constitution which serve to illustrate this subject.

It is declared that "no tax or duty shall be laid on articles exported from any State." Suppose a duty on the export of cotton, of tobacco, or of flour, and a suit instituted to recover it. Ought judgment to be rendered in such a case? ought the judges to close their eyes on the Constitution, and only see the law?

The Constitution declares that "no bill of attainder or *ex post facto* law shall be passed."

If, however, such a bill should be passed and a person should be prosecuted under it, must the Court condemn to death those victims whom the Constitution endeavours to preserve?

"No person," says the Constitution, "shall be convicted of treason unless on the testimony of two witnesses to the same overt act, or on confession in open court."

Here, the language of the Constitution is addressed especially to the Courts. It prescribes, directly for them, a rule of evidence not to be departed from. If the Legislature should change that rule, and declare one witness, or a confession out of court, sufficient for conviction, must the constitutional principle yield to the legislative act?

From these and many other selections which might be made, it is apparent that the framers of the Constitution contemplated that instrument as a rule for the government of courts, as well as of the Legislature.

Why otherwise does it direct the judges to take an oath to support it? This oath certainly applies in an especial manner to their conduct in their official character. How immoral to impose it on them if they were to be used as the instruments, and the knowing instruments, for violating what they swear to support!

The oath of office, too, imposed by the Legislature, is completely demonstrative of the legislative opinion on this subject. It is in these words:

> I do solemnly swear that I will administer justice without respect to persons, and do equal right to the poor and to the rich; and that I will faithfully and impartially discharge all the duties incumbent on me as according to the best of my abilities and understanding, agreeably to the Constitution and laws of the United States.

Why does a judge swear to discharge his duties agreeably to the Constitution of the United States if that Constitution forms no rule for his government? if it is closed upon him and cannot be inspected by him?

If such be the real state of things, this is worse than solemn mockery. To prescribe or to take this oath becomes equally a crime.

It is also not entirely unworthy of observation that, in declaring what shall be the supreme law of the land, the Constitution itself is first mentioned, and not the laws of the United States generally, but those only which shall be made in pursuance of the Constitution, have that rank.

Thus, the particular phraseology of the Constitution of the United States confirms and strengthens the principle, supposed to be essential to all written Constitutions, that a law repugnant to the Constitution is void, and that courts, as well as other departments, are bound by that instrument.

Marshall's interpretation of judicial authority within a blended power structure of government has largely been followed as if a scientific truth. However, modern challenges have brought the certainty of judicial wisdom into question. In the following reading, you should apply your new understanding of interpretation very carefully. Review Article Three of the Constitution and see whether your interpretation is similar or different than Marshall's. Pay close attention to the Judiciary Act and the power of the supreme court to issue a Writ of Mandamus under original jurisdiction. Finally, think about how Marshall invented a new power for the court: the power to strike down congressional legislation.

As social problems and political controversies continue to be brought to courts for resolution, it is important to recall the historical-structural conditions that constituted the contradiction between rights claims and social control. In the next two readings that follow pay close attention to the arguments. Try to practice close reading in order to examine how constitutional interpretation is being applied and what philosophical differences would be relevant when considering controversies today.

The powers of interpretation articulated by Marshall have been used by judges to prioritize the stability of state–economic relations over the liberty interested of groups suffering injustice. Moreover, many common sense explanations of legality, including fairness and accountability, can be contradicted by courts using arbitrary methods when judges interpret what they think legislative bodies meant. Thus, even when groups mobilize against injustice they might not find justice through the courts. Still, sociolegal scholars McCann and Lovell (2020) found that the way in which those who experience injustice mobilize and come to understand rights within historical narratives of labor struggles for example are still important, especially to highlight the common sense knowledge of unequal social relations and how dominant groups evade legal accountability. This ability to apply critical sociolegal analysis to common struggles is important to those who experience injustice. In this final excerpt, consider how McCann and Lovell frame the case. In what ways does it draw upon the contextual framework you have developed throughout this reader? In what ways does it differ or add to the framework?

WARDS COVE V. ATONIO (1989)

MR. JUSTICE WHITE delivered the opinion of the Court.

Title VII of the Civil Rights Act of 1964, 78 Stat. 253, as amended, 42 U.S.C. § 2000e et seq., makes it an unfair employment practice for an employer to discriminate against any individual with respect to hiring or the terms and condition of employment because of such individual's race, color, religion, sex, or national origin; or to limit, segregate, or classify his employees in ways that would adversely affect any employee because of the employee's race, color, religion, sex, or national origin.

Griggs v. Duke Power Co., 401 U.S. 424, 431, 91 S.Ct. 849, 853, 28 L.Ed.2d 158 (1971), construed Title VII to proscribe "not only overt discrimination but also practices that are fair in form but discriminatory in practice." Under this basis for liability, which is known as the "disparate-impact" theory and which is involved in this case, a facially neutral employment practice may be deemed violative of Title VII without evidence of the employer's subjective intent to discriminate that is required in a "disparate-treatment" case.

The claims before us are disparate-impact claims, involving the employment practices of petitioners, two companies that operate salmon canneries in remote and widely separated areas of Alaska. The canneries operate only during the salmon runs in the summer months. They are inoperative and vacant for the rest of the year. In May or June of each year, a few weeks before the salmon runs begin, workers arrive and prepare the equipment and facilities for the canning operation. Most of these workers possess a variety of skills. When salmon runs are about to begin, the workers who will operate the cannery lines arrive, remain as long as there are fish to can, and then depart. The canneries are then closed down, winterized, and left vacant until the next spring. During the off-season, the companies employ only a small number of individuals at their headquarters in Seattle and Astoria, Oregon, plus some employees at the winter shipyard in Seattle.

In 1974, respondents, a class of nonwhite cannery workers who were (or had been) employed at the canneries, brought this Title VII action against petitioners. Respondents alleged that a variety of petitioners' hiring/promotion practices—e.g., nepotism, a rehire preference, a lack of objective hiring criteria, separate hiring channels, a practice of not promoting from within—were responsible for the racial stratification of the work force and had denied them and other nonwhites employment as noncannery workers on the basis of race. Respondents also complained of petitioners' racially segregated housing and dining facilities. All of respondents' claims were advanced under both the disparate-treatment and disparate-impact theories of Title VII liability.

Under the Court of Appeals' theory, simply because nonwhites comprise 52% of the cannery workers at the cannery in question, see App. to Brief for Respondents B-1, respondents would be successful in establishing a prima facie case of racial discrimination under Title VII. Such a result cannot be squared with our cases or with the goals behind the statute. The Court of Appeals' theory, at the very least, would mean that any employer who had a segment of his work force that was—for some reason—racially imbalanced, could be haled into court and forced to engage in the expensive and time-consuming task of defending the "business necessity" of the methods used to select the other members of his work force. The only practicable option for many employers would be to adopt racial quotas, insuring that no portion of their work forces deviated in racial composition from the other portions thereof; this is a result that Congress expressly rejected in drafting Title VII.

The Court of Appeals also erred with respect to the unskilled noncannery positions. Racial imbalance in one segment of an employer's work force does not, without more, establish a prima facie case of disparate impact with respect to the selection of workers for the employer's other positions, even where workers for the different positions may have somewhat fungible skills (as is arguably the case for cannery and unskilled noncannery workers).

Consequently, we reverse the Court of Appeals' ruling that a comparison between the percentage of cannery workers who are nonwhite and the percentage of noncannery workers who are nonwhite makes out a prima facie case of disparate impact.

SUMMARY

You have read cases using a sociolegal analytical framework that centered the intersections of race, gender, and class injustice. You have considered how formal law tends to construct abstract ideals that mask the everyday experience of those who do not get the benefit of power. You have also learned about the polyvocality of legality or how different individuals and groups form ideas about what law is and should be. Finally, you have considered the role of the judge in this complicated social structure. When judges promote legality narratives that come from elites and the wealthiest, they are maintaining an unequal power system that benefits the haves over the have-nots. This contradicts other legality narratives that stress fairness and equality. Judges do have the ability to protect the interests of the poor, the less powerful, and the most vulnerable. They simply need to the courage to act and the ability to empathize with those that have different experiences than their own.

You have learned that different approaches to controversies will produce different interpretations of constitutional rights. These cases form part of our legal imagination. Controversy is a necessary part of the democratic process as different people will hold strong opinions about what is right and wrong. When judges routinely side with one class, racial, or ethnic group, or gender identity, political tensions will rise and we all lose a common sense of what justice means. This has been true throughout the history of the US constitutional law. In closing, consider scholar Robert Cover's (1975) analysis of how the antislavery judge engaged with law and constitutional controversies throughout history and how that might apply to future cases and controversies:

The judge is "educated to think in terms of the values underlying legality and ordered processes … education, colleagueship with others of similar training, day-to-day experience with those processes lead (them) to be more alert than most to the dangers to law … the prominent, antislavery judge thus found (themself) in a particularly critical role in the posited system … a greater than average say in the direction that law might take."

REFERENCES

Chamblis, W. J. 1993. "On Law Making." In *Making Law: The State, the Law, and Structural Contradictions.* Bloomington and Indianapolis: Indiana University Press. 35.

Cover, R. M. 1975. *Justice Accused: Antislavery and the Judicial Process,* 224.

McCann, M. W., and G. I. Lovell. 2020. *Union by Law: Filipino American Labor Activists, Rights Radicalism, and Racial Capitalism,* 158–159, 390.